THE KING

and His

GLORY

FROM HIS RETURN TO EARTH
INTO THE ETERNAL STATE

GREG HARRIS

KRESS
BIBLICAL
RESOURCES

Kress Biblical Resources
The Woodlands, Texas
www.kressbiblical.com

ISBN: 978-1-934952-62-7

Scripture taken from the NEW AMERICAN STANDARD BIBLE®, Copyright © 1960,1962,1963,1968,1971,1972,1973,1975,1977 by The Lockman Foundation. Used by permission.

Scripture quotations marked HCSB are taken from the Holman Christian Standard Bible®, Used by Permission HCSB ©1999,2000,2002,2003,2009 Holman Bible Publishers. Holman Christian Standard Bible®, Holman CSB®, and HCSB® are federally registered trademarks of Holman Bible Publishers.

Lift up your heads, O gates,
And be lifted up, O ancient doors,
That the King of glory may come in!

Who is the King of glory?
The LORD strong and mighty,
The LORD mighty in battle.
Lift up your heads, O gates,
And lift them up, O ancient doors,
That the King of glory may come in!

Who is this King of glory?
The LORD of hosts,
He is the King of glory

—Psalm 24:7–10

CREDITS

Dr. Greg Harris' personal editor: Rebecca R. Howard

Dr. Greg Harris' website: www.glorybooks.org

TMS consulting class: "The Master's Seminary consulting class," Spring 2020 (We didn't actually have a TMS consulting class this time around, but I went ahead and used the term anyway): Bob and Julie Fanciullacci, Becky Howard, Bullwinkle, Nancy Anderson, Tricia [T the D] Steiger, Andre Randolph [Emeritus], Faly Ravoahangy [Emeritus], Premend Choy [Emeritus] Bill and Lalanne Barber, Dave Owen, Chad Tucker and Chris Fowler (problem child).

—And those untimely born and grafted in: Kevin Laymon, Rob Thurman, Aaron Filburn, H. Chris E. Bush, Chazz ("Two Golden Calves") Anderson, and King Charles Clemmons.

A Special thanks for Pat Rotisky and her godly expertise on this project.

BOOK DEDICATION

The King and His Glory: From His Return to Earth Into the Eternal State is dedicated to two of God's most choice vessels: Drs. William (Bill) Barrick and Robert (Bob) Provost, whose lives have touched so many—mine at the forefront.

For so many times their brotherhood/friendship and godly wisdom were so needed by me at that time, and God used them both deeply and repeatedly in my life, especially these last six of many years.

I am a better Christian and my writings are better because of these two men. If God said "I'll let you have any two men (other than Jesus and the Apostles)," from the first century up to the present time to be alongside of me to help me in your studies, books, and journal articles—plus my walk with the Lord—I'd choose Bob Provost and Bill Barrick—no question about and an easy decision to make. We will leave it at that until the Lord does His unveiling.

May they bless many more people God sovereignly places them with and may they bear much fruit with their multiplicity of ministries.

CONTENTS

THE KING AND HIS GLORY:
FROM HIS RETURN TO EARTH
INTO THE ETERNAL STATE

INTRODUCTION AND A FORMATION DILEMMA

Many people throughout the world have read verses from the Book of Isaiah. Maybe you are like I was when I read it at a younger age. I knew a few verses taken from Isaiah, but I could not view the book as a whole—much less walk someone else through Isaiah. But now I can. I have found over almost forty years of study and ministry that most people who love the LORD go to this beloved biblical book, and while they may not necessarily be able to view Isaiah as a whole, they know from their New Testament readings and cross references that many Messianic quotes emerge from this book. In fact, no other prophet who wrote what became Holy-Spirit-inspired books of the Bible is quoted more in the New Testament than Isaiah. This does not mean that the prophets who never wrote books of the Bible had a less effective ministry. If they were walking with Him (consider Elijah and Elisha), each godly prophet was doing what God wanted him to do, whether it is someone such as Micaiah in 1 Kings 22, standing bravely and alone as he publicly denounced the hundreds of false prophets and the king foolish enough to have such reprobates with them in the first place, or whether they were part of a select group, moved by the Holy Spirit to write, such as the Apostle Peter in 2 Peter 1:12–21, writing from death row in Rome:

> Therefore, I shall always be ready to remind you of these things, even though you already know them, and have been established in the truth which is present with you. And I consider it right, as long as I am in this earthly dwelling, to stir you up by way of reminder, knowing that the

laying aside of my earthly dwelling is imminent, as also our Lord Jesus Christ has made clear to me [*decades earlier, in John 21:19*]. And I will also be diligent that at any time after my departure you may be able to call these things to mind.

For we did not follow cleverly devised tales when we made known to you the power and coming of our Lord Jesus Christ, but we were eyewitnesses of His majesty. For when He received honor and glory from God the Father, such an utterance as this was made to Him by the Majestic Glory, "This is My beloved Son with whom I am well-pleased"—and we ourselves heard this utterance made from heaven when we were with Him on the holy mountain.

So we have the prophetic word made more sure, to which you do well to pay attention as to a lamp shining in a dark place, until the day dawns and the morning star arises in your hearts. But know this first of all, that no prophecy of Scripture is a matter of one's own interpretation, for no prophecy was ever made by an act of human will, but men moved by the Holy Spirit spoke from God.

Some of those who spoke for God also wrote for God/from God, such as Peter did in the last chapter he wrote shortly before his execution, reminding his beloved readers in 2 Peter 3:1–2, "This is now, beloved, the second letter I am writing to you in which I am stirring up your sincere mind by way of reminder, that you should remember the words spoken beforehand by the holy prophets and the commandment of the Lord and Savior spoken by your apostles." And no other Old Testament book written by God's prophets has as many messianic prophecies/promises as does the Book of Isaiah. However, many believers are still somewhat hesitant to read all of Isaiah, if for no other reason than its daunting size of 66 chapters.

And one other incentive for reading any of the Old Testament writings is that Jesus twice on the day He was resurrected showed us the treasured value—and usefulness—of all the Old Testament books. The first instance is Jesus' encounter with two disciples on the road to Emmaus. Luke 24:25–27 tells what Jesus said to them at the end, using the two-fold division of the Scriptures that was accepted at the time:

And He said to them, "O foolish men and slow of heart to believe in all that the prophets have spoken! Was it not necessary for the Christ to suffer these things and to enter into His glory?" Then beginning with Moses and with all the prophets, He explained to them the things concerning Himself in all the Scriptures."

"All the Scriptures" would at this time have been what Christians and others call the Old Testament. (Most of the Jews of Jesus' day up through the present time would not call it such; they would have no reason to do so.)

No doubt in wonder and astonishment, "they got up that very hour and returned to Jerusalem, and found gathered together the eleven and those who were with them" (Luke 24:33). Luke 24:36 explains, "While they [*the two disciples mentioned previously*] were telling these things, He Himself stood in their midst."

When He appeared to those gathered in Luke 24:44–47, He used the then-accepted threefold division of the Scriptures, the same Scriptures He used before, only with a slightly different categorizing of them:

Now He said to them, "These are My words which I spoke to you while I was still with you, that all things which are written about Me in the Law of Moses and the Prophets and the Psalms must be fulfilled." Then He opened their minds to understand the Scriptures, and He said to them, "Thus it is written, that the Christ should suffer and rise again from the dead the third day, and that repentance for forgiveness of sins should be proclaimed in His name to all the nations, beginning from Jerusalem."

So, no doubt as He had already done earlier with the two disciples on the road to Emmaus, after "He opened their minds to understand the Scriptures" (Luke 24:45), "beginning with Moses and with all the prophets, He explained to them the things concerning Himself in all the Scriptures" (Luke 24:27). Obviously, Jesus would have used the Book of Isaiah to explain much of who He is and what He had just accomplished in Jerusalem, facts concerning His death, burial, and resurrection. In addition to using Isaiah, He would have begun with Moses and used all the prophets until the end of the biblical verses written about Him. He would also deal with many of the prophecies that have not yet taken place.[1]

Imagine how large a gap would be in your theology if you did not know or believe verses from Isaiah. And just for the record, the Trinity does not *believe* in the divine inspiration of Scripture; they worked—especially the Holy Spirit—to make sure that Scripture is truly the unique, true, and only Word of God. Many people do not realize it, but just as 2 Peter was Peter's death-row epistle, 2 Timothy was Paul's death-row epistle. And 2 Timothy 3:16–17 clearly presents the Bible as uniquely "God-breathed," a doctrine scoffed at by liberal theologians, atheists and agnostics:

> "All Scripture is inspired by God [*literally "God-breathed"*] and profitable for teaching, for reproof, for correction, for training in righteousness; that the man of God may be adequate, equipped for every good work."

In Peter's death-row epistle, the Holy Spirit inspired the soon-to-be martyr to write these opening verses of what would eventually be called Second Peter:

> Simon Peter, a bond-servant and apostle of Jesus Christ,

---

1   In fact, because so many citations in the Bible from Isaiah play a major role, when it came time to do the chapter divisions for *The Bible Expositor's Handbook (OT/NT)*, I put an entire chapter *in the New Testament section about Isaiah*—not the Old Testament section—and appropriately entitled chapter 16 "The Gospel According to Isaiah." And for time's sake and not to make the book too large, we had to put in at least some incredibly important verses—some irreplaceable Scripture—so that we could understand some of the great truths of the Bible. One illustration will suffice for now, Matthew 1:18–23:

> "Now the birth of Jesus Christ was as follows. When His mother Mary had been betrothed to Joseph, before they came together she was found to be with child by the Holy Spirit. And Joseph her husband, being a righteous man, and not wanting to disgrace her, desired to put her away secretly.
> "But when he had considered this, behold, an angel of the Lord appeared to him in a dream, saying, 'Joseph, son of David, do not be afraid to take Mary as your wife; for that which has been conceived in her is of the Holy Spirit. And she will bear a Son; and you shall call His name Jesus, for it is He who will save His people from their sins.'
> "Now all this took place that what was spoken by the Lord through the prophet might be fulfilled, saying, 'BEHOLD, THE VIRGIN SHALL BE WITH CHILD, AND SHALL BEAR A SON, AND THEY SHALL CALL HIS NAME IMMANUEL,' which translated means, 'GOD WITH US.'"

Consequently, "[n]ow all this took place that what was spoken by the Lord [*the true source*] through the prophet [*the human source*] might be fulfilled"—and the scriptural citation was Isaiah 7:14, appropriately taken from the Immanuel portion of the Book of Isaiah (Isa 7–12).

To those who have received a faith of the same kind as ours, by the righteousness of our God and Savior, Jesus Christ: Grace and peace be multiplied to you in the knowledge of God and of Jesus our Lord; seeing that His divine power has granted to us everything pertaining to life and godliness, through the true knowledge of Him who called us by His own glory and excellence. For by these He has granted to us His precious and magnificent promises, so that by them you may become partakers of the divine nature, having escaped the corruption that is in the world by lust.

Zechariah is the second-most-quoted prophetic book in the New Testament, and yet many Word-loving worshipers of God would be virtually clueless in regard to the theological importance, the historical landscape, and the order in which the Book of Zechariah fits in Scripture. But it is eternally important that what is contained within this wonderful God-given book be distributed and known by Christians and those who will be saved during the Tribulation. The Messianic verses that are cited in the New Testament and are used at some of the most important events in the words and work of Jesus Christ during His incarnation, should be motivation enough to study Zechariah carefully. There is even more reason when one considers truths about His second coming (eschatological doctrines) the verses and where they occur *and* why they occur where they do in Scripture. That gives one an appreciation of reasons to study the book of Zechariah in detail: (1) Jesus would have cited or quoted (in Luke 24) verses from Zechariah that are written about Him, and connected with this, (2) in Zechariah there are truths about the attributes and activities of Jesus Christ at His First and Second Coming, that are not found elsewhere, and (3) As Jesus worked his way from Moses and all the prophets until the end of the referenced biblical verses, He would also have dealt with many of the prophecies that have not yet taken place. Although numerous God-given biblical prophesies had already been fulfilled—and these are vitally important to know—*more* prophecies remain unfulfilled at the present time and will be completed at the Second Coming of the Lord Jesus Christ to earth, and some of the most important and staggering prophesies in all of Scripture are in Zechariah. (4) The verses from Zechariah that Jesus used—unless they were fulfilled in His life, death or resurrection—are just as true and doctrinally important today as they were when Jesus used them to point to Himself.

I hope you will be able to watch the Bible unfold as we study it together.

A FEW IMPORTANT ITEMS TO NOTE

First, while Zechariah will play an important part of our study in this book, this is not a study on the Book of Zechariah, rather it is a study about this book's title: *The King and His Glory: From His Second Coming to Earth Into the Eternal State.* The Eternal State includes the New Heavens and a New Earth, and these are (even though we presently see in a mirror only dimly) what we generally consider by the word "heaven." By the time of Revelation 21–22, all evil will have been properly defeated, all evil will have been judged by Jesus the Messiah, and those at the great white throne judgment will have been cast into the lake of fire/hell (Rev. 20:11–15). After the final judgment, there will be no more Satan to battle. Sin and sinners will have been eradicated, and the redeemed will be rewarded by Jesus Christ. These attributes belong to the Godhead eternally: holiness, love, glory, and the fulness of the joy of the Trinity. There will be a resurrected body for each the redeemed, and God's holy angels will be present—and this is just the short list of future blessings for the redeemed. Another great enticement exists, mentioned in 1 John 3:1–2: "See how great a love the Father has bestowed upon us, that we should be called children of God; and such we are. For this reason the world does not know us, because it did not know Him. Beloved, now we are children of God, and it has not appeared as yet what we shall be. We know that, when He appears, *we shall be like Him*, because we shall see Him just as He is."

Second, one more caveat: *many* biblical studies have been done by this time, and that includes studies done in the five "Glory Books." *The King and His Glory* will take excerpts from or refer especially to *The Stone and the Glory: Lessons on the Temple Presence and the Glory of God and His Temple Presence* (written mainly for Gentiles) and *The Stone and the Glory of Israel: An Invitation for the Jewish People to Meet Their Messiah* (written mainly for the Jewish people). Those two books can be used currently. *The Stone and the Glory of Israel* can be a valuable gift to a Jewish friend or relative, or by your having this knowledge, you will be able to converse with Jewish people about these eternally important biblical truths. Though I know that God has absolutely no obligation to use the books, I wrote both versions for those in the great Tribulation. In some of my other writings you can see details about that wicked time, which will be unlike any other time in history past or future. Yet a tremendous blessing for those who find themselves in the Tribulation is that it will be a time of unparalleled evangelism and salvation for both Jews and Gentiles, for the Gospel will go to the utter ends of the earth, as Jesus declared in Matthew 24:14, speaking in the context of His second coming, "And this gospel of the kingdom shall be preached in the whole world for a witness to all the nations, and then the end shall come."

We will also refer to *The Face and the Glory: Lessons on the Invisible and Visible God and His Glory* a few times, and lastly we will point people to the combined printed edition (which also has Kindle and other such digital formats) of *The Bible Expositor's Handbook (OT/NT)*. I thank B & H Academic for granting permission to use those quotes. On many occasions we'll refer to something biblically important that is covered in much more detail in one of these books; where that occurs, you will be given the specific book and the chapter of that book.

One final thought: while we cannot cover everything, we will cover many incredible and irreplaceable biblical doctrines—especially in the Old Testament. Those who want to begin their study of the Bible in Matthew, and never go back to trace such foundational doctrinal truths, must remember this: as we saw twice in Luke 24, the LORD Jesus Christ Himself worked His way to—and through—every book in the Old Testament and showed that many passages were specifically and directly related to Him. Many of those truths would be foundational for Jesus to establish His church and its biblical doctrine. After all, we would never start at the Gospel of Matthew (or at even at Zechariah) without knowing at least broadly the biblical trail that tells so wondrously of the King—and especially about His Glory.

THE KING AND HIS GLORY:
From His Return to Earth Into the Eternal State

ONE FORMATTING DECISION

As I was praying through the book, its contents and arrangement, I had a dilemma before me: is this current work a Glory Book, and should I use the formatting that I have used for the previous five Glory Books, or should the format for this book be the one we used for the 30 chapters of *The Bible Expositor's Handbook (OT/NT)*? Basically the answer is, this is another Glory Book in content, but written in the Handbook style. I did this because (1) it allows me more freedom of movement, so to speak, in using longer titles and subdivisions than fit in the Glory Books style; (2) I think you will discover that this biblical material will be easier to convey using the Handbook format; (3) Each of the 30 chapters of *The Bible Expositor's Handbook (OT/NT)* has an introductory paragraph, a Summary and Conclusion section (for reinforcement of what we studied, and these summaries can be used for quick review, if needed).

When this book is published, it will become the next 12 chapters as supplemental chapters to add to the other 30 chapters of what now becomes unofficially the 42 chapters of *The Bible Expositor's Handbook (OT/NT)*—or it can be read easily as a stand-alone book, apart from any of the other books mentioned.

To me, these benefits of doing the formatting made it an easy call, and I hope that it will greatly enrich our study of *The King and His Glory: From His Return to Earth Into the Eternal State*. All royalties from the books are signed over to the Master's Academies International for them to use however they see fit.

CHAPTER ONE

BROADLY SETTING THE BIBLICAL TABLE (PART 1):

THE FIRST TWO BOOKS OF MOSES: GENESIS AND EXODUS

INTRODUCTION

The Bible's passages about the Lord Jesus Christ are a feast for the Christian's spirit. In order to enjoy them, we need to "set the table" by looking at previous passages to establish the biblical context. Let's remember again what Jesus said in reference to Himself in all the Scriptures, as we saw twice in Luke 24. Verse 27, "And beginning with Moses and with all the prophets, He explained to them the things concerning Himself in all the Scriptures." Later that same day, to those who had gathered together with the eleven Apostles, verse 44, "Now He said to them, 'These are My words which I spoke to you while I was still with you, that all things which are written about Me in the Law of Moses and the Prophets and the Psalms must be fulfilled.'" Earlier in His life and ministry, Jesus had communicated something similar in condemning His critics, John 5:44-47:

> "How can you believe, when you receive glory from one another, and you do not seek the glory that is from the one and only God? Do not think that I will accuse you before the Father; the one who accuses you is Moses, in whom you have set your hope. For if you believed Moses, you would

THE KING AND HIS GLORY

believe Me; for he wrote of Me. "But if you do not believe his writings, how will you believe My words?"

Whether these questions are for denominations, seminaries, colleges, and churches, or are limited to individuals, they are just as valid today, and how these questions are answered—or simply ignored—has eternal consequences and ramifications for both the redeemed and the lost. As with my other books, I have written this one for those who believe (or who eventually will believe) the Bible as God's inerrant Word. And while entire books or a series of books answer or attempt to answer these questions, we will do the same, but in this study, and as always, we will try to "answer Scripture with Scripture" when possible. Also, while not underplaying its importance to anyone ever born, so many prophecies appropriately relate to the Incarnation and to the salvation Jesus won at the Cross— which is, of course, eternally valuable—but these prophecies have already been fulfilled. And while not trying to avoid verses completely about Jesus' Incarnation, **in this book we'll study the Second Coming of Jesus and matters related to His return and reign as King.** The Holy Spirit reveals stunning prophecies about the Lord Jesus' return to earth in the Old Testament—not just the New Testament nor only in the Book of Revelation, as some claim. Many of these verses that we will study tie in with all the other Glory Books (especially *The Stone and the Glory*, *The Stone and the Glory of Israel*, and *The Face and the Glory)*, and/or the printed volume of *The Bible Expositor's Handbook (OT/NT)*. In this book, in the four chapters on "Broadly Setting the Biblical Table," we will look at verses from the Old Testament that highlight the King aspects of Messiah Jesus' return to earth and His rule thereafter. Since many of these verses are made in the covenants of God, we will examine those promises and the people they are made to. Finally, we will see that not only are there prophecies that have not yet been fulfilled, but that there are many verses about the Second Coming of Jesus Christ to reign and rule, beginning first with the earth. We will track much of the biblical trail that Jesus used in John 5 and Luke 24.

One additional note before going further: citations or references to my *The Bible Expositor's Handbook (OT/NT)* (Nashville: B & H Academic, 2020) will have a chaper number and the page number(s) in the printed version. Those who have read that book and any of the Glory Books will be familiar with parts of what we cover. But for those who have read none of these books, we have laid at least enough groundwork for them to see how vital some of the biblical truths within these books are to understanding the rest of the Bible. Prayerfully, we look for God to "hook" people with a deeper love—and ideally to worship the Trinity in Spirit and in truth. So, if you have read all the books already or are familiar with the core Bible verses, there are things that you can use for review, and hopefully there are things that "stir you up by way of reminder," as Peter purposely did in 2 Peter 1:12–14:

> Therefore, I will always be ready to remind you of these things, even though you already know them, and have been established in the truth which is present with you. I consider it right, as long as I am in this earthly dwelling, to stir you up by way of reminder, knowing that the laying aside of my earthly dwelling is imminent, as also our Lord Jesus Christ has made clear to me.

As we come to particular verses, we will often tell you which chapter in the previously mentioned books discusses them. If you have read any or all of the previous books, there will be *very much new material* that is not found in those books; *The King and His Glory: From His Return to Earth Into the Eternal State* stands alone as its own book. The full bibliographic information for the Glory Books is on the last page of this book.

BROAD SPECTRUM OF BIBLICAL MARKERS TO NOTE

Entire books have been written on each item, biblical passage or topic, so we will not elaborate on these but will point out a few irreplaceable places in the Scriptures. First, the Creation perfections lasted only through the first two chapters of Genesis. In Genesis 3, the unannounced evil one led Eve and then Adam into sin that precipitates the Fall and the curse that lasts even up to our present time. God, however, offered a glimmer of hope in Genesis 3:15: "And I will put enmity / Between you and the woman, / And between your seed and her seed; / He shall bruise you on the head,

/ And you shall bruise Him on the heel." God revealed that the One born of a woman—when there had been no normal births yet—would eventually crush the head of the evil one, but only after this evil one has inflicted severe pain on whoever the One to come would be. God said broadly who it would be—One born of a woman—but it would take the unfolding of God's divine revelation to specifically designate who this would be, where this would take place, how this One would suffer and—very importantly— why this unnamed One had to suffer. The principle question from Genesis 3:15 forward, from a human vantage point, is: who is this One who will crush the head of the true serpent Satan (Rev 12:9)?

Second, after previously announcing a worldwide flood, whereby God would destroy all the people of the earth with the exception of Noah and 7 others, <u>God used the word *covenant* for the first time in Genesis 6:18, where God Himself promised (and note the future tense) what He would do</u>: "But I will establish My covenant with you; and you shall enter the ark—you and your sons and your wife, and your sons' wives with you." The word *covenant* means a binding, legally recognized agreement between two or more parties. War treaties are examples of covenants, and so is the marriage ceremony a covenant, as Malachi 2:14 states to Jewish people living in sin: "Yet you say, 'For what reason [*is God displeased with us*]?' Because the LORD has been a witness between you and the wife of your youth, against whom you have dealt treacherously, though she is your companion *and your wife by covenant.*"

Third, <u>God is the One who ratified the Noahic Covenant, and whoever ratifies a covenant has certain responsibilities</u>. Since God speaks in Genesis 9:8–17, He alone ratified the covenant, and He alone has obligations to fulfill:

> Then God spoke to Noah and to his sons with him, saying, "Now behold, I Myself do establish My covenant with you, and with your descendants after you; and with every living creature that is with you, the birds, the cattle, and every beast of the earth with you; of all that comes out of the ark, even every beast of the earth. I establish My covenant with you; and all flesh shall never again be cut off by the water of the flood, neither shall there again be a flood to destroy the earth.

God said, "This is the sign of the covenant which I am making between Me and you and every living creature that is with you, for all successive generations; I set My bow in the cloud, and it shall be for a sign of a covenant between Me and the earth. It shall come about, when I bring a cloud over the earth, that the bow shall be seen in the cloud, and I will remember My covenant, which is between Me and you and every living creature of all flesh; and never again shall the water become a flood to destroy all flesh.

"When the bow is in the cloud, then I will look upon it, to remember the everlasting covenant between God and every living creature of all flesh that is on the earth." And God said to Noah, "This is the sign of the covenant which I have established between Me and all flesh that is on the earth."

God alone ratified the Noahic Covenant; God alone is the One responsible for the fulfillment of each item He mentioned. Those who believe the Bible accept the flood as the Bible presents it: it was a declaration of what God said He would do and was His fulfillment of these things. No forced allegorical interpretation needs to be hammered into it to make it fit; the language conveys accurately what God said and did. And while some groups have temporarily usurped the rainbow, it (1) is still His rainbow, and (2) remains the sign God gave of His covenant faithness to what He promised in the Noahic Covenant.

GOD'S PROMISES WITHIN THE ABRAHAMIC COVENANT[2]

With this background, we come to the second covenant of God.

Adapted from The Bible Expositor's Handbook (OT/NT) Chapter 3 (pp. 32–35):

---

2 Adapted from a truncated version of the Abrahamic Covenant, by Greg Harris, *The Bible Expositor's Handbook (OT/NT)* (Nashville: B & H Academic, 2020), in Chapter 3: "Why Are There so Many Different Interpretations of the Bible?" 27–39. Used by permission. See that chapter for much more important and relevant information that we do not cover here.

While we are not able to consider much of the total material in the Pentateuch, the second covenant of God occurs relatively quickly after Genesis 9, in Genesis 12:1–3:

Now the LORD said to Abram,
"Go forth from your country,
And from your relatives
And from your father's house,
To the land which I will show you;
And I will make you a great nation,
And I will bless you,
And make your name great;
And so you shall be a blessing;
And I will bless those who bless you,
And the one who curses you I will curse.
And in you all the families of the earth will be blessed."

Although the word covenant is not stated here, it will be used elsewhere in related passages. In Genesis 12:1–3, God promised three particular elements that He would give: a land (the boundaries were not yet given), a seed (or lineage), and a blessing for all the families of the earth. Notice that God used future tenses in promising the land, the seed, and the blessing; therefore, this is not the actual ratification of what would eventually be called the Abrahamic Covenant.

After his nephew Lot departed from Abram to go to more pleasant (at that time) Sodom and Gomorrah (Gen 13:8–13), Genesis 13:14 continues the account, picking up where the author left off in Genesis 12:

The LORD said to Abram, after Lot had separated from him, "Now lift up your eyes and look from the place where you are, northward and southward and eastward and westward; for all the land which you see, I will give it to you and to your descendants forever. I will make your descendants as the dust of the earth, so that if anyone can number the dust of the earth, then your descendants can also be numbered. Arise, walk about the land through its length and breadth; for I will give it to you." Then

Abram moved his tent and came and dwelt by the oaks of Mamre, which are in Hebron, and there he built an altar to the LORD (Gen 13:14–18).

In this account, not only did God have Abram look out over the land, seeing the four compass points; God also said, "I will give it to you and to your descendants forever" (Gen 13:15). Notice once more that God employed future tenses; this also is not the ratification of the covenant. Abram responded to God's commands by moving to a particular place in the land, the oaks of Mamre in Hebron and building an altar there. There is nothing so far in the account that indicates that the fulfillment of such promises was anything but literal and physical. God really did mean the land of which He spoke.

Genesis 15 is a major development in the unfolding of God's revelation. The first 11 verses show Abram's dilemma and God's answer and actions:

After these things the word of the LORD came to Abram in a vision, saying,

"Do not fear, Abram.
I am a shield to you;
Your reward shall be very great."

Abram said, "O Lord GOD, what will You give me, since I am childless, and the heir of my house is Eliezer of Damascus?" And Abram said, "Since You have given no offspring to me, one born in my house is my heir."

Then behold, the word of the LORD came to him, saying, "This man will not be your heir; but one who will come forth from your own body, he shall be your heir." And He took him outside and said, "Now look toward the heavens, and count the stars, if you are able to count them." And He said to him, "So shall your descendants be." Then he believed in the LORD; and He reckoned it to him as righteousness. And He said to him, "I am the LORD who brought you out of Ur of the Chaldeans, to give you this land to possess it." He said, "O Lord GOD, how may I know that I will possess it?" So He said to him, "Bring Me a three year old heifer, and a three year old female goat, and a three year old ram, and a turtledove, and a young pigeon." Then he brought all these to Him and cut them in two, and laid each half opposite the other; but he did not cut the birds. The birds of prey came down upon the carcasses, and Abram drove them away.

In light of this backdrop, God then ratified what would be known hereafter as the Abrahamic Covenant in Genesis 15:12–21:

> Now when the sun was going down, a deep sleep fell upon Abram; and behold, terror and great darkness fell upon him. God said to Abram, "Know for certain that your descendants will be strangers in a land that is not theirs, where they will be enslaved and oppressed four hundred years. But I will also judge the nation whom they will serve, and afterward they will come out with many possessions. As for you, you shall go to your fathers in peace; you shall be buried at a good old age. Then in the fourth generation they will return here, for the iniquity of the Amorite is not yet complete."
>
> It came about when the sun had set, that it was very dark, and behold, there appeared a smoking oven and a flaming torch which passed between these pieces.
>
> On that day the LORD made a covenant with Abram, saying,
>
> "To your descendants I have given this land,
>
> From the river of Egypt as far as the great river, the river Euphrates:
>
> the Kenite and the Kenizzite and the Kadmonite and the Hittite and the Perizzite and the Rephaim and the Amorite and the Canaanite and the Girgashite and the Jebusite."

It is important to remember that, just as with the Noahic Covenant, the one who ratifies the covenant has the responsibility of bringing about his part. Abram slept through the whole thing—just as God intended. God alone ratified this covenant; God alone has the responsibility to fulfill what He had covenanted. In this ratification of the Abrahamic Covenant, no more future tenses are used: "On that day the LORD made a covenant with Abram, saying, 'To your descendants I have given this land, /From the river of Egypt as far as the great river, the river Euphrates'" (Gen 15:18). Just to show by other means that God intended for these promises to be fulfilled literally and physically, God listed people groups who then had inhabited, or who would inhabit the land; these were real people with whom Abraham and his descendants had to deal.

Years later, after Lot and his family had departed for Sodom and Gomorrah, God reminded Abraham of His promise once again, in Gen 17:7–8:

> "I will establish My covenant between Me and you and your descendants after you throughout their generations for an everlasting covenant, to be God to you and to your descendants after you. I will give to you and to your descendants after you, the land of your sojournings, all the land of Canaan, for an everlasting possession; and I will be their God."

In this section, God is the One who described this as "My Covenant" and "an everlasting covenant" for the land that He gave Abram and his descendants "for an everlasting possession," along with God's own special relationship with them, "and I will be their God." Those who love God's Word fully accept this section and see no reason why God did not mean what He said He would do.

Further, those who accept the literal-grammatical interpretation of the flood account and accept that the Noahic Covenant is in effect must explain the following important question:

KEY THEOLOGICAL CONSIDERATION: The burden of proof is on those who will accept and interpret God's first covenant in Genesis 9 (i.e., the Noahic Covenant) in a literal fashion for everything about it and then switch the hermeneutic so that some or much of the next covenant of God is allegorical. This second covenant is from the same God, the same author, the same book, and the same genre. How, other than a presupposition imposed on the text, could one arrive at and thrust into the text a hermeneutic that does not allow the text to mean anything?

THE INCREDIBLE BIBLICAL RELEVANCE OF GENESIS 49[3]

From The Stone and the Glory of Israel (pp. 14–17):

Genesis 49 begins with Jacob dying as an old man. As his father had done for him, he wanted to bequeath to his sons their proper portions. Because a father bequeathing to his children is a common occurrence, it is easy to see why this important event could be overlooked. However, this bequest is different because it will become part of God's holy and unbreakable promises in Scripture. So in a very real sense, these are not solely Jacob's words or thoughts; these are God's words and thoughts given by Jacob.

Genesis 49:1 begins, "Then Jacob summoned his sons and said, 'Assemble yourselves that I may tell you what will befall you in the days to come.'" Although it is easy to miss their importance, two biblical nuggets of pure gold have already been exposed. For instance, "the days to come" can also be translated as "the end of the days," or "the last days," and Genesis 49:1 is the first time that phrase appears in Scripture—but it will not be the last time. So God takes the original audience and all future readers all the way from the original utterances throughout thousands of years to the people and events in the last days.

The second revelatory nugget from God is likewise easy to miss. In Genesis 49:1, God gave Jacob words regarding future specific events as Jacob proclaimed, "Assemble yourselves that I may tell you what will befall you in the days to come." God clearly reveals the "you" whom He has in mind. At the end of Jacob's blessing, Genesis 49:28 summarizes: "All these are the twelve tribes of Israel, and this is what their father said to them when he blessed them. He blessed them, every one with the blessing appropriate to him." Genesis 49 makes it a biblical impossibility for the Jewish people to be eradicated by an enemy or by collective enemies. Genesis 49:1 and 28 *require* that the twelve tribes of Israel be living and functioning in the last days. Absolutely no one—from Haman to Hitler to anyone else—can

---

3   Adapted from Greg Harris', *The Stone and the Glory of Israel: An Invitation for the Jewish People to Meet Their Messiah* (The Woodlands, TX: Kress Christian Publications, 2016), Chapter One, "The Stone," 14–22. Used by permission. See that chapter for much more important and relevant information than we could cover here.

eradicate the Jews from the face of the earth. It is a biblical impossibility because God's Word clearly shows that the twelve tribes will be present in the last days.

Those two verses in Genesis would be enough, but there is more—much, much more. Not only does Genesis 49 contain the first reference to the last days during which the twelve tribes of Israel will be present; Genesis 49:8–12 gives one of the earliest prophecies of the coming Messiah and reveals new details that God had not yet disclosed elsewhere in Scripture:

> "Judah, your brothers shall praise you; your hand shall be on the neck of your enemies; your father's sons shall bow down to you. Judah is a lion's whelp; from the prey, my son, you have gone up. He couches, he lies down as a lion, and as a lion, who dares rouse him up?

> "The scepter shall not depart from Judah, nor the ruler's staff from between his feet, until Shiloh comes, and to him shall be the obedience of the peoples. He ties his foal to the vine, and his donkey's colt to the choice vine; he washes his garments in wine, and his robes in the blood of grapes. His eyes are dull from wine, and his teeth white from milk."

From this point forward, it becomes a biblical mandate that the Messiah, according to God's sovereign decree, must be from the tribe of Judah. So whoever the Messiah is, He must give clear documentation of His lineage—and it must be traced back to the tribe of Judah. Also, it should not be overlooked that the Messiah's reign will not be limited only to or over the nation of Israel. When God's Messiah reigns, "to Him shall be the obedience of the peoples" (Gen 49:10), which is another way of saying that His kingdom will be a worldwide kingdom over all the earth; no people groups, kingdoms, nor individuals will be exempt from His reign and rule.

We could conclude here with what we have already seen and marvel at what God has already promised, but we have still more to glean from this wonderful revelation from God. In Genesis 49 comes this double blessing to Joseph and his lineage due to his faithful walk of holiness and obedience to God. Verse 28 states, "All these are the twelve tribes of Israel, and this is what their father said to them when he blessed them. He blessed them, each one with the blessing appropriate to him." So, in verses 22–26 God blesses Joseph this way:

> "Joseph is a fruitful bough, a fruitful bough by a spring; its branches run over a wall. The archers bitterly attacked him, and shot at him and harassed him, but his bow remained firm, and his arms were agile, from the hands of the Mighty One of Jacob (from there is the Shepherd, the Stone of Israel).

> "From the God of your father who helps you, and by the Almighty who blesses you with blessings of heaven above, blessings of the deep that lies beneath, blessings of the breasts and of the womb. The blessings of your father have surpassed the blessings of my ancestors up to the utmost bound of the everlasting hills; may they be on the head of Joseph, and on the crown of the head of the one distinguished among his brothers."

So much is contained in this wonderful blessing of the Lord that it would be understandable how one could miss some of its significance. But as with any other truth that God reveals in this chapter, we *must* have within this background before us "the last days," and "what shall befall you," the twelve tribes of Israel (Gen 49:1, 28). With the promise of the Lion of the tribe of Judah being the Messiah who will reign over the entire world (Gen 49:8–12) come two further designations regarding God's future Messiah, in verse 24: "From the hands of the Mighty One of Jacob (from there is *the Shepherd, the Stone of Israel*)." Whoever the Messiah is, He must do the work of God's sent Shepherd and God's sent Stone of Israel, and—this is important—He must do so in the last days (Gen 49:1), with the twelve tribes of Israel (v. 28). The promised Messiah sent by God *must* fulfill these prophecies, or else He is *not* the promised Messiah.

(Ends this section from *The Stone and the Glory of Israel*, pp. 14–17)

Realizing that we are leaving out more than we can put in, we come to the Book of Exodus and the ratification of the covenant. This is really not the place to begin our study of Exodus, but we will begin by noting a few necessary doctrinal truths in the Book of Exodus. *The Stone and the Glory of Israel* has so much more to offer that would be beneficial to study before coming to the ratification of the Mosaic Covenant.

The Ratification of the Mosaic Covenant—and Beyond[4]

After God brought the newly redeemed people to Mount Sinai (Exodus 19), He further brought the people to Himself. Exodus 24:1–8 gives the account:

> Then He said to Moses, "Come up to the LORD, you and Aaron, Nadab and Abihu and seventy of the elders of Israel, and you shall worship at a distance. Moses alone, however, shall come near to the LORD, but they shall not come near, nor shall the people come up with him."
>
> Then Moses came and recounted to the people all the words of the LORD and all the ordinances; and all the people answered with one voice and said, "All the words which the LORD has spoken we will do!" Moses wrote down all the words of the LORD. Then he arose early in the morning and built an altar at the foot of the mountain with twelve pillars for the twelve tribes of Israel. He sent young men of the sons of Israel, and they offered burnt offerings and sacrificed young bulls as peace offerings to the LORD. Moses took half of the blood and put it in basins, and the other half of the blood he sprinkled on the altar. Then he took the book of the covenant and read it in the hearing of the people; and they said, "All that the LORD has spoken we will do, and we will be obedient!" So Moses took the blood and sprinkled it on the people, and said, "Behold the blood of the covenant, which the LORD has made with you in accordance with all these words."

A few matters stand out as extremely important in this account. First, the Mosaic Covenant is the only covenant of God so far where somebody else was present and active. Previously in the Noahic Covenant (Gen 9) and the Abrahamic Covenant (Gen 15), God alone ratified the covenant. Remember: those who ratify the covenant have a responsibility to do their

---

4   Material taken and adapted from *The Bible Expositor's Handbook (OT/NT)*, Chapter Five: "The Mosaic Covenant and Its Biblical Relevance," 58–63. Used by permission. See this chapter for a much more detailed account of the material we had to omit.

part. So in the Mosaic Covenant, God has a part and the nation of Israel has a part. Second, unlike the previous two covenants, the Mosaic Covenant is not stated as being everlasting. Third, the people claim twice, "All that the LORD has spoken we will do, and we will be obedient!" Yet, as the Bible clearly shows, rare are the times when the people are in covenant obedience to Yahweh. Fourth, from Exodus 24 onward, as long as the Mosaic Covenant is in effect, national Israel is under covenant obligation to do what God tells them to do. So this covenant relationship goes far beyond the events of Exodus 24 into Joshua, Judges, 1 Samuel, and so forth. Fifth, all Jewish people were as much under the Mosaic Covenant obligations as any of their ancestors on the day the covenant was ratified in Exodus 24, as long as that covenant was operative. Sixth, Exodus 24:4 reveals that Moses "arose early in the morning, and built an altar at the foot of the mountain with twelve pillars for the twelve tribes of Israel." Thus, the Mosaic Covenant was made only with the nation of Israel, not with all the nations of the world, and has items specifically for them alone.

> KEY TRUTH: As we will repeatedly see in upcoming verses, the Bible presents the Mosaic Covenant by various synonyms such as "the law of Moses," "Moses wrote," or just "the law."

Among other matters, the Mosaic Covenant establishes the basis for the tabernacle (and later the temple), the Levitical priesthood, the Holy of Holies, and the Ark of the Covenant. Right after the Mosaic Covenant was ratified, God made wonderful and personal promises. In Exodus 25:8, God commanded, "Let them construct a sanctuary for Me, that I may dwell among them." Exodus 25:20–22 adds:

> "The cherubim shall have their wings spread upward, covering the mercy seat with their wings and facing one another; the faces of the cherubim are to be turned toward the mercy seat. You shall put the mercy seat on top of the ark, and in the ark you shall put the testimony which I will give

to you. There I will meet with you; and from above the mercy seat, from between the two cherubim which are upon the ark of the testimony, I will speak to you about all that I will give you in commandment for the sons of Israel."

Later in the same context, God made a promise to do something that He had never done since Genesis 3: He consecrated a specific place with His own glory:

> "I will meet there with the sons of Israel, and it shall be consecrated by My glory. I will consecrate the tent of meeting and the altar; I will also consecrate Aaron and his sons to minister as priests to Me. I will dwell among the sons of Israel and will be their God. They shall know that I am the LORD their God who brought them out of the land of Egypt, that I might dwell among them; I am the LORD their God." (Exod 29:43–46)

FOUNDATIONAL TRUTH: For the first time since Genesis 3, God condescended to dwell among humanity. In Genesis 3, God expelled Adam and Eve from His presence. In Exodus 25, immediately after the ratification of the Mosaic Covenant, God promised His very presence among the people. This is not an Old Testament God of hate (as many claim); these are aspects of God's love and grace—and faithfulness.

Such was God's original plan—and joy and delight: to have fellowship with His people whom He had recently brought to Himself in a special, covenant relationship with Himself.

But Exodus 32:1–6 describes the wretched sin done by the Jewish people only a few days after the ratification of the Mosaic Covenant:

> Now when the people saw that Moses delayed to come down from the mountain, the people assembled about Aaron and said to him, "Come, make us a god who will go before us; as for this Moses, the man who

brought us up from the land of Egypt, we do not know what has become of him." Aaron said to them, "Tear off the gold rings which are in the ears of your wives, your sons, and your daughters, and bring them to me." Then all the people tore off the gold rings which were in their ears, and brought them to Aaron. He took this from their hand, and fashioned it with a graving tool and made it into a molten calf; and they said, "This is your god, O Israel, who brought you up from the land of Egypt."

Now when Aaron saw this, he built an altar before it; and Aaron made a proclamation and said, "Tomorrow shall be a feast to the LORD." So the next day they rose early and offered burnt offerings, and brought peace offerings; and the people sat down to eat and to drink, and rose up to play.

Exodus 32 shows several high-handed sins of covenant disobedience and rebellion under the Mosaic Covenant. God, being fully aware of Israel's sins, informed Moses accordingly:

> Then the LORD spoke to Moses, "Go down at once, for your people, whom you brought up from the land of Egypt, have corrupted themselves. They have quickly turned aside from the way which I commanded them.

> "They have made for themselves a molten calf, and have worshiped it and have sacrificed to it, and said, 'This is your god, O Israel, who brought you up from the land of Egypt!'" The LORD said to Moses, "I have seen this people, and behold, they are an obstinate people. Now then let Me alone, that My anger may burn against them and that I may destroy them; and I will make of you a great nation." (Exod 32:7–10)

Moses responded by interceding for the sinful nation:

> Then Moses entreated the LORD his God, and said, "O LORD, why does Your anger burn against Your people whom You have brought out from the land of Egypt with great power and with a mighty hand? Why should the Egyptians speak, saying, 'With evil intent He brought them out to kill them in the mountains and to destroy them from the face of the earth'? Turn from Your burning anger and change Your mind about doing harm to Your people. Remember Abraham, Isaac, and Israel,

Your servants to whom You swore by Yourself, and said to them, 'I will multiply your descendants as the stars of the heavens, and all this land of which I have spoken I will give to your descendants, and they shall inherit it forever.'"

So the LORD changed His mind about the harm which He said He would do to His people. (Exod 32:11–14)

CORE TRUTH: Moses pleaded with God based on His faithfulness to the Abrahamic Covenant, not the nation's sin under the Mosaic Covenant.

When God offered to Moses to destroy the nation of Israel and start over with him, Moses said in essence and reverently, "You cannot do that, God!" God knew about His covenant with Abraham and that, in spite of Israel's heinous sins, He would remain faithful and true to what He had promised. Moses did not instruct God in this account; this is very much like Jesus asking Philip where they would get enough to feed the multitudes (John 6:1–6), with Jesus fully knowing ahead of time what He would do. Jesus led Philip, and God led Moses into the deductions that each should have.

FOUNDATIONAL TRUTH: Evident in Moses'—and God's— understanding of the promises God had previously made under the Abrahamic Covenant is a literal-grammatical hermeneutic. God did not respond to Moses' interpretation by saying, "You have that all wrong! These are allegorical truths only."

FOUNDATIONAL TRUTH: If God had acted as He said, destroying Israel and starting over with Moses, making him a great nation, then the twelve tribes of Israel would have been destroyed—other than Moses, who was from the tribe of Levi—and thus there would be no Lion from the tribe of Judah, whom God had already promised in Genesis 49:8–12. We who are saved should be extremely thankful to God for being true to all His promises!

Even though Moses had made a successful intervention for the people, as an object lesson God removed His visible presence outside the camp because of this high-handed sin of the nation (Exod 33). Sin kills; it always kills. Sin separates; it always separates. Exodus 34–39 gives instructions for the building of God's tabernacle and the start of the Levitical priesthood. In keeping His word, God ultimately did consecrate His tabernacle with His glory, as seen in Exodus 40:34–38:

> Then the cloud covered the tent of meeting, and the glory of the LORD filled the tabernacle. Moses was not able to enter the tent of meeting because the cloud had settled on it, and the glory of the LORD filled the tabernacle. Throughout all their journeys whenever the cloud was taken up from over the tabernacle, the sons of Israel would set out; but if the cloud was not taken up, then they did not set out until the day when it was taken up. For throughout all their journeys, the cloud of the Lord was on the tabernacle by day, and there was fire in it by night, in the sight of all the house of Israel.

Thus, the book of Exodus ends on both a positive and a negative note. Positively, God is present, and He exhibits an aspect of His glory to the nation of Israel. Negatively, access to God is significantly limited given that His presence resides in the Holy of Holies, a place even Moses was not permitted to enter.

CORE TRUTH: What began in Exodus 40—God being in the Holy of Holies with very limited access to Him—will stay that same way until Matthew 27:50–51: "And Jesus cried out again with a loud voice and yielded up His spirit. And behold, the veil of the temple was torn in two from top to bottom; and the earth shook, and the rocks were split." Much more about this eternally life-altering biblical truth later.

(Ends this section from *The Bible Expositor's Handbook (OT/NT)*, pp. 58–63)

SUMMARY AND CONCLUSION

From this chapter we learned among other things, (1) three times in the Bible Jesus said that it was written about Him (John 5:45–47; Luke 24:27; Luke 24:44); (2) God offered a glimmer of hope in Genesis 3:15 of a future destroyer of the enemy; (3) God used the word *covenant* for the first time in Genesis 6:18, meaning it was a binding, legally recognized agreement between two or more parties. (4) God is the One who ratifies the Noahic Covenant, and each one who ratifies a covenant has responsibilities. Since God speaks in Genesis 9:8–17, He alone ratified the covenant, and He alone has obligations to fulfill; (5) although the word covenant is not stated here, it is used elsewhere. In Genesis 12:1–3, God promised three particular elements that He would give: a land (boundaries not yet given), a seed (or lineage), and a blessing for all the families of the earth; (6) in Genesis 13:14–15, "And the LORD said to Abram, after Lot had separated from him, 'Now lift up your eyes and look from the place where you are, northward and southward and eastward and westward; for all the land which you see, I will give it to you and to your descendants *forever*,'" and we noted that the future tense was used at this point. (7) In Genesis 15, God alone ratified this covenant; God alone has the responsibility to fulfill what He covenanted. In this ratification of the Abrahamic Covenant, no more future tenses are used: "On that day the LORD made a covenant with Abram, saying, 'To your descendants I have given this land, / From the river of Egypt as far as the great river, the river Euphrates'" (Gen 15:18); (8) in Genesis 17:7–8, God is the One who described this as "My Covenant" and "an everlasting covenant," for the land that He gave Abram and his descendants "for an everlasting possession," along with God's own special relationship with them, "and I will be their God; (9) and we saw the crucial truth that the burden of proof is on those who will accept and interpret God's first covenant in Genesis 9 (i.e., the Noahic Covenant) in a literal fashion for everything about it and then switch the hermeneutic so that some or much of the next covenant of God is allegorical. (10) This second covenant is from the same God, the same author, the same book, and the same genre. How, other than a predisposition to bring something to the text, could one arrive at and thrust into the text this new hermeneutic?

Genesis 49 is a chapter that will play a very important part of this book. In this quite-often-overlooked chapter we learned (11) Genesis 49 begins with Jacob being an old man, "Then Jacob summoned his sons and said, 'Assemble yourselves that I may tell you what will befall you in the days to come;'" (12) Genesis 49:28 summarizes: "All these are the twelve tribes of Israel, and this is what their father said to them when he blessed them. He blessed them, everyone with the blessing appropriate to him;" (13) Genesis 49 makes it a biblical impossibility for the Jewish people to be eradicated by an enemy or by collective enemies. Genesis 49:1 and 28 *require* that the twelve tribes of Israel be living and functioning in the last days; (14) Genesis 49:8–12 gives one of the earliest prophecies of the coming Messiah and reveals new details that God had not yet disclosed elsewhere in Scripture, namely, (15) from this point forward, it becomes a biblical mandate that the Messiah, according to God's sovereign decree, must be from the tribe of Judah. So whoever the Messiah is, He must give clear documentation of His lineage—and it must be traced back to the tribe of Judah; (16) this is the first chapter that reveals God's Messiah reigns—"to Him shall be the obedience of the peoples" (Gen 49:10), which is another way of saying that His kingdom will be a worldwide kingdom over all the earth; no people groups, kingdoms, nor individuals will be exempt from His reign and rule; (17) in Genesis 49:22–26 a double blessing comes to Joseph and his lineage due to his faithful walk of holiness and obedience to God. (18) With the promise of the Lion of the tribe of Judah being the Messiah who will reign over the entire world (Gen 49:8–12), come these two further designations regarding God's future Messiah in verse 24: "From the hands of the Mighty One of Jacob (from there is *the Shepherd, the Stone of Israel*);" so two additional descriptions of the Messiah are given in this one verse. (19) Whoever the Messiah is, He must do the work of God's sent Shepherd and God's sent Stone of Israel, and—this is important—He must do so in the last days (Gen 49:1), with the twelve tribes of Israel (v. 28); (20) the promised Messiah sent by God *must* fulfill these prophecies, or else He is *not* the promised Messiah.

For the Mosaic Covenant: (1) the Mosaic Covenant is the only covenant of God so far where somebody else was present and active; (2) unlike the previous two covenants, the Mosaic Covenant is not stated as being everlasting; (3) twice the people claim, "All that the LORD has spoken we will do, and we will be obedient!" yet, as the Bible clearly shows, rare are the times when the people are in covenant obedience to Yahweh; (4) from Exodus 24 onward, as long as the Mosaic Covenant is in effect, national Israel is under covenant obligation to do what God tells them to do. (5) The Mosaic Covenant was made with the twelve tribes of Israel, and thus made with the nation of Israel and not the Gentiles; (6) right after the Mosaic Covenant was ratified in Exodus 24, God made these wonderful promises, beginning with Exodus 25:8, where God commanded, "Let them construct a sanctuary for Me, that I may dwell among them;" (7) For the first time since Genesis 3, God condescended to dwell among humanity. In Genesis 3, God expelled Adam and Eve from His presence. In Exodus 25, immediately after the ratification of the Mosaic Covenant, God promised His very presence among the people. (8) This is not an Old Testament God of hate (as many claim); these are aspects of God's love and grace—and faithfulness.

Sadly, (9) in the Golden Calf rebellion of Exodus 32, when God told Moses that He would wipe out the Jewish people and go through him, (10) Moses reverently argued based on what God had already promised in the Abrahamic Covenant—not on the basis of the Mosaic Covenant. (11) Evident in Moses'—and God's—understanding of the promises God had previously made under the Abrahamic Covenant is a literal-grammatical hermeneutic. God did not respond to Moses' interpretation by saying, "You have that all wrong! These are allegorical truths only." (12) If God had acted as He said, destroying Israel and starting over with Moses, making him a great nation, then the twelve tribes of Israel would have been destroyed—other than Moses, who was from the tribe of Levi—and thus there would be no Lion from the tribe of Judah, whom God had already promised in Genesis 49:8–12. (13) Exodus ends with God's presence in manifestation of God's Glory, but the sad part is no one had free access to Him. Finally, (14) the separation between God and people that began in Exodus 40—God being in the Holy of Holies with very limited access to Him—will stay that same way until Matthew 27:50–51: "And Jesus cried out again with a loud voice and yielded up His spirit. And behold, the veil of the temple was torn in two from top to bottom; and the earth shook, and the rocks were split."

DEEPER WALK STUDY QUESTIONS

1) State five biblical truths about the Noahic Covenant and five about the Abrahamic Covenant. Tell why both of these covenants are so important in understanding Bible interpretation. Be specific.

2) Why does it matter that the words "eternal" or "everlasting" are important to what God promised with the Noahic and Abrahamic covenants? List 10 ways in which this is important theologically.

3) Why is Genesis 49 important? List 10 theological reasons.

4) What prophecies specifically relate to the Messiah in Genesis 49? Name 10 reasons why they matter later on as the biblical account unfolds over the centuries.

5) Name five similarities between the Abrahamic Covenant and the Mosaic Covenant. Why do they matter theologically? Explain in detail. What are five differences between these two covenants? List them very specifically and explain in detail why they matter.

6) Explain in detail why God instructing the people to build His tabernacle in Exodus 25 is important. Give six biblical truths to take from this account.

7) Why did God not destroy the nation of Israel after the Golden Calf rebellion? List four reasons and explain why they matter theologically. How does this account support a literal-grammatical hermeneutic? Give five reasons and be specific about each one.

8) List 10 ways from this chapter that God shows His faithfulness.

9) Make up your own question from the material covered in this chapter. What is the question, and what is the answer, and why are they important biblically? Explain in detail.

CHAPTER TWO

BROADLY SETTING THE BIBLICAL TABLE (PART 2):

THE LAST THREE BOOKS OF MOSES: LEVITICUS, NUMBERS, AND DEUTERONOMY

INTRODUCTION

We began our study by reminding people what Jesus said in reference to Himself in all the Scriptures, as we saw twice in Luke 24 and once again in John 5.

Luke 24:27, "And beginning with Moses and with all the prophets, He explained to them the things concerning Himself in all the Scriptures."

Luke 24:44, "Now He said to them, 'These are My words which I spoke to you while I was still with you, that all things which are written about Me in the Law of Moses and the Prophets and the Psalms must be fulfilled.'"

John 5:45–47, "How can you believe, when you receive glory from one another, and you do not seek the glory that is from the one and only God?

"Do not think that I will accuse you before the Father; the one who accuses you is Moses, in whom you have set your hope. For if you believed Moses, you would believe Me; for he wrote of Me.

"But if you do not believe his writings, how will you believe My words?"

We could not include everything that we wanted to, even in a very broad setting. This chapter begins where we ended last time and continues with vital truths from the last three books of Moses. They will play a significant place in the life of Jesus the Messiah.

THE BLESSING AND THE CURSE[5]

In the ratification of the Mosaic Covenant, when the people of Israel said twice in Exodus 24 (:3 and :7), "All that Yahweh says to do we will do," the people were bound to do anything that Yahweh commanded them to do as long as they were under the Mosaic Covenant. So when God established the sacrifices, the Day of Atonement, and other matters, He was adding these to the long commands or directives of things He would have national Israel observe or do. Once these commands—not suggestions—were given by God, the outcome depended on whether national Israel would be obedient to the LORD. As Scripture and history repeatedly show, the collective Jewish people were usually far from being faithfully obedient.

The term/title "the blessing and the curse"—which will play an incredibly important role in the protection or danger of national Israel—occurs only three times in the Bible, and every time there is *the* definite article in front of each part: "So it shall be when all of these things have come upon you, *the blessing and the curse* which I have set before you, and you call them to mind in all nations where the LORD your God has banished you." (Deut 30:1). These commands are not something broad and evasive; as we will see, they are very specific commands from God and He will use the resulting responses for or against national Israel. The second usage is in the same chapter: "I call heaven and earth to witness against you today, that I have set before you life and death, *the blessing and the curse*. So choose life in order that you may live, you and your descendants" (Deut 30:19). We see in Joshua 8:34, "Then afterward he read all the words of the law, *the blessing and the curse*, according to all that is written in the book of the law." As

---

5   Adapted from *The Bible Expositor's Handbook (OT/NT)*, "The Mosaic Covenant," chapter 5 "The Blessing and the Curse" subsection, 64–68. Used by permission.

we will see, this is essential to national Israel, and they would know what it meant even without having the actual term used.

Even though other parts of the Mosaic Covenant do not have the words "the blessing and the curse," they certainly decribed it in detail, but, as we saw, it will not yet be called "the blessing and the curse" until Deuteronomy 30. Further, these are very specific offers of blessings promised for obedience or very strong warnings that will *come on national Israel* in this section of Scripture—not to the Gentiles at this point—if the Jewish people continued to rebel against Yahweh and His Word. He promised the Jewish people tremendous blessings if they obeyed Him, in Leviticus 26:1–13:

> "You shall not make for yourselves idols, nor shall you set up for yourselves an image or a sacred pillar, nor shall you place a figured stone in your land to bow down to it; for I am the LORD your God. You shall keep My sabbaths and reverence My sanctuary; I am the LORD.

> "If you walk in My statutes and keep My commandments so as to carry them out, then I shall give you rains in their season, so that the land will yield its produce and the trees of the field will bear their fruit. Indeed, your threshing will last for you until grape gathering, and grape gathering will last until sowing time. You will thus eat your food to the full and live securely in your land. I shall also grant peace in the land, so that you may lie down with no one making you tremble. I shall also eliminate harmful beasts from the land, and no sword will pass through your land. But you will chase your enemies, and they will fall before you by the sword; five of you will chase a hundred, and a hundred of you will chase ten thousand, and your enemies will fall before you by the sword.

> "So I will turn toward you and make you fruitful and multiply you, and I will confirm My covenant with you. And you will eat the old supply and clear out the old because of the new. Moreover, I will make My dwelling among you, and My soul will not reject you. I will also walk among you and be your God, and you shall be My people.

> "I am the LORD your God, who brought you out of the land of Egypt so that you would not be their slaves, and I broke the bars of your yoke and made you walk erect."

This blessing section specifically given by God for national Israel included, among many other wonderful blessings from God: bountiful crops, abundant rains, peace in the land, and victories over their enemies. And beyond all these important but subsidiary blessings, God promised to dwell in their midst in rich fellowship.

But none of these blessings were automatic. Leviticus 26:14–39 contains the items pertaining to "the curse" section under the Mosaic Covenant:

> "But if you do not obey Me and do not carry out all these command-ments, if, instead, you reject My statutes, and if your soul abhors My ordinances so as not to carry out all My commandments, and so break My covenant, I, in turn, will do this to you: I will appoint over you a sudden terror, consumption and fever that shall waste away the eyes and cause the soul to pine away; also, you shall sow your seed uselessly, for your enemies shall eat it up. And I will set My face against you so that you shall be struck down before your enemies; and those who hate you shall rule over you, and you shall flee when no one is pursuing you." (Lev 26:14–17)

God foretold that enemies would rule over the nation of Israel if they dis-obeyed Him; if His strong punishment did not draw the sinful people back to Him in repentance and obedience, He promised an intensification of His cursing on them, including severe drought and falling into the hands of their enemies:

> "If also after these things, you do not obey Me, then I will punish you seven times more for your sins. And I will also break down your pride of power; I will also make your sky like iron and your earth like bronze. Your strength shall be spent uselessly, for your land will not yield its produce and the trees of the land will not yield their fruit.

> "If then, you act with hostility against Me and are unwilling to obey Me, I will increase the plague on you seven times according to your sins. I will let loose among you the beasts of the field, which will bereave you of your children and destroy your cattle and reduce your number so that your roads lie deserted.

"And if by these things you are not turned to Me, but act with hostility against Me, then I will act with hostility against you; and I, even I, will strike you seven times for your sins. I will also bring upon you a sword which will execute vengeance for the covenant; and when you gather together into your cities, I will send pestilence among you, so that you shall be delivered into enemy hands. 'When I break your staff of bread, ten women will bake your bread in one oven, and they will bring back your bread in rationed amounts, so that you will eat and not be satisfied.

"Yet if in spite of this, you do not obey Me, but act with hostility against Me, then I will act with wrathful hostility against you; and I, even I, will strike you seven times for your sins." (Lev 26:18–28)

God even promised cannibalism of their own children as part of His curse in Leviticus 26:29–31:

"Further, you will eat the flesh of your sons and the flesh of your daughters you will eat. I then will destroy your high places, and cut down your incense altars, and heap your remains on the remains of your idols; for My soul shall abhor you. I will lay waste your cities as well, and will make your sanctuaries desolate; and I will not smell your soothing aromas."

Although the nation of Israel was not yet in the land God had promised them, God pointed to exile from that land as part of the curse for national Israel if they did not obey Him:

"And I will make the land desolate so that your enemies who settle in it shall be appalled over it. You, however, I will scatter among the nations and will draw out a sword after you, as your land becomes desolate and your cities become waste.

"Then the land will enjoy its sabbaths all the days of the desolation, while you are in your enemies' land; then the land will rest and enjoy its sabbaths. All the days of its desolation it will observe the rest which it did not observe on your sabbaths, while you were living on it. As for those of you who may be left, I will also bring weakness into their hearts in the lands of their enemies. And the sound of a driven leaf will chase them and even when no one is pursuing, they will flee as though from the sword, and they will fall. They will therefore stumble over each other as if running from the sword, although no one is pursuing; and you will have no strength to stand up before your enemies.

"But you will perish among the nations, and your enemies' land will consume you. So those of you who may be left will rot away because of their iniquity in the lands of your enemies; and also because of the iniquities of their forefathers they will rot away with them." (Lev 26:32–39)

The blessing-or-the-curse section was an either/or choice for national Israel; God proposed no additional options to the Jewish people: obey Me, and I will bless you; disobey Me, and these are the curses that will most certainly come upon you. As you read through the Old Testament, virtually every item of God's promised curse is shown in the Bible's account of sinful national Israel, especially in books such as Judges and 1 and 2 Kings. What's more, these promises make perfect sense within a literal-grammatical hermeneutic—not with an allegorical interpretation.

However, the blessing section of Leviticus 26:1–13 and the curse section in 26:14–39 are not the only parts of what God promised. In Leviticus 26:43–46, God looked many centuries beyond and made additional promises to the same Jewish people, even after He had sent them into exile:

"For the land will be abandoned by them, and will make up for its sabbaths while it is made desolate without them. They, meanwhile, will be making amends for their iniquity, because they rejected My ordinances and their soul abhorred My statutes. Yet in spite of this, when they are in the land of their enemies, I will not reject them, nor will I so abhor them as to destroy them, breaking My covenant with them; for I am the LORD their God.

"But I will remember for them the covenant with their ancestors, whom I brought out of the land of Egypt in the sight of the nations, that I might be their God. I am the LORD.'"

These are the statutes and ordinances and laws which the LORD established between Himself and the sons of Israel through Moses at Mount Sinai.

FOUNDATIONAL TRUTHS: The blessing or the curse became a spiritual barometer for national Israel as long as they were under the Mosaic Covenant. Nothing merely happened; God remained true to His Word. If the nation was under famine, such as in Ruth 1:1 ("Now it came about in the days when the judges governed, that there was a famine in the land"), the problem was not a weather problem. The true problem was lack of obedience to Yahweh. In the same way, whenever Israel was defeated in battle (such as at Ai, in Joshua 7), the problem was not a military problem; the problem was a lack of covenant obedience to Yahweh under the Mosaic Covenant.

NOTE AS WELL: Since "the blessing and the curse" is under the Mosaic Covenant and is limited to national Israel, famines or military defeats anywhere else or at any other time in history are totally unrelated. For instance, a famine in Egypt or Ethiopia in biblical times or a famine in the United States or elsewhere has nothing to do with the Mosaic Covenant promises that God made to national Israel under "the blessing and the curse."

A STAR! A STAR! SHINING IN THE NIGHT!

When I started writing *The Bible Expositor's Handbook (OT)*, this chapter was—and it remains—one of my all-time favorite chapters of anything I have ever written. Thank you again, B & H Academic, for letting me use some of the abbreviated material for this current chapter. If I were forced somehow to narrow down to only one chapter to read from the Old Testament edition—which is incredibly difficult to do—it would be from be from pp. 73–87, *The Bible Expositor's Handbook (OT/NT)*, "A Star! A Star! Shining in the Night!" I strongly urge everyone to read this biblical gold mine that God gave us in His Word.

Anyone who has ever preached about the spectacular events associated with the birth of Jesus or has participated in a nativity scene or has been in a Christmas pageant is aware of the account of the wise men who followed a revelatory star. Matthew 2:1–2 states, "Now after Jesus was born in Bethlehem of Judea in the days of Herod the king, magi from the east arrived in Jerusalem, saying, 'Where is He who has been born King of the Jews? For we saw His star in the east and have come to worship Him.'" Those who check biblical cross-references or read commentaries will see that most scholars link this verse with one in the Old Testament, Numbers 24:17, "I see him but not now; / I behold him, but not near; / A star shall come forth from Jacob, / A scepter shall rise from Israel." To preach about the wise men and the star they followed and to cross-reference it to Numbers 24:17 is certainly valid. But one should not overlook other prophetic Scriptures that likewise point to the person and work of Jesus Christ. Numbers 24:17 comes toward the end of a section of promises; we risk leaving out so much God-given gold if we start and end with that one verse. In this chapter we will explore the ways in which Scripture progressively builds upon itself by harmonizing with, and expanding upon, previous promises that God has given. This broader view of Scripture, then, will expand our understanding of the fulfillment of God's promises through Christ. (p. 73)

We will include some of the biblical truth that we covered, but there is much more left out, so I highly recommend that you read the entire chapter of *The Bible Expositor's Handbook (OT/NT)* version. Below is an abbreviated synopsis of the truths within:

As was noted in a previous chapter, there is clear biblical evidence that the reference to Judah as a lion refers specifically to Jesus Christ. In Revelation 5, after the apostle John has been transported in a vision to heaven, he sees a sealed scroll and somehow knows that until that scroll is opened and completed, Satan will still continue his work, and the Messiah's reign will never come. John is instructed by one of the twenty-four elders in this vision in Revelation 5:5, "Stop weeping; behold, the Lion that is from the tribe of Judah, the Root of David, has overcome so as to open the book and its seven seals." Those of us who accept the inerrancy of God's Word know that this description of Jesus comes directly from the prophetic truths in Genesis 49, and these things must come to pass in the end of the days or the last days. (p. 75)

THE THEOLOGICAL
SIGNIFICANCE OF NUMBERS 22–24

We started in Numbers 24:17, but Numbers 22–24 is one section of Scripture that contains four separate prophetic sections. Taken together, these chapters record the attempt of a Gentile king—Balak—to hire a "somewhat-of-a-prophet" named Balaam to curse Israel for him. Within this context, God chose to reveal sublime prophecies of the coming Messiah. While we cannot here deal with all the particulars of Numbers 22–24, four vital truths are easily seen in this section of Scripture: (1) The oracles in Numbers 22–24 are God's Word, not Balaam's word. (2) The text repeatedly refers to national Israel as a people. (3) The blessing or cursing of Numbers 22–24 is based on the Abrahamic Covenant promises. (4) The unfolding revelatory light concerning the promised Messiah expands and harmonizes with God's previous promises.

#1: THE ORACLES IN NUMBERS 22–24 ARE
YAHWEH'S WORD—NOT BALAAM'S WORD

Although it is common to label these chapters as "Balaam's Oracles" or "the Oracles of Balaam," this is not how God viewed these prophecies. The wonderful promises and revelation that occur in these chapters are neither Balaam's thoughts nor his opinions, nor do they transpire by means of any learned technique on his part; he was simply a mouthpiece for God to communicate these holy truths. Repeatedly, the text emphasizes that these are the very words of God. For instance, God told Balaam to go with the king's emissaries, "but only the word which I speak to you shall you do" (Num 22:20). After Balaam's terrifying experience with the Angel of the Lord (the same Angel of the Lord we have previously seen in Genesis 16 and 22 and Exodus 3), God warned Balaam, "Go with the men, but you shall speak only the word which I tell you" (Num 22:35). Numbers 23:5 states, "The LORD put a word in Balaam's mouth and said ..." concurring with Numbers 23:16, "The LORD met Balaam and put [an oracle] in his mouth," again instructing him precisely what he must speak to Balak. In Numbers 24:2 the text states that "the Spirit of God came upon [Balaam]," so when Balaam spoke the word of God, he spoke just what the text says: the word of God. Consequently, any attempts to downplay the importance of what is revealed in these chapters should not be accepted; they are the very words of God Himself. The word of God given by means of Balaam in Numbers 22–24 should be received as you would receive any other part of the word of God elsewhere in Scripture.

KEY TRUTH: God is not limited by the frail and sinful human containers in the giving and receiving of God's Word. Paul wrote in 2 Corinthians 4:7, "But we have this treasure in earthen vessels, so that the surpassing greatness of the power will be of God and not from ourselves." No matter who the best holy prophet or apostle of God was, it would still require divine inspiration to bring into being God's Word, because His Word would never originate in the hearts or minds of fallen humanity.

CONSIDER ALSO: When giving His revelation, neither is God limited by fallen humans who oppose Him and are lost and dead in their sins. Anyone who thinks it is impossible for God to use someone such as Balaam as a means of receiving and expressing His divine revelation should consider the account given in John 11:47–52:

Therefore the chief priests and the Pharisees convened a council, and were saying, "What are we doing? For this Man is performing many signs.

"If we let Him go on like this, all men will believe in Him, and the Romans will come and take away both our place and our nation." But one of them, Caiaphas, who was high priest that year, said to them, "You know nothing at all, nor do you take into account that it is expedient for you that one Man die for the people, and that the whole nation not perish." Now he did not say this on his own initiative; but being high priest that year, he prophesied that Jesus was going to die for the nation, and not for the nation only, but in order that He might also gather together into one the children of God who are scattered abroad."

#2 NATIONAL ISRAEL AS A PEOPLE OCCURS REPEATEDLY WITHIN THE TEXT

Many believe there is no indication in the text of Genesis 12:1–3 that the promise to bless the ones who blessed Abraham and the warning about those who cursed him was ever intended to extend beyond Abraham. However, this is a presupposition forced on the text and certainly not one derived from it. The designation of the nation of Israel as a people occurs frequently in Numbers 22–24. For instance, in the immediate context there was a "great fear because of the people" [of Israel] (Num 22:3). Numbers 22:5 gives this description by King Balak: "a people came out of Egypt; behold, they cover the surface of the land, and they are living opposite me," following this request for Balaam to "come, curse this people" (Num 22:6, 17). Before beginning one of the God-given oracles, Balaam saw "a portion of the people" (Num 22:41). Elsewhere, God by means of Balaam describes Israel as "a people who dwells apart" (Num 23:9) and "a people [that] rises like a lioness" (Num 23:24).

Of infinitely more importance was Yahweh's own statement in Numbers 22:12 as He instructed Balaam concerning the nation of Israel's present status before Him, "God said to Balaam, 'Do not go with them; you shall not curse the people, for they are blessed.'" God considered the blessing that He had given Abraham as still operative for the Jewish nation at this time and certainly not restricted only to Abraham. The nation of Israel's current status was that "they are blessed" before Him because of the unfailing love and the covenant promises given by Yahweh.

Finally, beyond the present, God, by means of Balaam, informed Balak and others what would transpire in the future: "And now, behold, I am going to My people; come, and I will advise you what this people will do to your people in the days to come" (Num 24:14). The significance of this verse will be developed in chapter 10 of this book. Suffice it to say, the burden of proof is on those who want to remove any of the references made to the people of Israel instead of understanding the verse in its normative way.

#3 THE BLESSING OR CURSING OF NUMBERS 22–24 IS THE HEART OF THE ABRAHAMIC COVENANT PROMISES

Balak's request to have Balaam curse Israel is more than just an inappropriate choice of words: this story would reveal the very heart of whether God's promises to national Israel were still in force. Based on the three victories found in Numbers 21, Numbers 22–24 is one unit that develops in more detail the same theology with the repeated emphasis throughout this account of either blessing or cursing.

While the immediate context for Numbers 22–24 is the three military victories that God granted in Numbers 21, the earlier context from the Exodus onward has not spoken well of Israel as a whole. It includes such things as the evil reporting by the spies and God's subsequent judging of that generation (Num 13–14), Korah's rebellion (Num 16), and Moses' sinning by striking the rock the second time (Num 20). Thus, this important theological issue should not be overlooked: in spite of Israel's sins, Yahweh still would honor His Word. Even more to the point, Genesis 12:3 ("And I will bless those who bless you, / And the one who curses you I will curse. / And in you all the families of the earth shall be blessed") becomes the basis for the Balak-Balaam encounter and an indicator of whether God considered the promises He had previously made to be understood in a literal or spiritual fashion.

Numbers 22:1–3 explains Moab's fear, after the victories Yahweh had recently given Israel:

> Then the sons of Israel journeyed, and camped in the plains of Moab beyond the Jordan opposite Jericho. Now Balak the son of Zippor saw all that Israel had done to the Amorites. So Moab was in great fear because of the people, for they were numerous; and Moab was in dread of the sons of Israel.

Balak's invitation to Balaam came with a specific purpose: "Now, therefore, please come, curse this people for me since they are too mighty for me; perhaps I may be able to defeat them and drive them out of the land. For I know that he whom you bless is blessed, and he whom you curse is cursed" (Num 22:6). This statement cannot be true, for Genesis 12:3 has already indicated that blessing and cursing are exclusively reserved to be pronounced by Yahweh, especially as it relates to national Israel.

God appeared to Balaam warning him, "Do not go with them; you shall not curse the people; for they are blessed" (Num 22:12). Notice that Yahweh considered the Jewish people then currently blessed, with the basis of this blessing originating from the Abrahamic Covenant, not the people's repeated failure at keeping the Mosaic Covenant. So Balak's second plea for Balaam to curse the people was met by Balaam's response in Numbers 22:18: "I could not do anything, either small or great, contrary to the command of the LORD my God" which, as subsequent events will show, was not a true indication of Balaam's spiritual status. Nonetheless, Balaam was accurate in his statement about not being able to speak contrary to God's Word or God's will.

Balak's second attempt to have Balaam curse Israel follows the episode of Balaam, his donkey, and the terrifying presence of the Angel of the Lord, with drawn sword in hand (Num 22:22–34). The Angel sent Balaam to Balak, but strongly warned him to speak only what God revealed to him (Num 22:35–41). Thus, Balaam pronounced a discourse directly from the Lord (Num 23:5). When Balak requested, "Come curse Jacob for me" (Num 23:7), Balaam had no response other than "How shall I curse whom God has not cursed? / And how can I denounce whom the LORD has not denounced?" (Num 23:8). Consequently, Numbers 22–24 should not be considered as some minor offense against Yahweh, but rather as an attempt to encroach on the domain and territory—and attributes—of God.

Another attempt at cursing Israel was just as futile as the others (Num 23:11–30). Again, "the LORD met Balaam and put a word in his mouth" (Num 23:16). Within the discourse that follows, the famous verse Numbers 23:19 occurs: "God is not a man, that He should lie, / Nor a son of man, that He should repent; / Has He said, and will He not do it? / Or has He spoken, and will He not make it good?" From Genesis 1:1 through Numbers 23:19, other than items yet to be fulfilled (e.g., Lev 26:40–45), God has done all that He has promised and has made good every bit of His Word. Not only has Yahweh repeatedly done what He said He would do, but He Himself is the One who said, "You shall not curse the people, for they are blessed" (Num 22:12), based on His own previous blessing of them.

#4 THE UNFOLDING REVELATORY LIGHT CONCERNING THE PROMISED MESSIAH EXPANDS AND HARMONIZES WITH GOD'S PREVIOUS PROMISES

Time and space limitations do not permit a fuller treatment of all pertinent texts up through Numbers 24 regarding God's promises. However, three chapters in particular relate to God's promises in Numbers 24: Genesis 22, 27, and 49.

First, Genesis 22:16–18 recounts the additional revelation from God regarding the promised seed, after the Angel of the Lord abruptly stopped Abraham from sacrificing his own son:

> "By Myself I have sworn," declares the LORD, "because you have done this thing, and have not withheld your son, your only son, indeed I will greatly bless you, and I will greatly multiply your seed as the stars of the heavens and as the sand which is on the seashore; and your seed shall possess the gate of their enemies. In your seed all the nations of the earth shall be blessed, because you have obeyed My voice."

Years later Yahweh appeared to Abraham's son Isaac and made further promises in Genesis 26:24: "The LORD appeared to him the same night and said, 'I am the God of your father Abraham; / Do not fear, for I am with you. / I will bless you, and multiply your descendants, / For the sake of My servant Abraham.'" Isaac later reaffirmed to his son Jacob what God previously had promised:

> "Now may God give you of the dew of heaven,
> And of the fatness of the earth,
> And an abundance of grain and new wine;
> May peoples serve you,
> And nations bow down to you;
> Be master of your brothers,
> And may your mother's sons bow down to you.
> Cursed be those who curse you,
> And blessed be those who bless you." (Gen 27:28–29)

By the time of the events of Numbers, God has already revealed much more definitive information regarding His promised Messiah. For instance, as we saw, Genesis 49 adds additional revelation not only regarding Israel, but also regarding specific prophecies related to the future promised Messiah who will reign over the nations. These same truths are found and expanded in Numbers. Within these oracles that God gave came a developing clarity about the identity of the One to come. Numbers 23:21 states, "The LORD his God is with him, / And the shout of a king is among them." We should note the significance of this extremely important prophecy: centuries before Saul reigned as Israel's first king, God had already revealed in Numbers the future King/Messiah who would have an extremely close relationship with the LORD. Of course, God revealed more and more biblical truths about exactly how close that relationship was in eternity past and into eternity future.

With a glimpse into the future, God also explained how He currently viewed national Israel in spite of their multiple high-handed sins: "For there is no omen against Jacob, / Nor is there any divination against Israel; / At the proper time it shall be said to Jacob / And to Israel, what God has done!" (Num 23:23). Ever the slow learner, King Balak hoped that perhaps another change in location would render a different result (Num 23:25–30). This sets the stage for the magnificent divine revelation of Numbers 24, the emphasis again being that this is ultimately God's Word—not Balaam's—as "the Spirit of God came upon him" (Num 24:2).

Among other things, God through Balaam promised:

"He will devour the nations [Gentiles] who are his adversaries,
And will crush their bones in pieces,
And shatter them with his arrows.
He couches, he lies down as a lion,
And as a lion, who dares rouse him?" (Num 24:8–9)

Immediately after a pronouncement of what the Messiah will eventually do to His adversaries, we see the reiteration of God's earlier promise in Genesis 12:3, now stated in Numbers 24:9: "Blessed is everyone who blesses you, / And cursed is everyone who curses you." In Numbers 24, the focus turns to God's promise to deliver Israel in the future, especially by means of His own deliverer (see Num 24:8).

Within this same passage another marvelous Messianic preview occurs:

"I see him, but not now;
I behold him, but not near.
A star shall come forth from Jacob,
A scepter shall rise from Israel,
And shall crush through the forehead of Moab,
And tear down all the sons of Sheth.
Edom shall be a possession,
Seir, its enemies, also will be a possession,
While Israel performs valiantly.
One from Jacob shall have dominion,
And will destroy the remnant from the city." (Num 24:17–19)

The tremendous significance of these verses should not be understated, particularly as it relates to the future work of the One of whom the prophecy speaks. Again, the future aspect reveals not only that the Messiah will fight; it also reveals the enemies against whom He and His descendants will fight.

If we keep the promises made by God from Genesis through Numbers 24 in mind, a composite sketch of the promised Messiah emerges. The future King will have the service of an obedient Israel (Gen 27:29; 49:8) whom He has brought back into the land in accordance with His covenant faithfulness (Lev 26:40–45). This King will ultimately rule over the nations as well (Gen 49:10; Num 24:17–19), will possess the gates of His enemies (Gen 22:17), will have His hand on the neck of His enemies (Gen 49:8), and will exercise dominion over them (Num 24:19). Both Genesis 49 and Numbers 24 depict the promised King as fierce, crouching and lying down like a lion whom no one will dare to rouse (Gen 49:9; Num 24:9), and—most significantly—it is through this promised individual King that both the blessing and the cursing will come in its fullness (Gen 12:3; 27:29; Num 24:9).

It is difficult to argue that God considered His promise to curse those who curse Israel as having been completed during Abraham's lifetime, since the core issue to bless or curse national Israel occurs repeatedly in Numbers 22–24 and is part of the rationale for God's instruction to Balaam and the revelation about the nation, the coming Messiah, and His future reign as King. Not only is the Genesis 12:3 promise to bless or curse still present and operative, but God also expands His previous revelation to include the Messiah as both a beneficiary of the promise *and* the ultimate means by which these prophetic promises will be fulfilled. Those who would spiritualize these promises would have to answer the following questions: (1) Should all, any, or only some of the promises that God gave in Numbers 22–24 be taken as literal promises? (2) On what basis should they be considered as either literal or spiritual? (3) Most important, if the promises that God made and expanded in these chapters are not literal truths regarding the nation of Israel and the Messiah, exactly what did God mean by reaffirming and expanding the promises in these passages, using language very similar or identical to that used previously?

KEY CONSIDERATION: Those who take Numbers 24:17 to be a reference to Jesus the Messiah and the star announcing His birth must give a good biblical reason not to understand the other elements of this prophecy through a literal-grammatical hermeneutic as well.

These wonderful chapters of Numbers 22–24, although unknown to most Christians, would have been a significant part of John 5:46, "Moses wrote about Me," and part of the teaching mentioned twice in Luke 24: Jesus "beginning with Moses" and speaking of things concerning Himself.

THE SPIRITUAL RESULTS
IN THE FUTURE FOR NATION ISRAEL
IN DEUTERONOMY 30:1–10

The opening verse contains the phrase we should be used to by now, namely "the blessing and the curse" (Deut 30:1), and we will deal more with this information later. God gave His Word concerning the promised land in Leviticus 26:40–46, but Deuteronomy 30 reveals the spiritual condition necessary for God to bless national Israel. Deuteronomy 30 (unlike Lev 26) includes the words "the blessing and the curse" and also looks to the effects of the New Covenant at some undisclosed point in the future. In future chapters, we will tie these verses in with more information.

> "So it shall be when all of these things have come upon you, the blessing and the curse which I have set before you, and you call them to mind in all nations where the LORD your God has banished you, and you return to the LORD your God and obey Him with all your heart and soul according to all that I command you today, you and your sons, then the LORD your God will restore you from captivity, and have compassion on you, and will gather you again from all the peoples where the LORD your God has scattered you. If your outcasts are at the ends of the earth, from there the LORD your God will gather you, and from there He will bring you back.

And the LORD your God will bring you into the land which your fathers possessed, and you shall possess it; and He will prosper you and multiply you more than your fathers.

"Moreover the LORD your God will circumcise your heart and the heart of your descendants, to love the LORD your God with all your heart and with all your soul, in order that you may live.

"And the LORD your God will inflict all these curses on your enemies and on those who hate you, who persecuted you.

"And you shall again obey the LORD, and observe all His commandments which I command you today. Then the LORD your God will prosper you abundantly in all the work of your hand, in the offspring of your body and in the offspring of your cattle and in the produce of your ground, for the LORD will again rejoice over you for good, just as He rejoiced over your fathers; if you obey the LORD your God to keep His commandments and His statutes which are written in this book of the law, if you turn to the LORD your God with all your heart and soul."

All of these remain unfulfilled promises for now, until God sees fit to fulfill them in the future, mostly through the Person and work of God's future Messiah.

SUMMARY AND CONCLUSION

From this chapter, we learned among other things: (1) The term/title "the blessing and the curse"—which will play an incredibly important role in the protection or danger of national Israel—occurs only three times where the Bible actually uses this description, and every time there is *the* definite article in front of each part: "So it shall be when all of these things have come upon you, *the blessing and the curse* which I have set before you, and you call them to mind in all nations where the LORD your God has banished you…" (Deut 30:1); (2) For instance, Leviticus 26 is the first detailed issuing of "the blessing and the curse" as part of the Mosaic Covenant, but, as we saw, it will not yet be called "the blessing and the curse" until Deuteronomy 30; (3) These are very specific offers for blessings promised for obedience or very strong warnings of what will come on national Israel if they continue to rebel against Yahweh and His Word; (4) This blessing section specifically given by God for national Israel included bountiful crops, abundant rains, peace in the land, and victories over their enemies, among many other wonderful blessings from God; (5) Leviticus 26:14–39 contains the items pertaining to "the curse" section of the Mosaic Covenant: God foretold that enemies would rule over the nation of Israel if they disobeyed Him; if His strong punishment did not draw the sinful people back to Him in repentance and obedience, He promised an intensification of His cursing on them, including severe drought and falling into the hands of their enemies; (6) Although the nation of Israel was not yet in the land God had promised them, God pointed to exile from that land as part of the curse for national Israel if they did not obey Him; (7) The "blessing and the curse" section was an either/or choice for national Israel; God proposed no additional options to the Jewish people—simply obey Me, and I will bless you; disobey Me, and these are the curses that will most certainly come upon you; (8) However, the blessing section of Leviticus 26:1–13 and the curse section in 26:14–39 are not all that God promised. In Leviticus 26:40–46, God looked many centuries beyond and made additional promises to the same Jewish people, even after He had sent them into exile. He promised to bring them back to the land He had promised them in the Abrahamic Covenant; (9) The blessing or the curse became a spiritual barometer for national Israel as long as the Jewish people were under the Mosaic Covenant.

In the "A Star! A Star!" section is the account where the magi asked, (10) "Where is He who has been born King of the Jews? For we saw His star in the east, and have come to worship Him." (11) Those who check biblical cross-references or read commentaries will see that most scholars link this verse with Numbers 24:17, "I see him but not now; / I behold him, but not near; / A star shall come forth from Jacob, / A scepter shall rise from Israel." (12) But, one should not overlook other prophetic Scriptures that likewise point to the person and work of Jesus Christ. Numbers 24:17 comes toward the end of a section of promises; we risk leaving out much God-given gold if we start and end with that one verse; (13) While we were not able to deal with all the particulars of Numbers 22–24, four vital truths are easily seen in this section of Scripture: (a) The oracles in Numbers

22–24 are God's Word, not Balaam's word; (b) The text repeatedly refers to national Israel as a people; (c) The blessing or cursing of Numbers 22–24 is the heart of the Abrahamic Covenant promises; (d) The unfolding revelatory light concerning the promised Messiah expands and harmonizes with God's previous promises.

(14) Yahweh's own statement is in Numbers 22:12 as He instructed Balaam concerning the nation of Israel's present status before Him. "God said to Balaam, 'Do not go with them; you shall not curse the people, for they are blessed.'" (15) The nation of Israel's current status was that "they are blessed" before Him because of the unfailing love and the covenant promises given by Yahweh. (16) Balak's invitation to Balaam came with a specific purpose: "Now, therefore, please come, curse this people for me since they are too mighty for me; perhaps I may be able to defeat them and drive them out of the land. For I know that he whom you bless is blessed, and he whom you curse is cursed" (Num 22:6). This statement cannot be true, for Genesis 12:3 has already indicated that blessing and cursing are exclusively in purview of the Godhead. (17) Numbers 23:21 states, "The LORD his God is with him, / And the shout of a king is among them." We should note the significance of this extremely important prophecy: centuries before Saul reigned as Israel's first king, God had already revealed in Numbers the future King/Messiah who would have an extremely close relationship with the Lord.

Ever the slow learner, King Balak hoped that perhaps another change in location would render a different result (Num 23:25–30). (18) This sets the stage for the magnificent divine revelation of Numbers 24, the emphasis again being that this is ultimately God's word—not Balaam's—as "the Spirit of God came upon him" (Num 24:2). (19) Among other things, God through Balaam promised:

"He will devour the nations [Gentiles] who are his adversaries,
And will crush their bones in pieces,
And shatter them with his arrows.
He couches, he lies down as a lion,
And as a lion, who dares rouse him?" (Num 24:8–9)

(20) Immediately after a pronouncement of what the Messiah will eventually do to His adversaries, we see the reiteration of God's earlier promise in Genesis 12:3, now stated in Numbers 24:9: "Blessed is everyone who blesses you, / And cursed is everyone who curses you."

Finally, (21) if we keep the promises made by God from Genesis through Numbers 24 in mind, a composite sketch of the promised Messiah emerges. The future King will have the service of an obedient Israel (Gen 27:29; 49:8) whom He has brought back into the land in accordance with His covenant faithfulness (Lev 26:40–45). This King will ultimately rule over the nations as well (Gen 49:10; Num 24:17–19), will possess the gates of His enemies (Gen 22:17), will have His hand on the neck of His enemies (Gen 49:8), and will exercise dominion over them (Num 24:19). Both Genesis 49 and Numbers 24 depict the promised King as fierce, crouching and lying down like a lion whom no one will dare to rouse (Gen 49:9; Num 24:9), and—most significantly—it is through this promised individual King that both the blessing and the cursing will come in its fullness (Gen 12:3; 27:29; Num 24:9).

So (22) in the section of Numbers 22–24 not only is the Genesis 12:3 promise to bless or curse still present and operative, but also God expands His previous revelation to include the Messiah as both a beneficiary of the promise *and* the ultimate means by which these prophetic promises will be fulfilled.

DEEPER WALK STUDY QUESTIONS

1) The term/title "the blessing and the curse"—which will play an incredibly important role in the protection or danger of national Israel—occurs in the Bible only three times, and every time there is *the* definite article in front of each part. List five reasons how/why this wording is important.

2) Why are "the blessing and the curse" not for other nations? Explain. Name seven positive ways and seven negative ways the promises of God here affect Israel. Be specific.

3) How is the exile specifically related to the blessing and the curse of Leviticus 26/Deuteronomy 28? Give five specific doctrinal truths regarding this and especially how this would relate to Israel's future.

4) Where was the nation geographically when God gave the people "the blessing and the curse?" Why was this important for the children of the wilderness generation? Also, how many options did God give to national Israel about "the blessing and the curse"? Write five spiritual lessons that can be learned from this.

5) Name 8 biblical truths from Genesis 26:40–45 and why this is important to future biblical studies. Be specific.

6) Name 10 biblical truths from Numbers 22–24 and explain why they are important even today.

7) How does Balak's desire for Balaam to curse Israel infringe on God's domain? List six reasons why this is important, and be specific.

8) From Genesis up to Numbers 24, give 10 points of what the Word of God promises the future King/Messiah will do. Be specific and write a brief summary paragraph of why these truths are important to know.

9) Ask your own question and then write an answer to that question.

CHAPTER THREE

BROADLY SETTING THE BIBLICAL TABLE (PART 3):

FROM THE ESTABLISHMENT OF THE KINGSHIP UNTIL THE BABYLONIAN EXILE

INTRODUCTION

When God ratified the Mosaic Covenant with newly-redeemed national Israel in Exodus 24:1–8, the Jewish people said twice (paraphrasing), "All that Yahweh/the Lord has spoken, we will do." As we saw, that was an extremely short-lived promise, as the people became involved in the "golden calf" rebellion (Exod 32), and God punished them accordingly. As we saw in the last chapter, although it is not until Deuteronomy 30:1 that it is called "*the* blessing and *the* curse"—and remember: not "*a* blessing and *a* curse"—God was very specific with what He promised national Israel in both, at first, to the ones redeemed from Egypt (Lev 26), and then later, after the wilderness generation died away because of their high-handed sins. God gave their children virtually the same option and obligation (some of Deut 27; all of Deut 28): obey the Lord and be blessed by Him, or live in covenant disobedience and be cursed by God. As is true so many times in Scripture, God offered the people two options only—not twenty. It is also vital to note that God made the Mosaic Covenant only with the national Jewish people/Israel, not with the Gentiles, as Exodus 24:4 clearly shows:

> And Moses wrote down all the words of the LORD. Then he arose early in the morning, and built an altar at the foot of the mountain with twelve pillars for the twelve tribes of Israel.

We also saw the blessing that would come for national Israel when they obeyed the LORD. His promise to them in Leviticus 26:6–8 was the basis for Israel's peace and victories over their enemies:

> "I shall also grant peace in the land, so that you may lie down with no one making you tremble. I shall also eliminate harmful beasts from the land, and no sword will pass through your land. But you will chase your enemies, and they will fall before you by the sword; five of you will chase a hundred, and a hundred of you will chase ten thousand, and your enemies will fall before you by the sword."

Deuteronomy 28:7 repeats the promise by God when Israel is in obedience: "The LORD will cause your enemies who rise up against you to be defeated before you; they shall come out against you one way and shall flee before you seven ways." And, Deuteronomy 28:11 shows again how God viewed His land and to whom He had promised it: "And the LORD will make you abound in prosperity, in the offspring of your body and in the offspring of your beast and in the produce of your ground, in the land which the LORD swore to your fathers to give you."

Victory in warfare against national Israel's enemies was never intended to be automatic nor did Yahweh promise it if the nation lived in a sinful state before Him—and, in fact, certain defeat was guaranteed in that situation. Just a few references from "the curse section" of Leviticus 26 and Deuteronomy 28 plainly show this. God promised: "And I will set My face against you so that you shall be struck down before your enemies; and those who hate you shall rule over you, and you shall flee when no one is pursuing you" (Lev 26:17), and from the same curse section came this similar promise from God: "I will also bring upon you a sword which will execute vengeance for the [Mosaic] covenant; and when you gather together into your cities, I will send pestilence among you, so that you shall be delivered into enemy hands" (Lev 26:25). Deuteronomy 28:25–26 reveals with no hidden language some of the consequences if Israel rebelled against Yahweh:

> "The LORD will cause you to be defeated before your enemies; you shall go out one way against them, but you shall flee seven ways before them, and you shall be an example of terror to all the kingdoms of the earth. And your carcasses shall be food to all birds of the sky and to the beasts of the earth, and there shall be no one to frighten them away."

Even the curse section, or such other verses that talk about the destruction of national Israel, must be viewed through the lens of what God had already promised, such as the eternal promises of the Abrahamic Covenant, in Genesis 17:7–8:

> "And I will establish My covenant between Me and you and your descendants after you throughout their generations *for an everlasting covenant*, to be God to you and to your descendants after you.

> "And I will give to you and to your descendants after you, the land of your sojournings, all the land of Canaan, *for an everlasting possession*; and I will be their God."

Add to this messianic promises made specifically for the twelve tribes of Israel in the last days, which include the Lion from the tribe of Judah, and the Shepherd, the Stone of Israel (Gen. 49:1, 28, 8–12, 24). Based totally on God's mercy, His eternal plans for the Jews, and ultimately the entire world, are all done only by God's grace and His faithfulness to His Word, especially the covenants He made.

So, Israel did not need a king, for God would lead them to battle and to victory if they obeyed Him, and the same God would stand as their enemy to defeat them if they lived in disobedience to the Mosaic Covenant. Consequently, and of great importance, for national Israel, military victory or defeat was always a spiritual matter. So not only did the Jewish people not need a king, it would be a high-handed sin of blatant rebellion if they even asked for one.

And then—that is precisely what the Jewish people did.

THE INITIAL INSTRUCTIONS ABOUT THE KINGSHIP FOR THE JEWISH PEOPLE ARE FOUND IN THE PENTATEUCH

As long as the Jewish people were under the Mosaic Covenant, it meant that they were responsible to obey Yahweh completely in everything He commanded until He told them otherwise. So the "whatever the LORD said we will do," did not stop at Exodus 24 but went all the way over to the New Testament. Still speaking to those under the Mosaic Covenant, God directed them thusly, in Deuteronomy 17:14–15:

> "When you enter the land which the LORD your God gives you, and you possess it and live in it, and you say, 'I will set a king over me like all the nations who are around me,' you shall surely set a king over you whom the LORD your God chooses, one from among your countrymen you shall set as king over yourselves; you may not put a foreigner over yourselves who is not your countryman."

Fast forward a few centuries to 1 Samuel 8:1–5, and it reads like it was only a few days rather than hundreds of years between the accounts:

> And it came about when Samuel was old that he appointed his sons judges over Israel. Now the name of his first-born was Joel, and the name of his second, Abijah; they were judging in Beersheba. His sons, however, did not walk in his ways, but turned aside after dishonest gain and took bribes and perverted justice.
>
> Then all the elders of Israel gathered together and came to Samuel at Ramah; and they said to him, "Behold, you have grown old, and your sons do not walk in your ways. Now [*just as God in Deuteronomy 17:14 had said they would do*] appoint a king for us to judge us like all the nations."

First Samuel 8:6 states: "But the thing was displeasing in the sight of Samuel when they said, 'Give us a king to judge us.' And Samuel prayed to the LORD"—this should have been displeasing not only to Samuel, but to the people as well. This request for a king was a brazen and heinous sin against Yahweh and their agreement *and* obligations under the Mosaic covenant, for asking for a king in order to be like other nations was a rejection of God's rule over them. If I were Samuel, I would have asked them which of the pagan nations surrounding them they wanted to be like. All of them had pagan deities and many had child sacrifices to their gods. When the nation was living in national covenant disobedience—which they were—the curse part of "the blessing and the curse" promised them certain defeat. The *only* possibility for national Israel was being obedient to Him, and He would lead them in victory.

Back to the original verses we saw in Deuteronomy 17:14–15:

> "When you enter the land which the LORD your God gives you, and you possess it and live in it, and you say, 'I will set a king over me like all the nations who are around me,' you shall surely set a king over you whom the LORD your God chooses, one from among your countrymen you shall set as king over yourselves; you may not put a foreigner over yourselves who is not your countryman."

The LORD God alone claims, pledges, and reveals in His holy Word that He Himself would select their king for them. Maybe you have read Psalm 2 before, but not with this background, how verse 6 refers to a future king: "But as for Me, I have installed *My King* / Upon Zion, My holy mountain."

Continuing the account in 1 Samuel 8:6–9:

> But the thing was displeasing in the sight of Samuel when they said, "Give us a king to judge us." And Samuel prayed to the LORD. And the LORD said to Samuel, "Listen to the voice of the people in regard to all that they say to you, **for they have not rejected you, but they have rejected Me from being king over them**. Like all the deeds which they have done since the day that I brought them up from Egypt even to this day—in that they have forsaken Me and served other gods—so they are doing to you also.
>
> "Now then, listen to their voice; however, you shall solemnly warn them and tell them of the procedure of the king who will reign over them."

Tragically for the future Jewish people, as God told Samuel the prophet in 1 Samuel 8:7—"for they have not rejected you, but they have rejected Me from being king over them." This would not be the last time they would reject the One who would be God's choice. Much more will be written about this crucial account in an upcoming chapter of the book.

The account continues in 1 Samuel 8:10–22, as Samuel plainly told them what the reality of having a king would mean for most of the Jewish people:

> So Samuel spoke all the words of the LORD to the people who had asked of him a king.
>
> And he said, "This will be the procedure of the king who will reign over you: he will take your sons and place them for himself in his chariots and among his horsemen and they will run before his chariots. And he will appoint for himself commanders of thousands and of fifties, and some to do his plowing and to reap his harvest and to make his weapons of war and equipment for his chariots. He will also take your daughters for perfumers and cooks and bakers. And he will take the best of your fields and your vineyards and your olive groves and give them to his servants. And he will take a tenth of your seed and of your vineyards and give to his officers and to his servants. He will also take your male servants and your female servants and your best young men and your donkeys and use them for his work. He will take a tenth of your flocks, and you yourselves will become his servants. Then you will cry out in that day because of your king whom you have chosen for yourselves, but the LORD will not answer you in that day."
>
> Nevertheless, the people refused to listen to the voice of Samuel, and they said, "No, but there shall be a king over us, that we also may be like all the nations, that our king may judge us and go out before us and fight our battles."
>
> Now after Samuel had heard all the words of the people, he repeated them in the LORD's hearing.
>
> And the LORD said to Samuel, "Listen to their voice, and appoint them a king." So Samuel said to the men of Israel, "Go every man to his city."

The people in their sinfulness did not fully believe what they were committing themselves to, but again, to show from what we saw previously in "the blessing and the curse," the core issue is not only their disobedience to the Word, but their total disbelief that God would fight their battles and lead them to victories, which is why in 1 Samuel 8:19–20 they are so brazenly wicked: "Nevertheless, the people refused to listen to the voice of Samuel, and they said, 'No, but there shall be a king over us, that we also may be like all the nations, that our king may judge us and go out before us and fight our battles.'"

For more verses and crucial doctrine concerning the blessed fact that the LORD God clearly, consistently and faithfully does what He says He will do, see *The Bible Expositor's Handbook (OT/NT)*, Chapter 10, "This Just In: David's Victory Over Goliath Was *Not* an Upset!"

Fast forward to 1 Samuel 13:13–14 where God's prophet rebukes Saul for his sinful activities, and shows the future consequences of his sins:

> And Samuel said to Saul, "You have acted foolishly; you have not kept the commandment of the LORD your God, which He commanded you, for now the LORD would have established your kingdom over Israel forever."

After another sinful act by King Saul, God instructed the reluctant—but still obedient—prophet to anoint a new king for Israel, as seen in 1 Samuel 16:1–3, because every true king of Israel/king of the Jews required that they (1) had to be selected only by God, and (2) anointed by God, usually through one of the prophets:

> Now the LORD said to Samuel, "How long will you grieve over Saul, since I have rejected him from being king over Israel? Fill your horn with oil, and go; I will send you to Jesse the Bethlehemite, for I have selected a king for Myself among his sons."
>
> But Samuel said, "How can I go? When Saul hears of it, he will kill me." And the LORD said, "Take a heifer with you, and say, 'I have come to sacrifice to the LORD.'
>
> "And you shall invite Jesse to the sacrifice, and I will show you what you shall do; and you shall anoint for Me the one whom I designate to you."

HOW GOD ASSESSES SOMEONE'S WORTH / A TREMENDOUS REMINDER FROM GOD (1 SAM 16:7)

First Samuel 16:7 reveals this sobering truth, yet one that is encouraging if you are walking with God: "But the LORD said to Samuel, 'Do not look at his appearance or at the height of his stature, because I have rejected him; for God sees not as man sees, for man looks at the outward appearance, but the LORD looks at the heart.'" Such news is good or bad for many of us depending on whether we have a heart for God and His Word.

First Samuel 16:12–13 gives the account of the anointing of Israel's second king, David:

> So he sent and brought him in. Now he was ruddy, with beautiful eyes and a handsome appearance. And the LORD said, "Arise, anoint him; for this is he." Then Samuel took the horn of oil and anointed him in the midst of his brothers; and the Spirit of the LORD came mightily upon David from that day forward. And Samuel arose and went to Ramah.

If I had been present at that occasion, I could not have resisted the temptation to ask the Jewish people who wanted a king and had Saul for 40 years, about how "that king fighting your own battles" thing was working out for them. God gave them whom the nation greatly wanted—and deserved—as their King, namely, Saul. With only a few exceptions under Saul's reign, Israel was generally in complete covenant disobedience before the LORD God. Using the shortened version, we will limit this to 1 Samuel 17:1–3:

> Now the Philistines gathered their armies for battle; and they were gathered at Socoh which belongs to Judah, and they camped between Socoh and Azekah, in Ephes-dammim. And Saul and the men of Israel were gathered, and camped in the valley of Elah, and drew up in battle array to encounter the Philistines. And the Philistines stood on the mountain on one side while Israel stood on the mountain on the other side, with the valley between them.

And resulting in 1 Samuel 17:8–11:

> And he [*the Philistine champion Goliath*] stood and shouted to the ranks of Israel, and said to them, "Why do you come out to draw up in battle array? Am I not the Philistine and you servants of Saul? Choose a man for yourselves and let him come down to me.

"If he is able to fight with me and kill me, then we will become your servants; but if I prevail against him and kill him, then you shall become our servants and serve us."

Again the Philistine said, "I defy the ranks of Israel this day; give me a man that we may fight together."

When Saul and all Israel heard these words of the Philistine, they were dismayed and greatly afraid.

Thus entered the anointed but not yet ruling King David into the public prominence among Israel. This is a final urging (for those who need it) to read Chapter 10, "This Just In: David's Victory Over Goliath Was *Not* an Upset!" for many biblical trails and connections.

JUST NOTING A FEW TRUTHS ABOUT THE ETERNALLY IMPORTANT DAVIDIC COVENANT (2 SAMUEL 7/PSALM 89)

Time does not permit a study of the eternal and extremely revealing covenant of God with David. The most cursory reading of the Davidic Covenant (2 Sam 7/Ps 89) covers just the broad basics here. There is another chapter worth noting here from *The Bible Expositor's Handbook (OT/NT)*, Chapter 11: "The Davidic Covenant and Its Theological Relevance." The chapter about the Davidic Covenant should be read, if only for its importance in the New Testament and the life and work of God's Messiah. From the two chapters already mentioned, 2 Samuel 7 and Psalm 89—there are many more biblical passages that factor into this—are glimpses of the far-reaching theological significances of the Davidic Covenant and its prophetic implications for the coming of God's Messiah. First, God used the historical account of David wanting to build God a house (a physical structure) (2 Sam 7:1-7) to, instead, promising David that God would build him a house (a lineage of descendants) in what would eventually become the Davidic Covenant (2 Sam 7:8-17). Second, the promises inherent in the Davidic Covenant included "concerning the distant future" (2 Sam 7:19). Third, God promised that He would establish the throne of His kingdom forever (2 Sam 7:13). Fourth, Psalm 89 repeatedly reaffirms "the forever promises" of the Davidic Covenant (Ps 89:1–2, 28–29, 30–37), even though no one sat on David's throne when the psalm was written (Ps 89:38–52). Fifth, the Davidic Covenant secures the Messiah's right to rule over all the world, as Psalm 2 shows. Sixth, the Davidic Covenant promises most certainly would have been something that Jesus taught concerning Himself in Luke 24.

THE (TEMPORARY) SPLITTING OF THE TWELVE TRIBES OF ISRAEL INTO TWO COUNTRIES

You can read all of First Kings, if you like, but 1 Kings 12:16 gives the division itself:

When all Israel [*the 10 northern tribes*] saw that the king [*Southern tribes Judah and Benjamin, Davidic Covenant heir King Rehoboam*] did not listen to them, the people answered the king, saying,

> "What portion do we have in David?
> We have no inheritance in the son of Jesse;
> To your tents, O Israel!
> Now look after your own house, David!"

So Israel [*the 10 northern tribes*] departed to their tents.

Further revelation from God shows both His will and His role in dividing the two countries, and adverting a civil war:

> But the word of God came to Shemaiah the man of God, saying,
> "Speak to Rehoboam the son of Solomon, king of Judah, and to all the house of Judah and Benjamin and to the rest of the people, saying,
> 'Thus says the LORD, "You must not go up and fight against your relatives the sons of Israel; return every man to his house, for this thing has come from Me."'
> So they listened to the word of the LORD, and returned and went their way according to the word of the LORD (1 Kgs 12:22–24).

There were so many wicked things about this kingdom that it is only by the tolerant forbearing of the LORD and His divine decrees that the northern kingdom lasted about as long as the United States has, namely a little over 200 years. We will let the Word speak for itself to explain the first exile of the 10 tribes to Nineveh, Assyria, where Jonah had previously and reluctantly gone. Second Kings 17:6–18 is not God acting in some arbitrary outbreak of anger. Here is the biblical account of why the first exile to Assyria in 722 B.C. occurred:

In the ninth year of Hoshea, the king of Assyria captured Samaria and carried Israel away into exile to Assyria, and settled them in Halah and Habor, on the river of Gozan, and in the cities of the Medes.

Now this came about, because the sons of Israel had sinned against the LORD their God, who had brought them up from the land of Egypt from under the hand of Pharaoh, king of Egypt, and they had feared other gods and walked in the customs of the nations whom the LORD had driven out before the sons of Israel, and in the customs of the kings of Israel which they had introduced. And the sons of Israel did things secretly which were not right, against the LORD their God. Moreover, they built for themselves high places in all their towns, from watchtower to fortified city. And they set for themselves sacred pillars and Asherim on every high hill and under every green tree, and there they burned incense on all the high places as the nations did which the LORD had carried away to exile before them; and they did evil things provoking the LORD. And they served idols, concerning which the LORD had said to them, "You shall not do this thing."

Yet the LORD warned Israel and Judah, through all His prophets and every seer, saying, "Turn from your evil ways and keep My commandments, My statutes according to all the law which I commanded your fathers, and which I sent to you through My servants the prophets."

However, they did not listen, but stiffened their neck like their fathers, who did not believe in the LORD their God. And they rejected His statutes and His covenant which He made with their fathers, and His warnings with which He warned them. And they followed vanity and became vain, and went after the nations which surrounded them, concerning which the LORD had commanded them not to do like them. And they forsook all the commandments of the LORD their God and made for themselves molten images, even two calves, and made an Asherah and worshiped all the host of heaven and served Baal. Then they made their sons and their daughters pass through the fire, and practiced divination and enchantments, and sold themselves to do evil in the sight of the LORD, provoking Him.

We have listed some—by no means all—of the key covenant disobedient sins from here.

CRUCIAL: All of the trangressions listed were (1) high-handed sins against God, (2) all put them into the "curse" category of the "the blessing and the curse," and (3) the last part of the curse—after all of the warnings and previous punishments—ends with exile.

NOTE: The Assyrian Exile of the 10 northern tribes is the beginning of the Samaritans, who exiled most of the defeated northern tribes to Assyrian, but left several to stay behind in the region named Samaria to intermarry with pagan Gentile women.

KEY: The 10 northern tribes at that time called *Israel will never again be a separate nation by itself.* The majority of them went in the Assyrian exile, but the 10 tribes did not go out of existence—they *must* be in existence for the last days of Genesis 49—which they will be. More about this in upcoming chapters of this book.

As before, we will let the Word speak for itself:

WHY THE SOUTHERN KINGDOM JUDAH FELL AND MORE REASONS FOR THE NORTHERN TRIBES GOING INTO ASSYRIAN EXILE—2 KINGS 17:19–23

Also Judah did not keep the commandments of the LORD their God but walked in the customs which Israel had introduced. And the LORD rejected all the descendants of Israel and afflicted them and gave them into the hand of plunderers, until He had cast them out of His sight.

When He had torn Israel from the house of David, they made Jeroboam the son of Nebat king. Then Jeroboam drove Israel away from following the LORD and made them commit a great sin. And the sons of Israel walked in all the sins of Jeroboam which he did; they did not depart from them, until the LORD removed Israel from His sight, as He spoke through all His servants the prophets. So Israel was carried away into exile from their own land to Assyria until this day.

THE EVENTUAL FALL OF JERUSALEM/JUDAH—2 KINGS 25:1–7

Now it came about in the ninth year of his reign, on the tenth day of the tenth month, that Nebuchadnezzar king of Babylon came, he and all his army, against Jerusalem, camped against it, and built a siege wall all around it. So the city was under siege until the eleventh year of King Zedekiah. On the ninth day of the fourth month the famine was so severe in the city that there was no food for the people of the land.

Then the city was broken into, and all the men of war fled by night by way of the gate between the two walls beside the king's garden, though the Chaldeans were all around the city. And they went by way of the Arabah.

But the army of the Chaldeans pursued the king and overtook him in the plains of Jericho and all his army was scattered from him. Then they captured the king and brought him to the king of Babylon at Riblah, and he passed sentence on him.

And they slaughtered the sons of Zedekiah before his eyes, then put out the eyes of Zedekiah and bound him with bronze fetters and brought him to Babylon.

JUDAH EXILED
TO BABYLON—2 KINGS 25:21-23

Then the king of Babylon struck them down and put them to death at Riblah in the land of Hamath. So Judah was led away into exile from its land.

Now as for the people who were left in the land of Judah, whom Nebuchadnezzar king of Babylon had left, he appointed Gedaliah the son of Ahikam, the son of Shaphan over them. When all the captains of the forces, they and their men, heard that the king of Babylon had appointed Gedaliah governor, they came to Gedaliah to Mizpah, namely, Ishmael the son of Nethaniah, and Johanan the son of Kareah, and Seraiah the son of Tanhumeth the Netophathite, and Jaazaniah the son of the Maacathite, they and their men.

The godly but weeping Jeremiah would be stuck with this sorry lot after the fall of Jerusalem and the Temple was ransacked.

This next part is a peek ahead and should be included in our studies. Though not stated nor named until Jesus said it in Luke 21:21-24 about six centuries later, a new term emerged that still describes the the present situation for both Jews and Gentiles:

"But when you see Jerusalem surrounded by armies, then recognize that her desolation is at hand.

"Then let those who are in Judea flee to the mountains, and let those who are in the midst of the city depart, and let not those who are in the country enter the city; because these are days of vengeance, in order that all things which are written may be fulfilled.

"Woe to those who are with child and to those who nurse babes in those days; for there will be great distress upon the land, and wrath to this people, and they will fall by the edge of the sword, and will be led captive into all the nations; *and Jerusalem will be trampled underfoot by the Gentiles **until the times of the Gentiles be fulfilled**.*

The verses above indicate that the fall of Jerusalem and no Davidic Covenant King sitting on David's throne to this day means that the times of the Gentiles had begun in 586 BC, and continue up to the present time. Yet even with the sad pillaging and terror, there came from the Holy Spirit His promise that this would not last forever; eventually "until the times of the Gentiles be fulfilled" (Luke 21:24). You will find much more detailed information given in *The Bible Expositor's Handbook (OT/NT)*, and in other chapters of this book.

SUMMARY AND CONCLUSION

From this chapter we learned, among other things, additional truths built on the ones revealed in the first two chapters: (1) Victory in warfare against national Israel's enemies was never intended to be automatic nor promised by Yahweh—and, in fact, certain defeat was guaranteed—if the nation lived in sinful state before Him. Just a few sources from "the curse section" of Leviticus 26 and Deuteronomy 28 plainly show this; (2) Deuteronomy 28:25–26 reveals with no hidden language some of the consequences if Israel rebelled against Yahweh: "The LORD will cause you to be defeated before your enemies;" (3) Even the curse section, or such other verses, that talk about the destruction of the national Israel, must be viewed through the lens of what God had already promised, such as the eternal promises of the Abrahamic Covenant in view, such as Genesis 17:7–8: *for an everlasting covenant/ for an everlasting possession of the land*; (4) Based totally on God's mercy, the eternal plans with the Jews, and ultimately the entire world, are all done only by the grace of God and the faithfulness to His Word, especially as seen in the covenants of God. So (5) Israel did not need a king, for God would lead them to battle and to victory if they obeyed Him, and the same God would stand as their enemy to defeat them if they lived in Mosaic Covenant disobedience.

(6) In Deuteronomy 17:14–15, under the Mosaic Covenant, national Israel is commanded by God "that they shall surely set a king over

themselves whom the LORD your God chooses;" never was the kingship of Israel supposed to be by any sort of general election where the people voted; (7) In 1 Samuel 8:6–9, God informs the prophet Samuel to listen to the people—under these circumstances—with the result that national Israel had not rejected Samuel, but tragically, "they have rejected Me from being king over them." (8) In 1 Samuel 13:13–14 Saul acted foolishly by not fully obeying God, resulting in "But now your kingdom shall not endure. The LORD has sought out for Himself a man after His own heart, and the LORD has appointed him as ruler over His people, because you have not kept what the LORD commanded you;" (9) We also saw that the biblical doctrine in 1 Samuel 16:7 reveals this sobering truth, yet one that is encouraging if you are walking with God: "But the LORD said to Samuel, 'Do not look at his appearance or at the height of his stature, because I have rejected him; for God sees not as man sees, for man looks at the outward appearance, but the LORD looks at the heart.'"

(10) From 2 Samuel 7 and Psalm 89 we saw that God used the historical account of David wanting to build God a house (a physical structure) (2 Sam 7:1–7) to, instead, promising David that God would build him a house (a lineage of descendants) in what would eventually become the Davidic Covenant (2 Sam 7:8–17); (11) God promised that He would establish the throne of His kingdom forever (2 Sam 7:13); (12) Psalm 89 reaffirms "the forever promises" of the Davidic Covenant (Ps 89:1–2, 28–29, 30–37), even though no one sat on David's throne when the psalm was written (Ps 89:38–52). (13) Psalm 2 secures in the Davidic Covenant the Messiah's right to rule over all the world, as Psalm 2 shows, and a promise we should remind ourselves of often, (14) Jesus would have taught much about the Davidic Covenant in the two Luke accounts.

(15) The Assyrian Exile of the 10 northern tribes was also the place for the origin of the Samaritans; (16) The majority of the northern tribes went in the Assyrian exile, but the 10 tribes did not go out of existence—they *must* be in existence for the last days of Genesis 49—which they will be; (17) Jeremiah was the prophet who was left behind to witness all the murders, rapes, and carnages from the Babylonians; (18) the fall of Jerusalem and no Davidic Covenant King to this day means that the times of the Gentiles had begun, (19) yet even with the sad pillaging and terror, there came from

the Holy Spirit His promise that this would not last forever; eventually "the times of the Gentiles be fulfilled" (Luke 21:24). Simply put—this is not the end of the story; the times of the Gentiles must eventually be defeated and Jerusalem will be at complete rest.

DEEPER WALK STUDY QUESTIONS

1) Name five ways that God made sure the military victories or defeats were directly related to national Israel's walk with the Lord—or lack thereof. Be specific.

2) Name seven reasons why Israel did not need a king. Be specific.

3) In Deuteronomy 17:14–15, under the Mosaic Covenant, national Israel is commanded by God that they shall surely set a king over themselves "whom the LORD your God chooses." Name five biblical doctrines from this first, and then five spiritual lessons from this. Be specific.

4) From 1 Samuel 8:6–9, God informs the prophet Samuel to listen to the people and tells him that Israel has not rejected him, but tragically, "for they have not rejected you, but they have rejected Me from being king over them." List ten biblical truths from this passage, especially how this relates to national Israel's spiritual condition and future events. Be specific.

5) Name eight biblical doctrinal truths from 1 Samuel 16:7 that reveal this sobering truth, yet one that is encouraging if you are walking with God: "But the LORD said to Samuel, 'Do not look at his appearance or at the height of his stature, because I have rejected him; for God sees not as man sees, for man looks at the outward appearance, but the LORD looks at the heart.'" What are five applications we can learn from this text?

6) Name twelve doctrinal truths from 2 Samuel 7 and Psalm 89. Why are these truths important, even up to the present time? Be specific.

7) Why do we know that the 10 northern tribes that went into Assyrian exile cannot be destroyed? Give 5 biblical answers for why this must happen and why this is important in understanding the Person and work of God.

8) Name seven biblical truths from Jesus' declaration in Luke 21:24. Be specific.

9) Make up your own study question, answer it, and be able to give people five reasons why your question was important.

CHAPTER FOUR

THESE ARE THE APPOINTED TIMES OF YAHWEH

INTRODUCTION

"The secret things belong to the LORD/Yahweh our God," is part of a verse taken from Deuteronomy 29:29 that is a favorite to both Jews and Gentiles alike. It is evident from this verse that at least for the present time, God holds secret things among the Trinity and probably the angels of God, at least the higher-ranked angels such as Michael or Gabriel. Paul likewise could bear testimony of this same truth of God maintaining restricted knowledge as He sees fit. Paul wrote of his experience, not knowing whether it was a vision, and showed the restricted nature of what he heard, in 2 Corinthians 12:1–3, and he somewhat reluctantly disclosed what took place in private:

> Boasting is necessary, though it is not profitable; but I will go on to visions and revelations of the Lord. I know a man in Christ who fourteen years ago—whether in the body I do not know, or out of the body I do not know, God knows—such a man was caught up to the third heaven. And I know how such a man—whether in the body or apart from the body I do not know, God knows—was caught up into Paradise and heard inexpressible words, which a man is not permitted to speak.

If people were to ask why God would allow such an experience, the answer could be for His overall enjoyment and sovereignty, but obviously God does not disclose all information that He could reveal because (1) we are fallen, sinful creatures who cannot fully comprehend God's thoughts or His ways, and (2) the complete disclosures will not be given until the redeemed are taken to heaven. God knows that we have enough divine revelation given to us for the present time, as 1 Corinthians 13:12 substantiates, "For now we see in a mirror dimly, but then face to face; now I know in part, but then I will know fully just as I also have been fully known." Also 2 Peter 1:2–4 encouragingly adds:

> Grace and peace be multiplied to you in the knowledge of God and of Jesus our Lord; seeing that His divine power has granted to us everything pertaining to life and godliness, through the true knowledge of Him who called us by His own glory and excellence. For by these He has granted to us His precious and magnificent promises, in order that by them you might become partakers of the divine nature, having escaped the corruption that is in the world by lust.

In this chapter we will see helpful, God-given time markers that most Bible readers ignore until it is pointed out to them. These markers are a great help in understanding Scripture. God gave them to us so that we may better understand Him, His Word, and His will—and often His timing of events that affect the entire world.

INTRODUCTION TO SOME VALUABLE TIME MARKERS FOR WHAT WE WILL STUDY IN THIS CHAPTER

APPOINTED TIMES AND EPOCHS OF GOD NOT REVEALED BY HIM

We know throughout history that God is the author of His Word, the controller of times and events, and the finisher of our faith. All such items are found in many places in Scripture, but we will limit our introductory verses for this section of the book to Hebrews 1:1–4:

God, after He spoke long ago to the fathers in the prophets in many portions and in many ways, in these last days has spoken to us in His Son, whom He appointed heir of all things, through whom also He made the world. And He is the radiance of His glory and the exact representation of His nature and upholds [*in the Greek means "to bring to a completion or fulfillment"*] all things by the word of His power. When He had made purification of sins, He sat down at the right hand of the Majesty on high; having become as much better than the angels, as He has inherited a more excellent name than they.

We will use just two more examples, but you should have no trouble finding other such verses that show that God is the author of history past, present, and future. Just moments before Jesus' Ascension, Luke begins his account in Acts 1:1–8:

The first account I composed, Theophilus, about all that Jesus began to do and teach, until the day when He was taken up to heaven [*ascension/ seated at God's right hand/Psalm 110:1*], after He had by the Holy Spirit given orders to the apostles whom He had chosen. To these He also presented Himself alive after His suffering, by many convincing proofs, appearing to them over a period of forty days and speaking of the things concerning the kingdom of God. Gathering them together, He commanded them not to leave Jerusalem, but to wait for what the Father had promised, "Which," He said, "you heard of from Me; for John baptized with water, but you will be baptized with the Holy Spirit not many days from now."

There are other verses we could add, but since Luke wrote Acts, returning where we almost started the book, namely Luke 24, only this time going to the last words Jesus said in Luke's Gospel, Luke 24:49: "And behold, I am sending forth the promise of My Father upon you; but you are to stay in the city until you are clothed with power from on high"—and the disciples have a logical question in Acts 1:6: "So when they had come together, they were asking Him, saying, "Lord, is it at this time You are restoring the kingdom to Israel?" It should be noted: the apostles clearly understood what Jesus had taught and what the OT prophets and psalms revealed about Himself and the Kingdom of God, because He was "appearing to them over a period of forty days and speaking of the things concerning the kingdom of God" (Acts 1:3). Their question was not a "what" in Acts 1:6—restoring the kingdom to Israel—but rather a "when" question: "Now?" Jesus answered, Acts 1:7–8: "He said to them, *It is not for you to know times or epochs which the Father has fixed by His own authority*; but you will receive power when the Holy Spirit has come upon you [*as we saw in Luke 24:49*]; and you shall be My witnesses both in Jerusalem, and in all Judea and Samaria, and even to the remotest part of the earth." So we know from these verses (1) times and epochs do exist, (2) God created the times and epochs, (3) He places these under His own authority to bring them to their fruition, and (4) ultimately (Rev 20), He brings everything to the closure that He desires.

Elsewhere, Paul's "Sermon on an Unknown God" while in Athens, as shown in Acts 17:24–26, reveals the same doctrine we saw in Acts 1, but under the inspiration of the Holy Spirit adds a massive truth concerning the sovereignty of God:

> He is Lord of heaven and earth [*not just God of the Jews*], and does not dwell in temples made with hands; nor is He served by human hands, as though He needed anything, since He Himself gives to all people life and breath and all things; and He made from one man every nation of mankind to live on all the face of the earth, *having determined their appointed times and the boundaries of their habitation* ...

This last report of God *having determined and having already established their appointed times and the boundaries of their* [every human nation's] *habitation,* clearly reveals what God has already done, not something He will do as things unfold; He does not use the future tense of the verb, which would then be translated as a work in progress. The Greek text looks back to the determining of their appointed times and boundaries as something which He has done long ago. The Holy Spirit through Paul does not specify names in revealing what the appointed times and boundaries are to be, but as we will see, these include national Israel. However, this should not be surprising to Bible readers; just the Book of Revelation shows multiple examples of such times and their sovereign control by God.

So Paul's sermon was very much in keeping with what Jesus had told the apostles—and eventually would tell the world, in Acts 1:7, "He said to them, *'It is not for you to know times or epochs which the Father has fixed by His own authority*;'" again, what Jesus is revealing is something having already been determined by the authority of God the Father but concealed by the Trinity for the present time.

Consider for a moment: What is the difference between a "time" and an "epoch?" Times are generally easier to recognize than epochs because the verses usually include the word "times," as we have repeatedly seen in Luke 21:24, "and Jerusalem will be trampled underfoot by the Gentiles until the times of the Gentiles are fulfilled." A similar usage in Romans 11:25 may be expressing a different vantage point; it is a biblical nugget that was not in Luke 21:24, and though this verse does not use the word "time," Paul proclaims this: "For I do not want you, brethren, to be uninformed of this mystery, lest you be wise in your own estimation, that a partial hardening has happened to Israel until the fulness of the Gentiles has come in." These two verses reveal biblical doctrinal truths—and one occurs in the doctrinal portion of Romans 1–11. "Times" focuses more on the beginning and the end of a time; again, only God knows these times as it relates to human history; we only know specifics about the times if the Trinity chooses to reveal what they are or were.

Epochs are distinctive periods in the history of someone or something important at the time. For example, both world wars would be epochs; 9/11 and related events from this would be an epoch. Most of us have lived through many epochs, but we'll probably have to wait to see all that transpired during them. Usually humanity recognizes epochs by looking back over them after they have taken place, but some epochs have been prophesied—such as the second destruction of God's Temple in Matthew 24:1–4. With epochs, the emphasis is more on the content of each epoch that includes events that transpired and persons who were prominent during them. All of these were strictly under God's sovereign watch and origin.

In a very encouraging passage of Scripture, having just written about the promise of the dead in Christ rising first and the Rapture of the Church, the Holy Spirit through Paul discloses in 1 Thessalonians 5:1–3:

Now as to the times and the epochs, brethren, you have no need of anything to be written to you [*and if you are saved now, that includes you*]. For you yourselves know full well that the day of the Lord will come just like a thief in the night. While they are saying, "Peace and safety!" then destruction will come upon them suddenly like labor pains upon a woman with child, and they will not escape.

These wonderful promises by God are given to the church, especially as these promises will be eventually written of in the last book of the Bible, in Revelation 6–18: the first part of the Tribulation (the first 3½ years), and the Great Tribulation (the last 3½ years of the Tribulation), when Satan and the Antichrist will have the height of their power and wickedness. The church has received another such promise in Revelation 3:10:

"Because you have kept the word of My perseverance, I also will keep you from the hour of testing, that hour, which is about to come upon the whole world, to test those who dwell on the earth."

CONSIDER: If God meant that the church had to be on guard for these particular times and epochs, it certainly would have been easy to say that with one or two words added. If Paul meant that the church had to be on guard for the coming times and epochs, why did he not just say so? Also, if Jesus did not promise, "I also will keep you from the hour of testing, that hour which is about to come upon the whole world" (Revelation 6–18), then why would He not say so, and how could you have any confidence in what either Jesus Christ or Paul meant by what they wrote or said? But their words are biblical doctrine and are irrevocable!

By the way, the part I quoted from Deuteronomy was the only part that many people quote, but the whole verse is necessary for understanding the accurate use of that verse. Here is the whole verse of Deuteronomy 29:29, originally written to the children of the wilderness generation before they entered the land God had repeatedly promised to them:

> The secret things belong to the LORD our God, but the things revealed belong to us and to our sons forever, that we may observe all the words of this law.

Let us go to where God has opened His Word for us—and it is His great pleasure that we do so, because the verses we will look at in this chapter have changed the way that many people view the text. For instance, Acts 1:7 very clearly shows that the Trinity did not at that time want the apostles to know the times or epochs that the Father has fixed by His own authority.

But how should we deal with the verses in which God does reveal the appointed times of Yahweh contained in His Scripture?

FIRST CORINTHIANS 10 HAS VERY HELPFUL VERSES ON USING SOME OT VERSES IN THE NT

First Corinthians 8:1–6 begins a larger discourse on Christian liberty that will not end until 11:1. In this case, one issue was whether a Christian could eat meat that had been sacrificed to pagan idols, and from there it seems that some of the Corinthian church members based their salvation on their profession of Jesus Christ rather than on the reality of what they claimed. Simply stated, as with most churches, there were sheep and goats—and the wolves of false apostles (2 Cor 11:13–15). Paul initially points to the argument among some of the Corinthian church members:

> Now concerning things sacrificed to idols, we know that we all have knowledge. Knowledge makes arrogant, but love edifies. If anyone supposes that he knows anything, he has not yet known as he ought to know; but if anyone loves God, he is known by Him.
>
> Therefore concerning the eating of things sacrificed to idols, we know that there is no such thing as an idol in the world, and that there is no God but one. For even if there are so-called gods whether in heaven or on earth, as indeed there are many gods and many lords, yet for us

there is but one God, the Father, from whom are all things and we exist for Him; and one Lord, Jesus Christ, by whom are all things, and we exist through Him.

Continuing his answer, Paul uses himself as an example in 1 Corinthians 9:1-5, and even more, as an apostle of Jesus Christ.

> Am I not free? Am I not an apostle? Have I not seen Jesus our Lord? Are you not my work in the Lord? If to others I am not an apostle, at least I am to you; for you are the seal of my apostleship in the Lord.
>
> My defense to those who examine me is this:
>
> Do we not have a right to eat and drink?
>
> Do we not have a right to take along a believing wife, even as the rest of the apostles and the brothers of the Lord and Cephas? [*The first alleged pope had a wife; interesting theology*]

Paul was attempting to teach the Corinthians that although he had the right to engage in many different behaviors, he may choose to act on all, some, or none of them, all contingent on the situation at hand—especially when those in the faith who were younger or weaker would be affected. Paul did not want to commit any act nor have any member of the Corinthian church practice any behavior that would offend someone of weaker faith or cause that one to stumble into sin, but rather that they all should be examples of Christ.

For the section germane to our present chapter, and one which we will come back to, is that Paul showed examples of the wilderness generation, who had certain rights and privileges, and yet, as far as we can tell, died unsaved, and they now await the Great White Throne judgment.

But before moving, there are verses in 1 Corinthians that will be useful for us in our study at hand. In 1 Corinthians 10:19–21, the Apostle Paul writes that eating things sacrificed to idols is a greater danger than some of them acknowledged:

> What do I mean then? That a thing sacrificed to idols is anything, or that an idol is anything? No, but I say that the things which the Gentiles sacrifice, they sacrifice to demons and not to God; and I do not want you to become sharers in demons.

> You cannot drink the cup of the Lord and the cup of demons; you cannot partake of the table of the Lord and the table of demons.

Paul continues his argument regarding things that are lawful or unlawful, but now includes other people as part of his biblical teaching:

> All things are lawful, but not all things are profitable. All things are lawful, but not all things edify.
>
> Let no one seek his own good, but that of his neighbor.
>
> Eat anything that is sold in the meat market without asking questions for conscience' sake; (1 Cor 10:23–25)

In 1 Corinthians 10:27–11:1 Paul gives his final answer and exhortation, using himself as an example, as long as Paul himself is in obedience to the Lord:

> If one of the unbelievers invites you and you want to go, eat anything that is set before you without asking questions for conscience' sake. But if anyone says to you, "This is meat sacrificed to idols," do not eat it, for the sake of the one who informed you, and for conscience' sake; I mean not your own conscience, but the other man's; for why is my freedom judged by another's conscience? If I partake with thankfulness, why am I slandered concerning that for which I give thanks?
>
> Whether, then, you eat or drink or whatever you do, do all to the glory of God. Give no offense either to Jews or to Greeks or to the church of God; just as I also please all men in all things, not seeking my own profit but the profit of the many, so that they may be saved.
>
> Be imitators of me, just as I also am of Christ.

Having established the proper context, we can return to the verses about things written in the Old Testament, but first, we need to add one more foundational truth, namely 2 Timothy 3:16–17:

> All Scripture is inspired by God and profitable for teaching, for reproof, for correction, for training in righteousness; so that the man of God may be adequate, equipped for every good work.

The context was the Old Testament, and the same truths apply now, making an accurate handler of God's Word even better-equipped with additional Holy-Spirit-inspired Scripture.

Just one quick reference before returning to 1 Corinthians 10. The Trinity does not start Their doctrine in Matthew 1; the Old Testament contains much doctrine, but not every part of it is still binding, even for the Jewish people under the Mosaic Covenant who were commanded for a while to do some things that they no longer do today. For instance, for a while the Jewish nation was commanded to gather a double portion of manna, as Exodus 16:5 instructs, "On the sixth day, when they prepare what they bring in, it will be twice as much as they gather daily"—and good luck to anyone who will be trying now to fulfill this Old Testament command from God. It is no longer relevant, and one not given to the New Testament church. Here are a couple of good tests to see whether a doctrine from God is still pertinent. (This is not a complete list.) First, is it still possible to fulfill? A second test is to see whether attributes and/or activities are an accurate depiction of Him, such as Genesis 1:1, "In the beginning God created the heavens and the earth" and Nehemiah 9:6: "You alone are the LORD. / You have made the heavens, / The heaven of heavens with all their host, / The earth and all that is on it, / The seas and all that is in them. / You give life to all of them. / And the heavenly host bows down before You." All of these are doctrinal truths and Godhead activities—and are still just as true as when they were first written centuries ago.

Just for time's sake we will temporarily leave the doctrinal part and look at applications of Old Testament truths. In 1 Corinthians 10:13, Paul writes one example of Jesus that is used in the New Testament—which was, is, and will be an eternal doctrine of God. Remember that this is in the middle of Paul's larger argument concerning whether the Corinthians should eat food sacrificed to idols. Paul uses the wilderness generation and the multiple miracles that they saw with their own eyes—and unless there were many deathbed receptions of the Gospel as they knew it up to that time, they died lost, are in Hades now, and await the final judgment. With that background knowledge, here is part of what Paul wrote in 1 Corinthians 10:1-13:

For I do not want you to be unaware, brethren, that our fathers were all under the cloud and all passed through the sea; and all were baptized into Moses in the cloud and in the sea; and all ate the same spiritual food; and all drank the same spiritual drink, for they were drinking from a spiritual rock which followed them; and the rock was Christ [*Messianic doctrinal truth*]. Nevertheless, with most of them God was not well-pleased; for they were laid low in the wilderness.

Now these things happened as examples for us, so that we would not crave evil things as they also craved. Do not be idolaters, as some of them were; as it is written, "THE PEOPLE SAT DOWN TO EAT AND DRINK, AND STOOD UP TO PLAY."

Nor let us act immorally, as some of them did, and twenty-three thousand fell in one day. Nor let us try the Lord, as some of them did, and were destroyed by the serpents.

Nor grumble, as some of them did, and were destroyed by the destroyer.

Now these things happened to them as an example, and they were written for our instruction, upon whom the ends of the ages have come.

Therefore let him who thinks he stands take heed that he does not fall.

No temptation has overtaken you but such as is common to man; and God is faithful, who will not allow you to be tempted beyond what you are able, but with the temptation will provide the way of escape also, so that you will be able to endure it.

This passage shows us that Old Testament verses can be used for application.

CAUTION: Be sure that your application doesn't become treated or viewed as doctrine by default. For instance, you can take the Genesis 6–9 judgment by God against a wickedly sinful world. You can ignore all the sin problems and God's solution of using the flood and go to Genesis 9 about the rainbow and fluff it up by preaching/teaching such things as, "God wants you to make rainbows out of your rain," i.e. make little good things out of going through hard times. Leaving out any of the attributes of God such as—short list—the holiness of God; His forbearance; the truthfulness of Him and His Word; His severe treatment of blasphemous sin; the real reason for God's rainbow, why He gave it, and what He said it meant, leave that out, and the fluff—by default—becomes taught as biblical truth, even holy doctrine. It is a sobering warning to follow, but needed and commanded by God (e.g., James 3:1–2).

THE HIDDEN BIBLICAL RICHES OF LEVITICUS 23

Ask many Christians who read their Bible to name their favorite chapter in the Bible, and very few will say—as I will—that Leviticus 23 is among their favorites. This chapter is one of my top ten favorites—as should be expected if you have read much of my work.

CRUCIAL: As we will see, God did something we would not know about other than by His divine disclosure: He appointed specific times for each of the seven items. In Acts 1:7, there are times (and epochs) *concealed*; in Leviticus 23 there were/are times *revealed*. And while most people might not realize this, God uses Leviticus 23 to mark special times that, in some cases, affect or will affect literally the entire world.

Twenty one times the plural of the Hebrew word *mo'ed* is used for "times" or "seasons." Translators and authors have had much debate over whether this word should be translated as *times* or *seasons* in certain verses. We will look at a few examples, beginning with the first usage in Genesis 1:14: "Then God said, 'Let there be lights in the expanse of the heavens to separate the day from the night, and let them be for signs and for seasons [*mo'ed*] and for days and years;'" It seems obvious that seasons was the intention God had for the Genesis 1 reference. Numbers 29:39 shows the difference in translations—only using the pertinent parts of this verse—the NASB translating *mo'ed* as "You shall present these to the LORD at your appointed times" while the ESV translates the same verse, "These you shall offer to the LORD at your appointed feasts" where, in this case, "feasts" fits better with what was being sacrificed at an appointed time—although the appointed time was important. And so go the remaining verses where *mo'ed* is used. It comes down to the author's emphasis on sacrifices/feasts or appointed times. As we will see later, some of the translations have theological baggage with them, especially in references to the future of Israel—or lack thereof.

We will examine six uses of *mo'ed*, and limiting ourselves to the ones referring specifically to the appointed feasts of Yahweh or to the appointed times of Yahweh—and this translation is not some minor item, as some of the other verses that use *mo'ed*—*because we have six uses of* mo'ed *either used in reference to God or God Himself speaking*, and Leviticus 23 stands alone in its importance, because it contains five of those six uses. We will present the material, and then reason biblically whether Yahweh meant this as an appointed feast or an appointed time—and the reasoning from Scripture should be tremendously important about which interpretational way to go with many related verses.

Yahweh ordained that this chapter contain some form of "the appointed times of Yahweh" *six times*, which is a large number of times for such usage in a chapter of the Bible. The first two of these are used ***in the introductory verses*** of Leviticus 23:1–2:

> The LORD spoke again to Moses, saying,
> "Speak to the sons of Israel, and say to them, '[**Yahweh's**] **The LORD's appointed times** [*mo'ed*] which you shall proclaim as holy convocations—**My appointed times** [*mo'ed*] are these:

Both times the ESV translates *mo'ed* as "appointed feasts."

We saw the sabbath mentioned in Exodus, and it is included in this chapter as well:

"For six days work may be done; but on the seventh day there is a sabbath of complete rest, a holy convocation. You shall not do any work; it is a sabbath to the LORD in all your dwellings" (Lev 23:3).

The third and fourth usage of some form of "the appointed times of the LORD," is the exact form used for the name of our current chapter. It's in Leviticus 23:4. "**These are the appointed times of [Yahweh] the LORD**, and the fourth usage described as **holy convocations** which you shall proclaim at the times appointed for them;" as would be expected, the ESV reads, "These are the appointed feasts of the LORD ...."

The fifth usage of such a designation is Leviticus 23:37, "These are **the appointed times of [Yahweh] the LORD,**" and the ESV translates it: "These are the appointed feasts of the LORD ... " The sixth and final usage of the phrase in Leviticus 23 is also *the last verse of that chapter*, Leviticus 23:44, "So Moses declared to the sons of Israel **the appointed times of [Yahweh] the LORD**"—with the ESV saying, "Thus Moses declared to the people of Israel the appointed feasts of the LORD." As we will see, there are tremendous interpretational issues in whether these are "appoint feasts of Yahweh" or "appointed times of Yahweh." Also, it is incredibly important—and consistent—to keep in the forefront of our thinking these biblical truths we have already noted: as with Acts 1:7, since these are seven appointed times of Yahweh, then the same description that Jesus gave to the apostles is true for these—"*which the Father has fixed by His own authority*." So the Father's own authority is the basis for the existence of appointed times, and His authority will be true for each of the seven appointed times of Yahweh; this was a major point of what the Apostle preached in Acts 17:24–27:

"The God who made the world and all things in it, since He is Lord of heaven and earth, does not dwell in temples made with hands; nor is He served by human hands, as though He needed anything, since He Himself gives to all people life and breath and all things; and He made from one man every nation of mankind to live on all the face of the earth, *having determined their appointed times and the boundaries of their habitation* that they would seek God, if perhaps they might grope for Him and find Him, though He is not far from each one of us;"

We are employing the seven appointed times of Yahweh, as found in Leviticus 23, by placing the application of the word to all the feasts mentioned in Leviticus 23, even though the word itself is not used in the description of each individual feast day—it is used as a title generically to identify all the feasts of Leviticus 23 as being "appointed times of Yahweh." As Acts 17:26 depicts broadly, "and He made from one man every nation of mankind to live on all the face of the earth, *having determined their appointed times and the boundaries of their habitation*." This is equally true for God's work of each the of the seven such appointed times in Leviticus 23.

The first of the seven appointed times of Yahweh commanded by God is **Passover**: "In the first month, on the fourteenth day of the month at twilight is the LORD's Passover (Lev 23:5). *The second of the seven appointed times of Yahweh* is **the Feast of Unleavened Bread** that follows immediately after the LORD's Passover, in Leviticus 23:6–8:

> "Then on the *fifteenth* day [noting that Passover took place the day before, on the *fourteenth* day] of the same month there is the Feast of Unleavened Bread to the LORD; for seven days you shall eat unleavened bread. On the first day you shall have a holy convocation; you shall not do any laborious work.
>
> But for seven days you shall present an offering by fire to the LORD. On the seventh day is a holy convocation; you shall not do any laborious work.'"

Since the LORD's Passover (Lev 23:5) and the Feast of Unleavened Bread (Lev 23:6–8) started on successive days, the two feasts were connected as one feast on their calendar, and these two gatherings were generally viewed as one gathering instead of two. Thus we find such usage in Mark 14:1–2:

> Now the Passover and Unleavened Bread was two days off; and the chief priests and the scribes were seeking how to seize Him by stealth, and kill Him; for they were saying, "Not during the festival [*singular use, not plural; they considered them both as one 8-day festival*], lest there be a riot of the people"

The third of the seven appointed times of Yahweh is **the Feast of the First Fruits of Your Harvest**, or just **Feast of First Fruits**

(Lev 23:9–14), that time of the year in the spring when the first fruits of the barley harvest are to be consecrated to the LORD:

> Then the LORD spoke to Moses, saying, "Speak to the sons of Israel, and say to them, 'When you enter the land which I am going to give to you and reap its harvest, then you shall bring in the sheaf of the first fruits of your harvest to the priest. And he shall wave the sheaf before the LORD for you to be accepted; on the day after the sabbath the priest shall wave it.
>
> Now on the day when you wave the sheaf, you shall offer a male lamb one year old without defect for a burnt offering to the LORD. Its grain offering shall then be two-tenths of an ephah of fine flour mixed with oil, an offering by fire to the LORD for a soothing aroma, with its libation, a fourth of a hin [gallon] of wine. Until this same day, until you have brought in the offering of your God, you shall eat neither bread nor roasted grain nor new growth. It is to be a perpetual statute throughout your generations in all your dwelling places.

God then gave instructions for ***the fourth of the seven appointed times of Yahweh,*** namely **the Feast of Weeks** for the last spring occasion in Leviticus 23:15–22:

> "You shall also count for yourselves from the day after the sabbath, from the day when you brought in the sheaf of the wave offering; there shall be seven complete sabbaths. You shall count fifty days to the day after the seventh sabbath; then you shall present a new grain offering to the LORD. You shall bring in from your dwelling places two loaves of bread for a wave offering, made of two-tenths of an ephah; they shall be of a fine flour, baked with leaven as first fruits to the LORD. Along with the bread, you shall present seven one year old male lambs without defect, and a bull of the herd, and two rams; they are to be a burnt offering to the LORD, with their grain offering and their libations, an offering by fire of a soothing aroma to the LORD. You shall also offer one male goat for a sin offering and two male lambs one year old for a sacrifice of peace offerings. The priest shall then wave them with the bread of the first fruits for a wave offering with two lambs before the LORD; they are to be holy to the LORD for the priest.

On this same day you shall make a proclamation as well; you are to have a holy convocation. You shall do no laborious work. It is to be a perpetual statute in all your dwelling places throughout your generations.

When you reap the harvest of your land, moreover, you shall not reap to the very corners of your field, nor gather the gleaning of your harvest; you are to leave them for the needy and the alien. I am the LORD your God.'"

The Feast of Weeks ultimately became called by its much more well-known designation, the holy convocation of **Pentecost**, originating from the word fifty, from the LORD's instructions in Leviticus 23:26, "You shall count fifty days to the day after the seventh sabbath," to arrive at the date God intended.

After all of the first four religious gatherings in the spring, there was "a long time of silence from God" from their vantage point. From the last of spring until about late September/October, nothing else was given to the people in this festival cycle from God. After a prolonged period of "silence of the LORD," the Jewish people were notified that there would be three festivals, all three occurring within a little over two weeks.

Yes, the dates of Leviticus 23 served as a base for the Jewish calendar (not the Gentile's solar calendar), but there is more.

Beyond all of this, and not noted by many, in Leviticus 23 are seven "these are the appointed times of Yahweh."

Not the appointed time of the Jews.

Not the appointed times for the Gentiles.

And certainly not the appointed times of the church, and although few people recognize this, the Holy Spirit being poured out and the beginning of the church becomes the fourth of seven appointments of Yahweh.

In another chapter we will see that the last three appointed times of Yahweh will affect the entire world history, past and present, and the reign of God's King forever and ever—but much more about that is covered in the upcoming chapters of this book. After the four spring convocations, there is a long time of silence, relatively speaking, before the last three appointed times of Yahweh, and these occur somewhere around October, as we will see later.

We have laid out God's Word of Leviticus 23 and have cited the first four of the seven designated times of Yahweh. We will examine the last three uses and the appointed times they delineate in an upcoming chapter. I think you will see why we waited to do the last three items later in the book, after we have gone through some pertinent biblical material.

THE FIRST FOUR TIMES OF YAHWEH HAVE NEW TESTAMENT CITATION/DOCUMENTATION

As we know, Leviticus 23 contains five times some form of "these are the appointed times of Yahweh" from the seven specific times noted by God. So God used the Jewish calendar and added eternal worth to the way that He used it. Four of the appointed times of Yahweh that are in the spring all have Scriptural fulfillment in the New Testament.

CRUCIAL: Let us be clear: The irrefutable fact that *God Himself* added significant truth for then or for far into the future can by no means have an allegorical interpretation—and God is allowed to do whatever He wants.

As we saw from 2 Timothy 3:16–17, that part of the Old Testament can be used for doctrine: "All Scripture is inspired by God and profitable for teaching, for reproof, for correction, for training in righteousness; so that the man of God may be adequate, equipped for every good work." We noted that the context of 2 Timothy 3 was the Old Testament. We also saw in 1 Corinthians 10:6, concerning the Old Testament, "Now these things happened as examples for us, so that we would not crave evil things as they also craved," and 10:11, "Now these things happened to them as an example, and they were written for our instruction, upon whom the ends of the ages have come."

Paul was forced by his love for the Corinthians to address the incestu-
ous relationship *inside the church*, and there were two problems with this: (1)
the actual sin continued, and (2) no one inside the church did anything to
eliminate this repetitive sin. Paul never directly addressed the elders or the
deacons, because they may have been there in name only and were not
performing the true work of a godly elder or deacon. Here was the sinful
situation at hand:

> It is actually reported that there is immorality among you, and immo-
> rality of such a kind as does not exist even among the Gentiles, that some-
> one has his father's wife. And you have become arrogant, and have not
> mourned instead, in order that the one who had done this deed might be
> removed from your midst.
>
> For I, on my part, though absent in body but present in spirit, have
> already judged him who has so committed this, as though I were present.
>
> In the name of our Lord Jesus, when you are assembled, and I with
> you in spirit, with the power of our Lord Jesus, I have decided to deliver
> such a one to Satan for the destruction of his flesh, that his spirit may be
> saved in the day of the Lord Jesus (1 Cor 5:1–5).

Only those who are saved should be trying to remove the leaven of sin from
their lives as part of their Christian walk, but in answering the questions at
Corinth, Paul cites ***the first of the seven appointed times of Yahweh***,
and he uses the 2 Timothy 3:16 doctrinal way in 1 Corinthians 5:7: "For
Christ our Passover also has been sacrificed." Returning to the context,
the next appointed time is there, as Paul taught that the consequences of sin
must be taken seriously. For the second appointed time of Yahweh, he used
the 1 Corinthians 10:6—not the 2 Timothy doctrinal part— as Paul uses
the Old Testament for life lessons, "Now these things happened as examples for us, so that we would not crave evil things as they also craved," and
10:11, "Now these things happened to them as an example, and they were
written for our instruction, upon whom the ends of the ages have come."

So in giving his rebuttal to the sin, the Holy Spirit inspires him to use 1
Corinthians 5:6–8, which includes ***the second of the seven appointed
times of Yahweh***:

Your boasting is not good. Do you not know that a little leaven [yeast] leavens the whole lump of dough? Clean out the old leaven, that you may be a new lump, just as you are in fact unleavened. For Christ our Passover also has been sacrificed. Let us therefore celebrate the feast [of leaven] not with old leaven, nor with the leaven of malice and wickedness, but with the unleavened bread of sincerity and truth.

Remember that Mark 14:1–2 reminds us that the Passover occurred one day before the seven-day Feast of Unleavened Bread, and even if they are connective festivals, they remain two separate parts of the seven "appointed times of Yahweh:"

> Now the Passover and Unleavened Bread was two days off; and the chief priests and the scribes were seeking how to seize Him by stealth, and kill Him; for they were saying, "Not during the festival, lest there be a riot of the people."

The Corinthian church was living a lifestyle—as they did most other things—backwards. Their lives were not devoid of sin even as they claimed to be attempting to live a godly lifestyle. Those who had already [allegedly] received the salvation offered in God's Passover Lamb, had bypassed that experience and were not living the Christian life at all. And unless this issue was fully addressed, the entire church body would ultimately be affected.

In the midst of this, two of the appointed times of Yahweh are mentioned in 1 Corinthians 5:6–8, the first two of the appointed times of Yahweh:

(1) "For Christ our Passover also has been sacrificed."
(2) Reference to the Feast of Unleavened Bread—although not named in the passage, being referred to in the context as just "feast:" "Let us therefore celebrate the feast ..." has to mean the one-week Feast of Unleavened Bread which began the day after the Passover.

IMPORTANT: The church was never commanded to celebrate the items listed in Leviticus 23. However, later, the Holy Spirit confirms that these are not insignificant events for the New Testament believer. For instance, the first and second "appointed times of Yahweh" are corroborated in the New Testament in 1 Corinthians 5. We know from Scripture that the Holy Spirit/the Apostle Paul did not command the Corinthian church to observe the Feast of Unleavened Bread, because first, they were mainly Gentiles and not Jews, after the resurrection. Second, they lived in Corinth, Greece, not Jerusalem. It is the spirit/Spirit of the celebration they were to honor by dealing with the permeating effect of unconfessed sin in the church. Third and finally, the Spirit explicitly identified this connection. We should be careful not to make assumptions about correlations in other passages that He does not make.

First Corinthians 15 is the chapter that Paul was expressly inspired to write to expound the irreplaceable doctrine of the resurrection of both the godly and the ungodly, and also of the Lord Jesus Himself, ***the third of the seven appointed times of Yahweh***:

Now I make known to you, brethren, the gospel which I preached to you, which also you received, in which also you stand, by which also you are saved, if you hold fast the word which I preached to you, unless you believed in vain. For I delivered to you as of first importance what I also received, that Christ died for our sins according to the Scriptures, and that He was buried, and that He was raised on the third day according to the Scriptures, and that He appeared to Cephas, then to the twelve.

After that He appeared to more than five hundred brethren at one time, most of whom remain until now, but some have fallen asleep; then He appeared to James, then to all the apostles; and last of all, as it were to one untimely born, He appeared to me also.

First Corinthians 15:12–14 plainly reveals the core of the problem:

> Now if Christ is preached, that He has been raised from the dead, how do some among you say that there is no resurrection of the dead? But if there is no resurrection of the dead, not even Christ has been raised; and if Christ has not been raised, then our preaching is vain, your faith also is vain.

In addressing the doctrine of the resurrection, the Holy Spirit through Paul gave this undeniable proof that the Lord Jesus Christ fulfilled the third appointed time of Yahweh, by citing it twice in 1 Corinthians 15:20–25:

> But now Christ has been raised from the dead, **the first fruits** of those who are asleep. For since by a man came death, by a man also came the resurrection of the dead.
>
> For as in Adam all die, so also in Christ all shall be made alive.
>
> But each in his own order: **Christ the first fruits**, after that those who are Christ's at His coming, then comes the end, when He delivers up the kingdom to the God and Father, when He has abolished all rule and all authority and power.
>
> For He must reign until He has put all His enemies under His feet.

The third appointed time of Yahweh: "Christ the first fruits," is described in Leviticus 23 as The Feast of the First Fruits of Your Harvest (Lev 23:9–14), the first fruits of the barley harvest, consecrated to the LORD.

We have already seen 3 appointed times of Yahweh revealed:

—Christ our Passover

—The Feast of Unleavened Bread: ideally, living a holy life after one is saved—which the Corinthians were not doing in 1 Corinthians 5.

—Christ is the first fruits of the Resurrection.

There is only one more New Testament citation or documentation revealed in Scripture—**the fourth appointed time of Yahweh, the Feast of Weeks**, more commonly called **Pentecost**, as Acts 2:1–5 so clearly reveals:

> And when the day of Pentecost had come, they were all together in one place.

And suddenly there came from heaven a noise like a violent, rushing wind, and it filled the whole house where they were sitting. And there appeared to them tongues as of fire distributing themselves, and they rested on each one of them. And they were all filled with the Holy Spirit and began to speak with other tongues, as the Spirit was giving them utterance.

Now there were Jews living in Jerusalem, devout men, from every nation under heaven.

We are currently in the long silence from God—relatively speaking—before He breaks the silence as it relates to the last three appointed times of Yahweh. Among other things, Luke 21:24 shows we are still in "the times of the Gentiles." The account in Acts 2 of the beginning of the church is also of tremendous importance.

KEY: If God minutely fulfilled the first four appointed times of Yahweh, and we are currently in the long period of silence, then why should we not expect Him to precisely fulfill in the future the final three of the seven that have no New Testament backing showing that they already have been fulfilled?

KEY: If your theology does not expound the fulfillment of the first four times of Yahweh, then you probably will not be looking for the same God to fulfill the last three of the appointed times, and you are omitting a large portion of biblical theology that God wants the world to know.

So, when will God break the silence and fulfill the last of the three appointed times of Yahweh? Well, the answer to that is the rest of the story about *The King and His Glory*.

SUMMARY AND CONCLUSION

In this chapter we learned, among other things: (1) Sometimes God does not want certain divine revelation known. "The secret things belong to the LORD/Yahweh our God," (Deuteronomy 29:29). Paul was prohibited from explaining what he had heard in what was likely a vision of heaven (2 Cor 12:1–30). (2) Verses such as 1 Peter 2:1–4 encourage us, "seeing that His divine power has granted to us everything pertaining to life and godliness, through the true knowledge of Him who called us by His own glory and excellence" (2 Pet 1:3). (3) Acts 1:3 eternally records that Jesus was "appearing to them over a period of forty days and speaking of the things concerning the kingdom of God." The questioning by the apostles concerning *when, but not what,* about the kingdom, shows they must have thought that Jesus would set up a literal restoration of the Kingdom with Him on the throne. (4) Instead of being told when, Jesus responded (Acts 1:7–8), saying, *"It is not for you to know times or epochs which the Father has fixed by His own authority*; but you will receive power when the Holy Spirit has come upon you; and you shall be My witnesses both in Jerusalem, and in all Judea and Samaria, and even to the remotest part of the earth." (5) Acts 17:26, In Paul's "Mars Hill Sermon," the Holy Spirit through Paul revealed the following doctrine regarding God and His times and epochs, "and He made from one man every nation of mankind to live on all the face of the earth, having determined their appointed times and the boundaries of their habitation ..." (Acts 17:26). (6) That verse clearly reveals what God has already done, not something He will do as things unfold; He does not use the future tense of the verb, which would then be translated as a work in progress.

We further learned that (7) times are generally easier to recognize than epochs because the verses usually include the word "times", as we have repeatedly seen in Luke 21:24, "and Jerusalem will be trampled underfoot by the Gentiles until the times of the Gentiles are fulfilled." (8) Epochs are historically a distinctive period in the history of someone or something important at the time, such as both world wars. (9) With epochs, the emphasis is more on the content of each epoch that includes events that transpired and persons who were prominent during them, and all were strictly under God's sovereign watch and ownership. (10) Just after writing about the promise of the dead in Christ rising first and the Rapture of the Church (1 Thes 4:13-18—a very encouraging passage), the Holy Spirit through Paul discloses in 1 Thessalonians 5:1–3: *"Now as to the times and the epochs, brethren, you have no need of anything to be written to you ... ."* because the saved living at that time will be Raptured, and will be taken home to be with the Lord at some undisclosed time before the Tribulation begins.

We also learned (11) Second Timothy 3:16–17, verses that many are familiar with, in context refer to the Old Testament: "All Scripture is inspired by God and profitable for teaching, for reproof, for correction, for training in righteousness; so that the man of God may be adequate, equipped for every good work." (12) Not all of the doctrinal commands for the Jews who were then under the Mosaic Covenant were still true for every later Jewish generation, but (13) other doctrines—especially the ones that show the activities or attributes of the Godhead—like Genesis 1:1—are usually eternal and still part of God's overall truths. (14) First Corinthians 10 uses two verses to show the application/use of Old Testament truths, namely, "Now these things happened as examples for us, so that we would not crave evil things as they also craved" (10:6), and "Now these things happened to them as an example, and they were written for our instruction, upon whom the ends of the ages have come" (10:11). (15) So, if the doctrinal part is the basis, biblical application is appropriate; however, people often ignore the doctrinal base and make sheer application, often teaching the *application* as doctrine, rather than correctly basing the application on the Old Testament doctrinal truths.

In this chapter, furthermore we learned, (16) in Leviticus 23, God then did something we would not know other than by His divine disclosure: He appointed seven specific times for the seven items listed in that one chapter. In Acts 1:7, these times and epochs are *concealed*; in Leviticus 23, these were/ are times *revealed*. (17) Leviticus 23 is the only Scripture that has the words "these are the appointed times of Yahweh," and God uses the seven items to disclose biblical doctrine—not application. (18) Leviticus 23 is the Jewish calendar, and it was used as such, but God Himself added extra emphasis to the calendar. (19) As with Acts 1:7, since these are seven appointed times of Yahweh, then the same description that Jesus gave to the apostles are true for these—"*which the Father has fixed by His own authority.*" (20) The seven appointed times of Yahweh qualify as Acts 17:26 depicts broadly, "and He made from one man every nation of mankind to live on all the face of the earth, *having determined their appointed times and the boundaries of their habitation.*"

(21) *The first of the seven appointed times of Yahweh* commanded by God is Passover: "In the first month, on the fourteenth day of the month at twilight is the LORD's Passover (Lev 23:5). *The second of the seven appointed times of Yahweh* is the Feast of Unleavened Bread, which follows immediately after the LORD's Passover, in Leviticus 23:6–8: "Then on the *fifteenth* day [noting that Passover took place the day before, on the *fourteenth* day] of the same month there is the Feast of Unleavened Bread to the LORD; for seven days you shall eat unleavened bread" (Lev 23:6). We also learned that (22) since the LORD's Passover (Lev 23:5) was on one day and the Feast of Unleavened Bread started the day after Passover (Lev 23:6–8), these two gatherings were generally viewed as one gathering instead of two (as Mark 14:1–2 shows). (23) *The third of the seven appointed times of Yahweh* is the Feast of the First Fruits of Your Harvest, or just Feast of First Fruits (Lev 23:9–14); that time of the year in the spring when the first fruits of the barley harvest shall be consecrated to the LORD, and (24) God then gave instructions for *the fourth of the seven appointed times of Yahweh,* namely the Feast of Weeks, for the last spring occasion in Leviticus 23:15–22. It will later pick up a new name, Pentecost. (24) After all of the first four religious gatherings in the spring, there was "a long time of silence from God," (from their vantage point). From the last of spring until about late September/October, nothing else was given to the people in this festival cycle from God. (25) After a prolonged period "of silence," the Jewish people were notified that there would be three festivals, all three occurring in a little over two weeks.

In conclusion, we learned (26) Leviticus 23 was the Jewish calendar used by the Jewish people, but God used it and made it His own: these are appointed time of Yahweh—not the appointed time for the Jews; not the appointed times for Gentiles. It was certainly not the appointed times of the church, and although few people recognize this, the Holy Spirit being poured and the beginning of the church becomes the fourth of seven appointments of Yahweh. (27) In an upcoming chapter of this book we will see that the last three appointed times of Yahweh will affect the entire world, history past and present, and the reign of God's King forever and ever. After the four spring convocations, there is a long time of silence, relatively speaking, before the last three appointed times of Yahweh, and these occur somewhere around October, as we will also see this later in the book. (28) The irrefutable fact that *God Himself* added significant truth for then or for far into the future can by no means have an allegorical interpretation— and God is allowed to do whatever He wants to do.

(29) As we saw from 2 Timothy 3:16–17, that part of the Old Testament can be used for doctrine: "All Scripture is inspired by God and profitable for teaching, for reproof, for correction, for training in righteousness; so that the man of God may be adequate, equipped for every good work." We noted that the context of 2 Timothy 3 was the Old Testament. (30) We also saw in 1 Corinthians 10:6, concerning the Old Testament, "Now these things happened as examples for us, so that we would not crave evil things as they also craved," and 10:11, "Now these things happened to them as an example, and they were written for our instruction, upon whom the ends of the ages have come." In 1 Corinthians 5:1–5, Paul had to address heinous sin issues inside the church. In answering the questions at Corinth, he cites **the first of the seven appointed times of Yahweh**, and does it in the 2 Timothy 3:16 doctrinal way in that he uses in 1 Corinthians 5:7: "For **Christ our Passover** also has been sacrificed." He used the second appointed time of Yahweh for life lessons from the Old Testament (not for direct doctrinal teaching), as 1 Corinthians 10:6 and 10:11 said should be done.

(31) So in giving his rebuttal to the sin, the Holy Spirit inspires him to write 1 Corinthians 5:6–8, which includes **the second of the seven appointed times of Yahweh**:

> Your boasting is not good. Do you not know that a little leaven [yeast] leavens the whole lump of dough? Clean out the old leaven, that you may be a new lump, just as you are in fact unleavened. For Christ our Passover also has been sacrificed. Let us therefore **celebrate the feast,** not with old leaven, nor with the leaven of malice and wickedness, but with the unleavened bread of sincerity and truth.

(32) In the midst of this, we have two of the appointed times of Yahweh referred to in 1 Corinthians 5:6–8. The first two of "the appointed times of Yahweh" is in the biblical record:

(1) "For Christ our **Passover** also has been sacrificed."

(2) Reference to **the Feast of Unleavened Bread**—although not named in the in the passage, referred to as just "the feast:" "Let us therefore celebrate the feast ...." This has to mean the one-week Feast of Unleavened bread, which began just after the Passover.

(33) These passages where God the Holy Spirit gives designations are not insignificant events, because the first and second of "the appointed times of Yahweh" now come with New Testament corroboration and Holy-Spirit-inspired certification.

In this chapter we additionally learned (34) that 1 Corinthians 15 is the chapter that Paul had to write to expound the irreplaceable doctrine of the resurrection of both the godly and the ungodly, and also of the Lord Jesus Himself, *the third of the seven appointed times of Yahweh*: "But now Christ has been raised from the dead, *the first fruits* of those who are asleep. For since by a man came death, by a man also came the resurrection of the dead. For as in Adam all die, so also in Christ all shall be made alive. But each in his own order: *Christ the first fruits... .*

(35) There is only one more of the seven feasts mentioned in the New Testament—*the fourth appointed time of Yahweh, the Feast of Weeks*, more commonly called **Pentecost**, as Acts 2:1–5 so clearly reveals:

And when the day of **Pentecost** had come, they were all together in one place.

And suddenly there came from heaven a noise like a violent, rushing wind, and it filled the whole house where they were sitting. And there appeared to them tongues as of fire distributing themselves, and they rested on each one of them. And they were all filled with the Holy Spirit and began to speak with other tongues, as the Spirit was giving them utterance.

Now there were Jews living in Jerusalem, devout men, from every nation under heaven.

Finally, two items: (36) if God minutely fulfilled the first four appointed times of Yahweh, and we are currently in the long period of silence, then why should we not look for Him to precisely fulfill in the future the final three of seven for which we have no New Testament evidence that they have already been fulfilled? And lastly, (37) if your theology does not expound the fulfillment of the first four times of Yahweh, then you most likely will not be looking for the same God to fulfill the last three of the appointed times as He so minutely fulfilled the first four, and you are omitting a large portion of biblical theology that God wants the world to know.

DEEPER WALK STUDY QUESTIONS

(1) What is the difference between a time and an epoch? Support your answer with four biblical examples.

(2) Name seven ways the New Testament can use the Old Testament for authentication. Use the 2 Timothy 3:16–17 passage and anything in 1 Corinthians.

(3) What are the first four appointed times of Yahweh? Write where each shows up biblically in the New Testament, and then write eight doctrinal truths about the significance of these first four of the appointed being cited in the New Testament. Explain your answer, be very specific, and support with Scripture.

(4) Write ten biblical truths from Acts 1:1–9. After the you have written your 10 biblical truths, write two or three sentences encapsulting why these truths are important.

(5) Write 10 doctinal truths from 1 Corinthians 10:1–9. Explain your answer, be very specific, and support with Scripture.

(6) Write 8 doctrinal truths from Acts 17:22–27. Explain your answer, be very specific, and support with Scripture.

(7) Of the seven times in Leviticus 23, only the first four feasts/ "appointed times of Yahweh" are cited in some manner in the New Testament. What are they, and why are they important?

(8) Why are the last appointed times of Yahweh not mentioned in the New Testament, and why is that important to know? List four reasons. Be specific, and support your answer biblically.

(9) Make up your own study question, answer it, and be able to give people five reasons why your question was important.

CHAPTER FIVE

BROADLY SETTING
THE BIBLICAL TABLE (PART 4):

RETURN FROM THE BABYLONIAN
EXILE—JUST AS GOD HAD PROMISED—
BUT NOW THE JEWS LIVE DURING
"THE TIMES OF THE GENTILES"

INTRODUCTION

We concluded the chapter entitled "Broadly Setting the Biblical Table (Part 3): From the Establishment of the Kingship Until the Babylonian Exile" which had Scripture verses showing the nation sinning time after time, and then—despite ongoing warnings to repent and walk with God—the ten northern tribes (also called Israel at that time) continually rebelling until they ultimately went into the Assyrian Exile in 722 BC. Approximately 150 years later, the two southern tribes—called Judah—were severely slaughtered, with many going into Babylonian exile. At that time, the Temple of the LORD was destroyed and Zedekiah was blinded (his eyes were gouged out), after he had first watched his sons murdered by the Babylonians. This means that the last thing the wicked king saw was the death of his children—something he would remember for the remainder of his life.

We know from the biblical account that those things happened. How could God do/allow such a slaughter and pillage?[6] If you start with that question and read 1 and 2 Kings, the question then becomes how could God wait so long before He judged the vile wickedness of His people? We know from previous studies that if all we had was the final part of "the blessing and the curse," and we were unaware of any exile(s), we also know that unless the ten tribes to the north and two tribes to the south repented and walked in covenant obedience, we should expect the exile part—and actually the exile is the last part—of the curse section. Leviticus 26:31–33 includes this earlier warning in the chapter:

> "I will lay waste your cities as well and will make your sanctuaries desolate; and I will not smell your soothing aromas. And I will make the land desolate so that your enemies who settle in it shall be appalled over it.
>
> "You, however, I will scatter among the nations and will draw out a sword after you, as your land becomes desolate and your cities become waste."

Leviticus 26:38–39 concludes the curse section with these last two warnings—and then a promise from the LORD:

> "But you will perish among the nations, and your enemies' land will consume you. So those of you who may be left will rot away because of their iniquity in the lands of your enemies; and also because of the iniquities of their forefathers they will rot away with them."

The warning section of "the blessing and the curse" concludes with these words and warnings from God in Deuteronomy 28:63–68:

> "And it shall come about that as the LORD delighted over you to prosper you, and multiply you, so the LORD will delight over you to make you perish and destroy you; and you shall be torn from the land where you are entering to possess it.

---

6 For many more details about this subject than we could cover in this chapter, see Greg Harris, *The Bible Expositor's Handbook (OT/NT)* (Nashville: B & H Academic, 2020), in Chapter 14: "Great is Thy Faithfulness?" 195–207. Used by permission.

"Moreover, the LORD will scatter you among all peoples, from one end of the earth to the other end of the earth; and there you shall serve other gods, wood and stone, which you or your fathers have not known.

"And among those nations you shall find no rest, and there shall be no resting place for the sole of your foot; but there the LORD will give you a trembling heart, failing of eyes, and despair of soul. So your life shall hang in doubt before you; and you shall be in dread night and day, and shall have no assurance of your life."

We know from our studies of the Davidic Covenant promises such as 2 Samuel 7 and Psalm 89, that eventually One with the attributes of God will come to reign, as seen in passages such as Isaiah 9:6:

For a child will be born to us, a son will be given to us;
And the government will rest on His shoulders;
And His name will be called Wonderful Counselor, Mighty God,
Eternal Father, Prince of Peace.

When this beloved promised Messiah is sent by God, the eternality of His rule can be seen in such passages as Isaiah 9:7:

There will be no end to the increase of His government or of peace,
On the throne of David and over his kingdom,
To establish it and to uphold it with justice and righteousness
From then on and forevermore.
The zeal of the LORD of hosts will accomplish this.

When Isaiah prophesied, it was during the reigns of four Davidic Covenant heirs, as Isaiah 1:1 confirms: "The vision of Isaiah the son of Amoz concerning Judah and Jerusalem, which he saw during the reigns of Uzziah, Jotham, Ahaz and Hezekiah, kings of Judah." These kings in David's line are part of the attested genealogy of Jesus the Messiah, as Matthew 1:8–9 bear witness:

Asa was the father of Jehoshaphat, Jehoshaphat the father of Joram, and Joram the father of Uzziah.
Uzziah was the father of Jotham, Jotham the father of Ahaz, and Ahaz the father of Hezekiah.

When Isaiah ministered and proclaimed by means of both voice and written communications, the Davidic Covenant was operative, and also the Levitical priesthood that functioned under the Mosaic Covenant with the appropriate sacrifices and other matters done at their appropriate times at the Temple of the LORD in Jerusalem.

So, the Messiah comes, but in order for Him to fulfill those promised attributes and activities, and in order for Him to sit "On the throne of David and over his kingdom, / To **establish** it and to **uphold** it with justice and righteousness"— that implies there would come a time when the Jewish people would have no Davidic Covenant heir sitting on David's throne. Along with the attributes of God, look at the same two verses and note that whenever this One takes His appropriate seat, it is permanent. So we will look afresh at these verses that mostly remain unfulfilled prophecy at the present time:

> For a child will be born to us, a son will be given to us;
> And the government will rest on His shoulders;
> And His name will be called Wonderful Counselor, Mighty God,
> Eternal Father, Prince of Peace. [**Attributes of the Godhead**]
> There will be no end to the increase of His government or of peace,
> On the throne of David and over his kingdom,
> To establish it and to uphold it with justice and righteousness
> From then on and forevermore. [**Attributes of eternality**]
> The zeal of the LORD of hosts will accomplish this. [**Attribute of Divine Passion to Fulfill these and other such promises related to these**]

How sure should we be that this will happen? —"The zeal of the LORD of hosts will accomplish this" could be translated that God will have a hot and holy passion to bring about everything *He Himself* has promised. He did not have to say this in order for it to come true, but you could rightly say this is similar to God underlining, highlighting, and placing exclamation points.

The last "son of David" to sit on David's throne, King Zedekiah, was captured and mutilated by Nebuchadnezzar's army. After about 600 years with no one sitting on the throne of David, these Davidic Covenant promises and pronouncements are very striking in Luke 1:26–35; after six centuries, there has been no change whatsoever in what God in Scripture wrote about the future King and His kingdom:

> Now in the sixth month the angel Gabriel was sent from God to a city in Galilee called Nazareth, to a virgin engaged to a man whose name was Joseph, of the descendants of David; and the virgin's name was Mary. And coming in, he said to her, "Greetings, favored one! The Lord is with you."
>
> But she was very perplexed at this statement, and kept pondering what kind of salutation this was.
>
> The angel said to her, "Do not be afraid, Mary; for you have found favor with God. And behold, you will conceive in your womb and bear a son, and you shall name Him Jesus. He will be great and will be called the Son of the Most High; and the Lord God will give Him the throne of His father David; and He will reign over the house of Jacob forever, and His kingdom will have no end."
>
> Mary said to the angel, "How can this be, since I am a virgin?"
>
> The angel answered and said to her, "The Holy Spirit will come upon you, and the power of the Most High will overshadow you; and for that reason the holy Child shall be called the Son of God."

Centuries earlier, in the Old Testament, Scripture repeatedly shows that one day God *must* have mercy on Israel—and ultimately the saved of all time—when He will rebuild the kingdom by sending His King, but only as Hosea 3:3–5 prophesies:

> Then I said to her, "You shall stay with me for many days. You shall not play the harlot, nor shall you have a man; so I will also be toward you."
>
> For the sons of Israel will remain for many days without king or prince, without sacrifice or sacred pillar and without ephod or household idols. [*At that time, there was no more functioning Levitical priesthood; the ephod was the sleeveless inner garment that the priests were supposed to wear, and the household idols were just another means of idolatry.*]
>
> Afterward the sons of Israel will return and seek the LORD their God and David their king; and they will come trembling to the LORD and to His goodness in the last days.

This incredible prophecy is in harmony with the first use of "the last days" in Gen 49:1 for the twelve tribes of Israel (Gen 49:28), the Lion from the tribe of Judah (Gen 49:8–12), and the Stone of Israel. Genesis 49:24: "From the hands of the Mighty One of Jacob (from there is the Shepherd, the Stone of Israel)." We'll see more about related items later, but if nothing else, *Scripture requires* that, as Hosea says, "the sons of Israel will remain for many days without king or prince"—and they have remained so since Zedekiah. Since 586 BC, no one—including Jesus in heaven—has sat on David's throne. But Jesus the Messiah will one day sit on the throne of David as we have seen in repeated prophecies of God recorded in the Scriptures. We have looked at this in the previous Glory Books, *The Bible Expositor's Handbook (OT/NT)*—and all the prophecies used in these books of the future King and His kingdom, which are direct quotes from a Godhead member, or are verses from the Holy-Spirit-inspired Word.

From *The Face and the Glory* (pp. 111–112):[7]

So what did these prophets prophesy concerning the future of the nation of Israel and its relationship to their God? The same God who had promised in Micah 3:4, "Then they [the wicked leaders of the rebellious nation] will cry out to the LORD, but He will not answer them. Instead, He will hide His face from them at that time, because they have practiced evil deeds," gives hope that this is not an eternal hiding of His face. Even more specific, note the future blessings eternally recorded at the end of Micah's prophecy based on God's covenant faithfulness:

> Who is a God like You, who pardons iniquity and passes over the rebellious act of the remnant of His possession? He does not retain His anger forever, because He delights in unchanging love. He will again have compassion on us; He will tread our iniquities under foot. Yes, You will cast all their sins into the depths of the sea. You will give truth to Jacob and unchanging love to Abraham, which You did swear to our forefathers from the days of old (Micah 7:18–20).

---

7   Greg Harris, *The Face and the Glory: Lessons on the Invisible and Visible God and His Glory* (The Woodlands, TX: Kress Biblical Resources, 2019). Used by permission.

The prophet Hosea would wholeheartedly concur with this teaching by revealing the future of national Israel regarding a prolonged vacancy of David's throne, followed by the advent of the One who would eventually come: "For the sons of Israel will remain for many days without king or prince, without sacrifice or sacred pillar, and without ephod or household idols. Afterward the sons of Israel will return and seek the Lord their God and David their king; and they will come trembling to the Lord and to His goodness in the last days" (Hos 3:4–5).

When Hosea prophesied this, both Israel and Judah had kings reigning in the two countries; they had not yet remained "many days without king or prince." Even though Hosea ministered to the ten northern tribes, he, too, was a Jew who looked for the fulfillment of the Davidic Covenant. The prophetic nature beyond the immediate events is clearly seen in the phrase that concludes this prophecy, noting that this will occur "in the last days" (Hos 3:5). God explains both the reason for His absence as well as the future remedy, promising in Hosea 5:15: "I will go away and return to My place until they acknowledge their guilt *and seek My face*; in their affliction they will earnestly seek Me." The prophet Isaiah also presents God in a prophecy as looking back on what He did to Israel and why, and how in His utter covenant faithfulness He will restore fellowship with the same Jewish nation He had previous punished, stating in Isaiah 54:7–10: "In an outburst of anger *I hid My face from you for a moment*; but with everlasting lovingkindness I will have compassion on you," says the Lord your Redeemer. "For this is like the days of Noah to Me; when I swore that the waters of Noah should not flood the earth again, so I have sworn that I will not be angry with you, nor will I rebuke you. For the mountains may be removed and the hills may shake, but My lovingkindness will not be removed from you, and My covenant of peace will not be shaken," says the Lord who has compassion on you.

(Ends the material from *The Face and Glory*)

CYRUS THE GREAT—
THE LORD GOD THE GREATER

Even secular historians agree that referring to a Persian king as Cyrus the Great is a fitting designation, because this great Gentile king decreed that the Jews were in Babylon because Yahweh had sent them into exile there. Many are the liberal critics—and there can be only one of two answers: God is a liar, or God is the author of all history past, present and future. The liberal critics maintain that the prophecies about Cyrus are so precise that they deem this to be a man-made book, but that is a lie, because it is presented as prophecy. Further, they conclude that even though it is presented as a prophecy, the passages from Isaiah can only be a fraud, because it was actually (according to them) written long after the facts, so regardless of what it says, it is a lie and no one needs to pay it any attention. That too is a lie!

That is one option—accept a fallen, man-centered, God-demeaning (temporarily, and in their thoughts only, not in reality) theology that is taught (sadly) in about 90% of "Christian schools," "Christian colleges," and "Christian seminaries." The other option—and it matters eternally which choice is made—is that this is the Holy-Spirit-inspired Word of God. Be forewarned that this is no minor matter of little theological significance. If this is a lie, then so is Isaiah 7:14 about the virgin birth recorded in Matt 1, the Messiah's reign, and the Book of Romans, because Paul quotes from Isaiah more than any other Old Testament source. So in essence, if the critics were to be believed, then throw away your Bible, or treat it as you would treat anything written by Shakespeare or one of the many atheistic philosophers.

Before looking at the verses most people turn to (as we will shortly), most people do not realize that Isaiah 40–48 concerns the "Theology Proper: The Doctrine of God." Much is written there about not just the Person of God, but also about the power of God's Word. He alone is the Author of History past, present, and future and dares people to tell Him what happened in history past. In this section on Theology Proper, every chapter has an emphasis on God and His power and God and His trustworthiness.

Here are just a few examples from God's Word in Isaiah 40–48 about the uniqueness of God's Word. In Isaiah 41:21–23, God issues a challenge and adds a little sarcasm in the last verse cited:

"Present your case," the LORD says.

"Bring forward your strong arguments,"

The King of Jacob says.

Let them bring forth and declare to us what is going to take place;

As for the former events, declare what they were,

That we may consider them and know their outcome.

Or announce to us what is coming;

Declare the things that are going to come afterward,

That we may know that you are gods;

Indeed, do good or evil, that we may anxiously look about us and fear together.

In Isaiah 42:9, the LORD God promises:

"Behold, the former things have come to pass,

Now I declare new things;

Before they spring forth I proclaim them to you."

A reminder again: this is either 100% demonic and Satanic and out of the pit, or it is the Holy and true Word of the Holy God. God offers no other options—and the decision that you make in regard to who is telling the truth and who is lying will literally affect your eternity.

In Isaiah 43:13-15, again from the wider "Theology Proper: The Doctrine of God" section of Isaiah (Isa 40–48), God reveals these attributes and activities about Himself:

"Even from eternity I am He;

And there is none who can deliver out of My hand;

I act and who can reverse it?"

Thus says the LORD your Redeemer, the Holy One of Israel,

"For your sake I have sent to Babylon,

And will bring them all down as fugitives,

Even the Chaldeans, into the ships in which they rejoice.

"I am the LORD, your Holy One,

The Creator of Israel, your King."

Remember that these verses are just a sampling; you can find more in the Theology Proper Section in Isaiah, or in correlating Scriptures that proclaim the same truths. In Isaiah 46:8–11, the LORD God declares and challenges anyone who opposes Him and His Word:

> "Remember this, and be assured;
> Recall it to mind, you transgressors.
> "Remember the former things long past,
> For I am God, and there is no other;
> I am God, and there is no one like Me,
> Declaring the end from the beginning
> And from ancient times things which have not been done,
> Saying, 'My purpose will be established,
> And I will accomplish all My good pleasure';
> Calling a bird of prey from the east,
> The man of My purpose from a far country.
> Truly I have spoken; truly I will bring it to pass.
> I have planned it, surely I will do it."

These worship-evoking verses—surely they are for you, and if not, they definitely should be—are in the context of Theology Proper, the Word and God Himself, before any talk of a pagan king He will use. Look Who is the first to say that Jerusalem will be rebuilt in Isaiah 44:24–26:

> Thus says the LORD, your Redeemer, and the one who formed you from the womb,
> "I, the LORD, am the maker of all things,
> Stretching out the heavens by Myself,
> And spreading out the earth all alone,
> Causing the omens of boasters to fail,
> Making fools out of diviners,
> Causing wise men to draw back,
> And turning their knowledge into foolishness,
> Confirming the word of His servant,
> And performing the purpose of His messengers.
> It is I who says of Jerusalem, 'She shall be inhabited!'

And of the cities of Judah, 'They shall be built.'
And I will raise up her ruins again.

With God first proclaiming that Jerusalem will be rebuilt, we will now turn to the human means that He will use, the king who is called by name about 150 years before he will be born, in Isaiah 44:28:

"It is I who says of Cyrus, 'He is My shepherd!
And he will perform all My desire.'
And he declares of Jerusalem, 'She will be built,'
And of the temple, 'Your foundation will be laid.'"

Isaiah 45:1–7 are great verses to show God's great power and sovereignty— as well as a beautiful love story:

Thus says the LORD to Cyrus His anointed [*messiah in the very broad sense and for a very specific purpose, but certainly not the promised Messiah to come*],
Whom I have taken by the right hand,
To subdue nations before him,
And to loose the loins of kings;
To open doors before him so that gates will not be shut:
"I will go before you and make the rough places smooth;
I will shatter the doors of bronze, and cut through their iron bars.
"And I will give you the treasures of darkness,
And hidden wealth of secret places,
In order that you may know that it is I,
"For the sake of Jacob My servant,
And Israel My chosen one,
I have also called you by your name;
I have given you a title of honor
Though you have not known Me.
"I am the LORD, and there is no other;
Besides Me there is no God.
I will gird you, though you have not known Me;
That men may know from the rising to the setting of the sun
That there is no one besides Me.
I am the LORD, and there is no other,

The One forming light and creating darkness,
Causing well-being and creating calamity;
I am the LORD who does all these.

We will let the words speak for themselves and say "Thank you, Beloved God, for being Truth and revealing Truth—and for all your innumerable attributes."

The LORD's Timeline for the Return of the Jewish People to Their Own Land from Babylon

About 150 years or so after many of Isaiah's prophecies, just a few years before the exile, Jeremiah wrote this (25:1–10):

> The word that came to Jeremiah concerning all the people of Judah, in the fourth year of Jehoiakim the son of Josiah, king of Judah (that was the first year of Nebuchadnezzar king of Babylon), which Jeremiah the prophet spoke to all the people of Judah and to all the inhabitants of Jerusalem, saying,
>
> "From the thirteenth year of Josiah the son of Amon, king of Judah, even to this day, these twenty-three years the word of the LORD has come to me, and I have spoken to you again and again, but you have not listened. And the LORD has sent to you all His servants the prophets again and again, but you have not listened nor inclined your ear to hear, saying, 'Turn now everyone from his evil way and from the evil of your deeds, and dwell on the land which the LORD has given to you and your forefathers forever and ever; and do not go after other gods to serve them and to worship them, and do not provoke Me to anger with the work of your hands, and I will do you no harm.' Yet you have not listened to Me," declares the LORD, "in order that you might provoke Me to anger with the work of your hands to your own harm.
>
> "Therefore thus says the LORD of hosts, 'Because you have not obeyed My words, behold, I will send and take all the families of the north,' declares the LORD, 'and I will send to Nebuchadnezzar king of Babylon, My servant, and will bring them against this land and against its inhabitants and against all these nations round about; and I will utterly

destroy them and make them a horror and a hissing, and an everlasting desolation. Moreover, I will take from them the voice of joy and the voice of gladness, the voice of the bridegroom and the voice of the bride, the sound of the millstones and the light of the lamp.'"

And then this final verse of this message—Jeremiah 25:11—is so revealing:

*"**This whole land will be a desolation and a horror, and these nations will serve the king of Babylon seventy years**."*

This is the first time the length of the Babylonian Exile is revealed, namely, 70 years.

To make sure that God really meant this, you could add Jeremiah 29:10–11 from Jeremiah 29:1–15:

> Now these are the words of the letter which Jeremiah the prophet sent from Jerusalem to the rest of the elders of the exile, the priests, the prophets and all the people whom Nebuchadnezzar had taken into exile from Jerusalem to Babylon. (This was after King Jeconiah and the queen mother, the court officials, the princes of Judah and Jerusalem, the craftsmen and the smiths had departed from Jerusalem.) The letter was sent by the hand of Elasah the son of Shaphan, and Gemariah the son of Hilkiah, whom Zedekiah king of Judah sent to Babylon to Nebuchadnezzar king of Babylon, saying,
>
> "Thus says the LORD of hosts, the God of Israel, to all the exiles whom I have sent into exile from Jerusalem to Babylon, build houses and live in them; and plant gardens and eat their produce. Take wives and become the fathers of sons and daughters, and take wives for your sons and give your daughters to husbands, that they may bear sons and daughters; and multiply there and do not decrease.
>
> Seek the welfare of the city where I have sent you into exile [*note who really sent them into* exile] and pray to the LORD on its behalf; for in its welfare you will have welfare.'
>
> "For thus says the LORD of hosts, the God of Israel, 'Do not let your prophets who are in your midst and your diviners deceive you, and do not

listen to the dreams which they dream. For they prophesy falsely to you in My name; I have not sent them,' declares the LORD.

"For thus says the LORD, 'When seventy years have been completed for Babylon, I will visit you and fulfill My good word to you, to bring you back to this place. For I know the plans that I have for you,' declares the LORD, 'plans for welfare and not for calamity to give you a future and a hope.

Then you will call upon Me and come and pray to Me, and I will listen to you. You will seek Me and find Me when you search for Me with all your heart. I will be found by you,' declares the LORD, 'and I will restore your fortunes and will gather you from all the nations and from all the places where I have driven you,' declares the LORD, 'and I will bring you back to the place *from where I sent you into exile.'*

For those who say it would be utter foolishness to believe in a literal-grammatical hermeneutic that would consider 70 years of exile to be a promise, saying instead that it should be interpreted as some allegorical promise to the church, we will limit this to two biblical individuals.

This is how "foolish" Daniel 9 began, Daniel 9:1–2:

In the first year of Darius the son of Ahasuerus, of Median descent, who was made king over the kingdom of the Chaldean—in the first year of his reign, I, Daniel, observed in the books the number of the years which was revealed as the word of the LORD to Jeremiah the prophet for the completion of the desolations of Jerusalem, namely, seventy years.

Would it not be wonderfully encouraging for Daniel to experience how Daniel 1:20 concludes: "And Daniel continued until the first year of Cyrus the king."

In Zechariah 1:12, we meet another "foolish individual" looking for the exile to be 70 years—and we will come back here later:

Then the angel of the LORD said, "O LORD of hosts, how long will You have no compassion for Jerusalem and the cities of Judah, with which You have been indignant these seventy years?"

Those who are so steeped in their allegorical interpretations can take it up with Daniel or the Angel of the Lord, if they can find them.

THE PROCLAMATION OF CYRUS FOR THE JEWS TO RETURN TO THEIR OWN LAND GIVEN THEM BY GOD

We will conclude this chapter with two versions of one proclamation that Cyrus the king—*prophesied by name by God* about 150 years earlier—and his earthly, kingly decree. Second Chronicles 36:11–23 hopefully can be read through clearer biblical lenses:

> Zedekiah [*the last man to sit on David's throne until the current time*] was twenty-one years old when he became king, and he reigned eleven years in Jerusalem. And he did evil in the sight of the LORD his God; he did not humble himself before Jeremiah the prophet who spoke for the LORD [*Therefore, with Zedekiah and those under his reign, being under the Mosaic Covenant, the curse part will apply to them severely*]. And he also rebelled against King Nebuchadnezzar who had made him swear allegiance by God. But he stiffened his neck and hardened his heart against turning to the LORD God of Israel.
>
> Furthermore, all the officials of the priests and the people were very unfaithful following all the abominations of the nations; and they defiled the house of the LORD which He had sanctified in Jerusalem. And the LORD, the God of their fathers, sent word to them again and again by His messengers, because He had compassion on His people and on His dwelling place; but they continually mocked the messengers of God, despised His words and scoffed at His prophets, until the wrath of the LORD arose against His people, until there was no remedy [*a sad, summary statement of such widespread wickedness*].
>
> Therefore He brought up against them the king of the Chaldeans who slew their young men with the sword in the house of their sanctuary, and had no compassion on young man or virgin, old man or infirm; He gave them all into his hand. And all the articles of the house of God, great

and small, and the treasures of the house of the LORD, and the treasures of the king and of his officers, he brought them all to Babylon.

Then they burned the house of God, and broke down the wall of Jerusalem and burned all its fortified buildings with fire, and destroyed all its valuable articles. And those who had escaped from the sword he carried away to Babylon; and they were servants to him and to his sons until the rule of the kingdom of Persia, to fulfill the word of the LORD by the mouth of Jeremiah, until the land had enjoyed its sabbaths. ***All the days of its desolation it kept sabbath until seventy years were complete***.

Now in the first year of Cyrus king of Persia—in order to fulfill the word of the LORD by the mouth of Jeremiah—the LORD stirred up the spirit of Cyrus king of Persia, so that he sent a proclamation throughout his kingdom, and also put it in writing, saying, "Thus says Cyrus king of Persia, 'The LORD, the God of heaven, has given me all the kingdoms of the earth, and He has appointed me to build Him a house in Jerusalem, which is in Judah. Whoever there is among you of all His people, may the LORD his God be with him, and let him go up!'"

All of the above Scripture makes perfect sense using the literal-grammatical hermeneutic, which is another way of using "the normative use of the language." Ezra 1:1–4 is the shorter version:

Now in the first year of Cyrus king of Persia, in order to fulfill the word of the LORD by the mouth of Jeremiah, the LORD stirred up the spirit of Cyrus king of Persia, so that he sent a proclamation throughout all his kingdom, and also put it in writing, saying, "Thus says Cyrus king of Persia, 'The LORD, the God of heaven, has given me all the kingdoms of the earth, and He has appointed me to build Him a house in Jerusalem, which is in Judah. Whoever there is among you of all His people, may his God be with him! Let him go up to Jerusalem, which is in Judah, and rebuild the house of the LORD, the God of Israel; He is the God who is in Jerusalem. And every survivor, at whatever place he may live, let the men of that place support him with silver and gold, with goods and cattle, together with a freewill offering for the house of God which is in Jerusalem.'"

SUMMARY AND CONCLUSION

Among other things in this chapter we saw: (1) sections from "the blessing and the curse" promises in Leviticus 26:31–33, and Deuteronomy 28:63–68 strongly promised the exile of the Jewish people unless they repented and walked with God; (2) yet even with exile looming, the Davidic Covenant offered many wonderful promises about the time of the Messiah's ultimate reign; (3) in Hosea 3:3–5, God prophesies and promises that in spite of their present situation, eventually He will fulfill His good Word to Israel in the last days; (4) God explains both the reason for His absence and the future remedy, promising in Hosea 5:15: "I will go away and return to My place until they acknowledge their guilt *and seek My face*; in their affliction they will earnestly seek Me." The prophet Isaiah also presents God in a prophecy as looking back on what He did to Israel and why, and how in His utter covenant faithfulness He will restore fellowship with the same Jewish nation He had previously punished, stating in Isaiah 54:7–10: "In an outburst of anger *I hid My face from you for a moment*; but with everlasting lovingkindness I will have compassion on you," says the LORD your Redeemer.

(5) In the theology proper section of Isaiah (40–48), God repeatedly challenges those who would attempt to demean Him; (6) One way He does it is with Isaiah 44:24–26, where God *before anyone else* says that Jerusalem will be rebuilt. (7) God even reveals the name of the Gentile king who was to be born about 150 years into the future, in Isaiah 48:28 and 45:1–7; (8) Critics of the Bible hate this section because (using their reasoning) this would mean there is a God who not only knows the future, but He brings the future into existence—which is exactly what He claims to do; (9) Sadly, the people do not repent, and God's promised exile will occur.

(10) The Babylonian Exile with Jerusalem and the Temple of the LORD being destroyed occurs—just as God repeatedly promised. (11) God made known to His godly prophet the answers as to how long the exile was to last: Jeremiah 25:11 and Jeremiah 29:10–11 limit the exile to 70 years. (11) Daniel understood this to be in the literal grammatical presentation, as we see in his responding to it (Dan 9:1-2):

In the first year of Darius the son of Ahasuerus, of Median descent, who was made king over the kingdom of the Chaldean—in the first year of his reign, I, Daniel, observed in the books the number of the years which was revealed as the word of the LORD to Jeremiah the prophet for the completion of the desolations of Jerusalem, namely, seventy years.

(12) Cyrus eventually arrived, just as God had said, (13) and in 2 Chronicles 36:11–23 and the shorter version in Ezra 1:1–4, Cyrus gave the decree to rebuild Jerusalem.

DEEPER WALK STUDY QUESTIONS

(1)   From "the blessing and the curse section" of Leviticus 26:31–33 and Deuteronomy 28:63–68, name 10 reasons for or characteristics of the promised exile and why the people should have heeded such a warning from God.

(2)   From Psalm 89 and Isaiah 9:6–7, give nine reasons why the Davidic Covenant promises from God were very important to the future of the Jewish people and ultimately to the future of the world.

(3)   What kind of promises did God make to Israel in Hosea 3:3–5? List six items and explain why they are important. Be specific.

(4)   Name five reasons why God's hiding His face would be horrible for national Israel, as well as five blessings when national Israel eventually seeks God's face when He allows the people to do so.

(5)   Name ten attributes about God found in Isaiah 44:24–26, 44:28, and 45:1–7. Be specific.

(6)   List eight attributes about Cyrus and show why critics of the Bible think this is a lie or forgery or both. Explain and defend your answer biblically.

(7) Name 7 ways Isaiah 45:1–7 is a love story. Be specific.

(8) Why are Jeremiah 25 and 29 important for understanding not only biblical history, but also the works of God? Explain with ten doctrinal points and be specific.

(9) List 15 biblical truths from the account of Cyrus as seen in 2 Chronicles 36:11–23.

(10) Make up your own study question, answer it, and be able to give people five reasons why your question was important.

CHAPTER SIX

A THEOLOGICAL WALK-THROUGH ZECHARIAH 1–6

INTRODUCTION

What the world at large and an ever-increasing number of those in the "Christian World" fail to acknowledge is that there exist behind the scenes spiritual realities that greatly affect the events of human history, and these realities are unknown and unseen unless God chooses to reveal them. In the Book of Zechariah, God's Word discloses several spiritual realities—both holy and evil. And while it may have seemed that God had done nothing and had allowed the Gentiles to win, indeed God had done just as He said He would do by punishing the nation of Israel for their willful and multiplied high-handed sins against Him due to their repeatedly breaking the Mosaic Covenant—God remained faithful doing exactly what He had promised to do by sending the people into Babylonian Exile.

When writing *The Bible Expositor's Handbook (OT/NT)*, Chapter 14, "Great Is Thy Faithfulness," (pp. 195–207), I spent an entire chapter discussing the details God had promised and fulfilled, and He did so with a literal-grammatical action that went precisely with what He had written. I think you will find that reading this chapter will be helpful, and while some people know—most do not—the beloved hymn that formed the title for the chapter in the *Handbook* comes in the midst of some of the harshest and most gruesome judgments given during the curse part of "the blessing and the curse" (Lev 26/Deut 28).

So what happens when the same God promises blessings to the same people that He had severely judged in accordance with His written Word? Will these blessings come true as well? The overwhelming majority of scholars, seminaries, pastors, and lay Christians declare that future blessings to Israel will never occur because they claim that God has replaced Israel with the church because of the multitude of Israel's sins—especially for the role they played in the crucifixion of Jesus the Messiah. Consequently—according to them—any promise of blessings to national Israel has been forfeited by the Jewish people, and because of this, the Jews play no significant role in eschatological/prophetic events.

There is only one major problem with such a theological position: God thinks/reasons/pronounces otherwise, and He does so repeatedly, persistently, and abundantly. The Book of Zechariah—among others—is one book wherein God Himself repeatedly makes very detailed promises both to national Israel and to the coming Messiah, who will conquer His foes and be the first to sit on David's throne in almost 3,000 years—and will have Jerusalem as the capital of His worldwide reign.

SETTING THE BIBLICAL TABLE FOR THE BOOK OF ZECHARIAH

Zechariah, whose name means "God Remembers," is in itself a verbal reminder in part of what the Holy Spirit will do throughout this book through the prophet: encourage the Jewish exiles returning from Babylon that God had not forgotten about them nor any of the multiplicity of promises that would affect them. We will learn more about him, but it is important to note that Zechariah was born in Babylon during the Babylonian Exile. So when he goes from Babylon to the land repeatedly promised to the Jews by God Himself, he is seeing for the first time what he had previously only heard stories about, or what he had learned about in reading the biblical account up to that time.

You can go back and review some of God's promises, but we will briefly call attention to a few pertinent ones in this chapter of our study. We have seen that centuries before in Isaiah 44–45 it was God Himself—Who had first said Jerusalem would be rebuilt—Who foretold the name of King Cyrus, about 150 years before raising up that Gentile king to a position of world prominence. When Cyrus came to power, God had already declared that it would be Cyrus who would give the decree for the Jews to return to their homeland. Before Cyrus appears in the biblical text (Isa 44:28), God declares in Isaiah 44:24–26:

> Thus says the LORD, your Redeemer, and the one who formed you from the womb,
> "I, the LORD, am the maker of all things,
> Stretching out the heavens by Myself
> And spreading out the earth all alone,
> Causing the omens of boasters to fail,
> Making fools out of diviners,
> Causing wise men to draw back
> And turning their knowledge into foolishness,
> Confirming the word of His servant
> And performing the purpose of His messengers.
> It is I who says of Jerusalem, 'She shall be inhabited!'
> And of the cities of Judah, 'They shall be built.'
> And I will raise up her ruins again."

There is no decree from Cyrus—nor Cyrus the King—without God bringing all the components into place. So when Cyrus first appears by name in Isaiah 44:28 ("It is I who says of Cyrus, 'He is My shepherd! / And he will perform all My desire.' / And he declares of Jerusalem, 'She will be built,' / And of the temple, 'Your foundation will be laid'"), (1) God declares that Cyrus will be the human means, (2) which God Himself will raise up at the proper time, and (3) foretells this 150 years or so before the event. You can also find a parallel account to Cyrus' decree for the Jews at the end of 2 Chronicles 36, but we will use the Ezra account because we will need to look at other verses in Ezra. Ezra 1:1–4 opens with Cyrus' decree, which is dated by historians to 538 BC:

> Now in the first year of Cyrus king of Persia, in order to fulfill the word of the LORD by the mouth of Jeremiah, the LORD stirred up the spirit of Cyrus king of Persia, so that he sent a proclamation throughout all his kingdom, and also put it in writing, saying, "Thus says Cyrus king of Persia, 'The LORD, the God of heaven, has given me all the kingdoms of the earth, and He has appointed me to build Him a house in Jerusalem, which is in Judah. Whoever there is among you of all His people, may his God be with him! Let him go up to Jerusalem which is in Judah, and rebuild the house of the LORD, the God of Israel; He is the God who is in Jerusalem. And every survivor, at whatever place he may live, let the men of that place support him with silver and gold, with goods and cattle, together with a freewill offering for the house of God which is in Jerusalem.'"

Not only did God stir the heart of the Gentile king, but the following verses in Ezra 1:5–9 show accompanying actions:

> Then the heads of fathers' households of Judah and Benjamin and the priests and the Levites arose, even everyone whose spirit God had stirred to go up and rebuild the house of the LORD which is in Jerusalem. And all those about them encouraged them with articles of silver, with gold, with goods, with cattle, and with valuables, aside from all that was given as a freewill offering.
>
> Also King Cyrus brought out the articles of the house of the LORD, which Nebuchadnezzar had carried away from Jerusalem and put in the house of his gods; and Cyrus, king of Persia, had them brought out by the hand of Mithredath the treasurer, and he counted them out to Sheshbazzar, the prince of Judah.

Ezra 2:64–65 shows that approximately 50,000 returned from Babylon to the land from where they were exiled, and they did not come back empty-handed. Zechariah was among the exiles who returned to his true homeland.

Ezra 3:8–20 records the beginning of rebuilding the Temple of Yahweh in 536 BC. For various reasons—most of them direct by-products of sins by the Jewish people—the Temple construction stopped, and the Jews started intermarrying with pagan Gentiles. God used the prophet Haggai as the human instrument to bring the nation into covenant obedience. We must remember that even though this is the times of the Gentiles, the nation of Israel is still under the benefits and obligations of the Mosaic Covenant.

Ezra 3:10–13 shows the contrast between the ornate splendor of the original Temple of Yahweh and the rather simple and modest restored foundation of the one these workers constructed:

> Now when the builders had laid the foundation of the temple of the LORD, the priests stood in their apparel with trumpets, and the Levites, the sons of Asaph, with cymbals, to praise the LORD according to the directions of King David of Israel. And they sang, praising and giving thanks to the LORD, saying, "For He is good, for His lovingkindness is upon Israel forever." And all the people shouted with a great shout when they praised the LORD because the foundation of the house of the LORD was laid.
>
> Yet many of the priests and Levites and heads of fathers' households, the old men who had seen the first temple, wept with a loud voice when the foundation of this house was laid before their eyes, while many shouted aloud for joy; so that the people could not distinguish the sound of the shout of joy from the sound of the weeping of the people, for the people shouted with a loud shout, and the sound was heard far away.

After the delays in building the Temple, the work began again in 520 BC, and Ezra 6:15 tells us exactly when the Temple of the Lord was finished: "And this temple was completed on the third day of the month Adar; it was the sixth year of the reign of King Darius"—the times of the Gentiles continuing—and to compare this with our modern calendar, the Temple was finished on 12 March 515 BC, a little over seventy years after it had been destroyed.

Declaration and Invitation and an Evaluation of the Truthfulness of God's Word (Zech 1:1–6):

With this background, the Book of Zechariah begins, having as its introduction:

> In the eighth month of the second year of Darius, the word of the LORD came to Zechariah the prophet, the son of Berechiah, the son of Iddo saying, "The LORD was very angry with your fathers."

We usually do not stop after only two sentences in our present biblical book to look elsewhere, but what Jeremiah wrote will help us to review pertinent knowledge that we will see in our study, and these newer truths will be based on the older ones. Jeremiah 29:1–10 reveals the prophet writing from Jerusalem to whoever the exiles already were in Babylon, but before Jerusalem and the Temple of the LORD were destroyed, by writing:

> Now these are the words of the letter which Jeremiah the prophet sent from Jerusalem to the rest of the elders of the exile, the priests, the prophets and all the people whom Nebuchadnezzar had taken into exile from Jerusalem to Babylon.
>
> (This was after King Jeconiah and the queen mother, the court officials, the princes of Judah and Jerusalem, the craftsmen and the smiths had departed from Jerusalem.)
>
> The letter was sent by the hand of Elasah the son of Shaphan, and Gemariah the son of Hilkiah, whom Zedekiah king of Judah sent to Babylon to Nebuchadnezzar king of Babylon, saying, "Thus says the LORD of hosts, the God of Israel, *to all the exiles whom I have sent into exile from Jerusalem to Babylon,*
>
> "Build houses and live in them; and plant gardens and eat their produce. Take wives and become the fathers of sons and daughters, and take wives for your sons and give your daughters to husbands, that they may bear sons and daughters; and multiply there and do not decrease. Seek the welfare of the city *where I have sent you into exile,* and pray to the LORD on its behalf; for in its welfare you will have welfare.'
>
> "For thus says the LORD of hosts, the God of Israel, 'Do not let your prophets who are in your midst and your diviners deceive you, and do not listen to the dreams which they dream. For they prophesy falsely to you in My name; I have not sent them,' declares the LORD.
>
> "For thus says the LORD, 'When seventy years have been completed for Babylon, I will visit you and fulfill My good word to you, to bring you back to this place.

The false prophets told the exiles that God had not been angry. Such brazen wickedness was in direct contradiction to the repeated proclamations of God through His holy prophets for centuries. The false prophets were wrong on many occasions; they said the exile was just a political event with no spiritual significance—God said that He Himself had sent the exiles to Babylon. The false prophets told the people not to unpack, that they would be going back soon—God counters this by declaring twice in Jeremiah 25 and 29 that it will be a 70 year exile—and a 70 year exile it was. Although those wretched false prophets claimed to speak for the LORD God, He had not sent them.

Repeating the verses to see them in context, here is Zechariah 1:1–6, God's declaration and invitation for the punished Jewish people to evaluate His Words:

> In the eighth month of the second year of Darius, the word of the LORD came to Zechariah the prophet, the son of Berechiah, the son of Iddo saying, "The LORD was very angry with your fathers [*contra the Jewish false prophets in Babylon*].
>
> "Therefore say to them, 'Thus says the LORD of hosts, "Return to Me," declares the LORD of hosts, "that I may return to you," says the LORD of hosts.
>
> "Do not be like your fathers, to whom the former prophets proclaimed, saying, 'Thus says the LORD of hosts, "Return now from your evil ways and from your evil deeds."' But they did not listen or give heed to Me," declares the LORD.
>
> "Your fathers, where are they? And the prophets, do they live forever?
>
> "But did not My words and My statutes, which I commanded My servants the prophets, overtake your fathers? Then they repented and said, 'As the LORD of hosts purposed to do to us in accordance with our ways and our deeds, so He, has dealt with us.'"

MARK THIS: The word "overtake" (Zech. 1:6) may not mean much to the casual reader of Scripture, depending on the culture or time when you lived, but it certainly did—or should—to the Jewish people under the Mosaic Covenant, being employed with both "the blessing and the curse." We will limit ourselves just to Deuteronomy. As God had promised earlier in "the blessing and the curse" of Deuteronomy 28, God did just as He said He would do. **The blessing part begins in Deuteronomy 28:1–2** "Now it shall be, if you will diligently obey the LORD your God, being careful to do all His commandments which I command you today, the LORD your God will set you high above all the nations of the earth. And all these blessings shall come upon you and **overtake** you, if you will obey the LORD your God." In the same manner, **the curse section** began this way in Deuteronomy 28:15: "But it shall come about, if you will not obey the LORD your God, to observe to do all His commandments and His statutes with which I charge you today, that all these curses shall come upon you and **overtake** you." One more usage in the curse section: "So all these curses shall come on you and pursue you and **overtake** you until you are destroyed, because you would not obey the LORD your God by keeping His commandments and His statutes which He commanded you (Deut 28:45). So in the verse that serves as the closing verse to the introduction, God uses both "the blessing and the curse" language, and "the blessing and the curse" outcome—just as He had repeatedly promised, and just as Zechariah 1:6 affirms, "But did not My words and My statutes, which I commanded My servants the prophets, **overtake** your fathers?"

After the introduction verses, Zechariah 1:1–7, the remaining part of Zechariah 1–6 is a series of eight night visions given to the prophet from the LORD. We will not try to explain nor explore each item. Instead, we will study especially those that will factor into later parts of *The King and His Glory*.

Since Yahweh had not only judged the Jewish people severely due to their hardness of heart and their many rebellious acts against Him, when God gave eight night—all eight night visions were given by God on the same night—He began with three visions speaking soothing words, healing words, and promises of future works that God will do for the Jewish people. Some people read these—and many other verses—and force on them the interpretation that this is replacement theology. They say the church replaces national Israel so that the church not only receives God's blessings, it also becomes a part of God's program wherever any positive promise is made by God about the Jewish people. Such theology is not found in these first three night visions—nor many other places. People see it only if they bring it to the Bible and force its interpretation and foregone conclusion upon the text. All God had to do was say, "That's it! I'm done with those sinful Jewish people forever and ever!"—and that would be enough. Let's look at the first three night visions and see if that is what Yahweh is attempting to convey in the plain sense of language.

CRUCIAL: When God used "the blessing and the curse" as a measure of increased increments of judgment, He fully expected the Jewish people to know what He spoke of, based on the Mosaic Covenant. He warned them through a myriad of prophets over the centuries, each understanding "the blessing and the curse" with a literal-grammatical "plain understanding of the text." Not only did God keep His promises, He further executed His judgments in full harmony and in a literal-grammatical hermeneutic fulfillment of judgments He did not desire to do, but knew that He had to in order to be true to His Word—and true to His character.

First of Eight Night Visions in Zechariah: 1:7–17: A Man in the Myrtles and a Vision of Angelic Riders on Horses to Patrol the Earth

On the twenty-fourth day of the eleventh month, which is the month Shebat, in the second year of Darius, the word of the LORD came to Zechariah the prophet, the son of Berechiah, the son of Iddo, as follows: I saw at night, and behold, a man was riding on a red horse, and he was standing among the myrtle trees which were in the ravine, with red, sorrel [*a light, reddish-brown*], and white horses behind him.

Then I said, "My lord, what are these?" And the angel who was speaking with me said to me, "I will show you what these are." And the man who was standing among the myrtle trees answered and said, "These are those whom the LORD has sent to patrol the earth."

So they answered the angel of the LORD who was standing among the myrtle trees, and said, "We have patrolled the earth, and behold, all the earth is peaceful and quiet."

Then the angel of the LORD answered and said, "O LORD of hosts, how long will You have no compassion for Jerusalem and the cities of Judah, with which You have been indignant these seventy years?"

And the LORD answered the angel who was speaking with me with gracious words, comforting words. So the angel who was speaking with me said to me, "Proclaim, saying, 'Thus says the LORD of hosts, "I am exceedingly jealous for Jerusalem and Zion.

"But I am very angry with the nations who are at ease; for while I was only a little angry, they furthered the disaster."

'Therefore, thus says the LORD, "I will return to Jerusalem with compassion; My house will be built in it," declares the LORD of hosts, "and a measuring line will be stretched over Jerusalem."'

"Again, proclaim, saying, 'Thus says the LORD of hosts, "My cities will again overflow with prosperity, and the LORD will again comfort Zion and again choose Jerusalem."'"

In response to the question they were asked in Zechariah 1:11–12, "So they answered the angel of the LORD [the preincarnate second member of the Godhead] who was standing among the myrtle trees, and said, 'We have patrolled the earth, and behold, all the earth is peaceful and quiet."

Then the angel of the LORD answered and said, "O LORD of hosts, how long will You have no compassion for Jerusalem and the cities of Judah, with which You have been indignant these seventy years?" Remember that Jeremiah 25:11; 29:10, and Dan 9:1–2, required the literal grammatical hermeneutic. Now the Angel of the LORD gives a fourth instance, with normal use of language to show (1) this is speaking in reference to Jerusalem, and (2) 70 years was what God repeatedly used about how long the Babylonian Exile was to last. (He only had to say it once, and it would be true.)

God used soothing words in Zechariah 1:13–14 and answered with His holy jealousy for Jerusalem and Zion: "And the LORD answered the angel who was speaking with me with gracious words, comforting words. So the angel who was speaking with me said to me, "Proclaim, saying, 'Thus says the LORD of hosts, "I am exceedingly jealous for Jerusalem and Zion."'" Earlier, God had promised the same thing very explicitly as part of the fulness of the benefits of the New Covenant (Jer 31:31–35). Here He spoke about Jerusalem in Jeremiah 31:38–40:

> "Behold, days are coming," declares the LORD, "when the city shall be rebuilt for the LORD from the Tower of Hananel to the Corner Gate. And the measuring line shall go out farther straight ahead to the hill Gareb; then it will turn to Goah.
>
> "And the whole valley of the dead bodies and of the ashes, and all the fields as far as the brook Kidron, to the corner of the Horse Gate toward the east, shall be holy to the LORD; it shall not be plucked up, or overthrown anymore forever."

Not only did the nations do what Yahweh raised them up to do for Him by destroying Jerusalem and the Temple of the LORD, they went beyond what He wanted, so the Genesis 12:3, "I will curse the ones who curse you" weighed on them:

"But I am very angry with the nations who are at ease; for while I was only a little angry, they furthered the disaster." 'Therefore, thus says the LORD, "I will return to Jerusalem with compassion; My house will be built in it," declares the LORD of hosts, "and a measuring line will be stretched over Jerusalem."'

"Again, proclaim, saying, 'Thus says the LORD of hosts, "My cities will again overflow with prosperity, and the LORD will again comfort Zion and again choose Jerusalem"'" (Zechariah 1:15–17).

Immanuel language—beyond the first advent!

CRUCIAL: What is God attempting to communicate to national Israel? Israel is the same nation He Himself sent into Babylonian exile, the nation He told that they would be there 70 years—and they were—because He was going to revisit them at that time and make the Gentile King Cyrus restore them. God said He would create Cyrus (Col. 1:26 "For by Him all things were created, both in the heavens and on earth, visible and invisible, whether thrones or dominions or rulers or authorities—all things have been created by Him and for Him)," and now says that He will comfort them by soothing words, *and* now He was no longer angry at national Israel. He was angry with the Gentiles, who were at that time at peace. History and later Scriptural books show that God was not talking about the immediate fulfillment of these blessings, if for no other reason than the coming King had not been born yet. But if you were to take this to be a blessing by God on the church—how could you possibly know how any Scripture should be interpreted? This is no minor issue; you/we teachers and preachers must consider also James 3. You/I will be held to higher standards for how we taught others the Word of God.

Second of Eight Night Visions in Zechariah 1:18–21:
Four Horns and Four Craftsman

> Then I lifted up my eyes and looked, and behold, there were four horns. So I said to the angel who was speaking with me, "What are these?" And he answered me, "These are the horns which have scattered Judah, Israel, and Jerusalem."
>
> Then the LORD showed me four craftsmen.
>
> And I said, "What are these coming to do?" And he said, "These are the horns which have scattered Judah, so that no man lifts up his head; but these craftsmen have come to terrify them, to throw down the horns of the nations who have lifted up their horns against the land of Judah in order to scatter it."

Another way of saying it, paraphrasing "I will bless the ones who bless you and curse the ones who curse you."

Third of Eight Night Visions in Zechariah 2:1–13:
A Man with a Measuring Line

Zechariah 2:1–5 discloses:

> Then I lifted up my eyes and looked, and behold, there was a man with a measuring line in his hand. So I said, "Where are you going?" And he said to me, "To measure Jerusalem, to see how wide it is and how long it is."
>
> And behold, the angel who was speaking with me was going out, and another angel was coming out to meet him, and said to him, "Run, speak to that young man, saying, 'Jerusalem will be inhabited without walls, because of the multitude of men and cattle within it.
>
> 'For I,' declares the LORD, 'will be a wall of fire around her, and I will be the glory in her midst.'"

Zechariah 2:6–13 starts the next paragraph, again with an emphasis on the presence of God in their midst:

> "Ho there! Flee from the land of the north," declares the LORD, "for I have dispersed you as the four winds of the heavens," declares the LORD.

"Ho, Zion! Escape, you who are living with the daughter of Babylon." For thus says the LORD of hosts, "After glory He has sent me against the nations which plunder you, for he who touches you, touches the apple of His eye.

"For behold, I will wave My hand over them, so that they will be plunder for their slaves. Then you will know that the LORD of hosts has sent Me.

"Sing for joy and be glad, O daughter of Zion; for behold I am coming and I will dwell in your midst," declares the LORD. "And many nations will join themselves to the LORD in that day and will become My people. Then I will dwell in your midst, and you will know that the LORD of hosts has sent Me to you.

"And the LORD will possess Judah as His portion in the holy land, and will again choose Jerusalem.

"Be silent, all flesh, before the LORD; for He is aroused from His holy habitation."

Fourth of Eight Night Visions in Zechariah 3:1–10: Cleansing of the High Priest

We will come back to these verses in another chapter, but let's look at the opening lines of the vision, Zechariah 3:1–2:

> Then he showed me Joshua the high priest standing before the angel of the LORD, and Satan standing at his right hand to accuse him.
>
> And the LORD said to Satan, "The LORD rebuke you, Satan! Indeed, the LORD who has chosen Jerusalem rebuke you! Is this not a brand plucked from the fire?"

Three important items to note before we move on: (1) Satan's name is used three times in these verses, and (2) Satan is present in this portion, but God does not allow him to speak. God very much wanted Satan to know the disclosure of this particular divine revelation. (3) This is the last time Satan appears in the OT. He will not show up again by name until Matthew 4/Mark 1/Luke 4 with the 40-day temptation of Jesus the Messiah.

Remember that Zech 3:8–10 connects with the context of the opening verses of this incredibly important prophecy because it has Satan standing there, not permitted to speak, but hearing some Messianic truths that will become clearer in the New Testament. Zechariah 3:8–10:

> Now listen, Joshua the high priest, you and your friends who are sitting in front of you—indeed they are men who are a symbol, for behold, I am going to bring in My servant the Branch.
>
> For behold, the stone that I have set before Joshua; on one stone are seven eyes. Behold, I will engrave an inscription on it,' declares the LORD of hosts, 'and I will remove the iniquity of that land in one day.
>
> In that day,' declares the LORD of hosts, 'every one of you will invite his neighbor to sit under his vine and under his fig tree.'"

In Zechariah 3:8, Joshua and his friends foreshadow coming events or persons—or, to narrow this down, they are foreshadowers of the One to come, Whom God will send. He is given very specific names/titles/roles: "for behold, I am going to bring in My Servant the Branch."

Both titles, "My Servant" and "the Branch," are used elsewhere in Scripture. Here are examples, first for the promised Servant of Yahweh (besides the fact that the entire Gospel of Mark presents and supports Jesus the Messiah as the prophesied Servant of Yahweh):

—Isaiah 42:1

"Behold, My Servant, whom I uphold; My chosen one in whom My soul delights. I have put My Spirit upon Him; He will bring forth justice to the nations.

—Isaiah 49:1–3

Listen to Me, O islands,
And pay attention, you peoples from afar.
The LORD called Me from the womb;
From the body of My mother He named Me.
He has made My mouth like a sharp sword,
In the shadow of His hand He has concealed Me; / And He has also made Me a select arrow, /He has hidden Me in His quiver.
He said to Me [singular—not plural], "You are My Servant, Israel,

In Whom I will show My glory."

—Isaiah. 49:5

"And now says the LORD, who formed Me from the womb to be His Servant,
To bring Jacob back to Him, so that Israel might be gathered to Him
(For I am honored in the sight of the LORD,
And My God is My strength),

—Isaiah 52:13–15:

Behold, My servant will prosper,
He will be high and lifted up and greatly exalted.
Just as many were astonished at you, My people,
So His appearance was marred more than any man
And His form more than the sons of men.
Thus He will sprinkle many nations,
Kings will shut their mouths on account of Him;
For what had not been told them they will see,
And what they had not heard they will understand.

—Isaiah 53:10–11

But the LORD was pleased
To crush Him, putting Him to grief;
If He would render Himself as a guilt offering,
He will see His offspring,
He will prolong His days,
And the good pleasure of the LORD will prosper in His hand.
As a result of the anguish of His soul,
He will see it and be satisfied;
By His knowledge the Righteous One,
My Servant, will justify the many,
As He will bear their iniquities.

Here are some samplings, first for the promised Branch of Yahweh:

(1) "the Branch"

—Isaiah 4:2–5 (context) the Righteous Rule of the Branch of the Redeemed (in the Panoramic Overview of Isaiah [1–5])

> In that day the Branch of the LORD will be beautiful and glorious, and the fruit of the earth will be the pride and the adornment of the survivors of Israel. It will come about that he who is left in Zion and remains in Jerusalem will be called holy—everyone who is recorded for life in Jerusalem.
>
> When the Lord has washed away the filth of the daughters of Zion and purged the bloodshed of Jerusalem from her midst, by the spirit of judgment and the spirit of burning, then the LORD will create over the whole area of Mount Zion and over her assemblies a cloud by day, even smoke, and the brightness of a flaming fire by night; for over all the glory will be a canopy.

Much more will be addressed about this important cleansing aspect only by means of the Branch, the Servant of Yahweh, later in the book.

—Isaiah 11:1–4, the Branch shows the lowliness of the Messiah, coming appropriately enough, written in "the Book of Immanuel" chapters of Isaiah 7–12:

> Then a shoot will spring from the stem of Jesse,
> And a branch from his roots will bear fruit.
> The Spirit of the LORD will rest on Him,
> The spirit of wisdom and understanding,
> The spirit of counsel and strength,
> The spirit of knowledge and the fear of the LORD.
> And He will delight in the fear of the LORD,
> And He will not judge by what His eyes see,
> Nor make a decision by what His ears hear;
> But with righteousness He will judge the poor,
> And decide with fairness for the afflicted of the earth;
> And He will strike the earth with the rod of His mouth,
> And with the breath of His lips He will slay the wicked.

Remember that chapter divisions are the works of human hands and not inspired, though most of the chapter markers are accurate and helpful. But Isaiah 53 is a terrible Servant of the LORD marker because, first, it omits the last three verses of Isaiah 52 which begins with, "Behold, My servant will prosper," second, Isaiah 53:1 does not use the word "Servant" then, and asks "Who has believed our report?" What report? The report that started in Isaiah 52:13–15, and the one that includes the utter unworldly brutality that will affect the Servant of Yahweh "So His appearance was marred more than any man / And His form more than the sons of men." See *The Darkness and the Glory* for more details of what made the cup that Jesus drank and His death different from that of anyone else, as well as from the collective whole of all humanity past, present, and future.

Isaiah 53:2–4, seen in its proper context, makes perfect sense as it is:

For He grew up before Him like a tender shoot,
And like a root out of parched ground;
He has no stately form or majesty
That we should look upon Him,
Nor appearance that we should be attracted to Him.
He was despised and forsaken of men,
A man of sorrows and acquainted with grief;
And like one from whom men hide their face
He was despised, and we did not esteem Him.
Surely our griefs He Himself bore,
And our sorrows He carried;
Yet we ourselves esteemed Him stricken,
Smitten of God, and afflicted.

Jeremiah 23:5–6 tells about the future reign of the Branch of Yahweh, a Davidic Covenant "qualifier." In the upcoming chapters we will see much more of the means of cleansing that God has chosen to use with some future remnant of Israel, also using the same means with Gentiles who will be saved during the Tribulation. This description of the Branch of Yahweh states:

"Behold, the days are coming," declares the LORD,

"When I will raise up for David a righteous Branch;
And He will reign as king and act wisely
And do justice and righteousness in the land.
"In His days Judah will be saved,
And Israel will dwell securely;
And this is His name by which He will be called,
'The LORD our righteousness.'

After 14 condemnation and judgement messages in Jeremiah 2–29, it sounds like God is done with national Israel forevermore, but Jer 30–33 erupts in an oasis of future blessings by God—and should be read as a four-chapter section of Scripture. It gives us, among other things, the first time that the New Covenant is designated by name (Jer 31:31–35). And since we are in the "Branch" verses about the Messiah, we will limit our study of these four chapters to Jeremiah 33:15, where He is called by God a righteous Branch. Adding the context of Jeremiah 33:1-22 will make it a much richer read for us:

> Then the word of the LORD came to Jeremiah the second time, while he was still confined in the court of the guard, saying, "Thus says the LORD who made the earth, the LORD who formed it to establish it, the LORD is His name, 'Call to Me and I will answer you, and I will tell you great and mighty things, which you do not know.'
>
> "For thus says the LORD God of Israel concerning the houses of this city, and concerning the houses of the kings of Judah which are broken down to make a defense against the siege ramps and against the sword, while they are coming to fight with the Chaldeans [*virtually another name for the Babylonians*] and to fill them with the corpses of men whom I have slain in My anger and in My wrath, and I have hidden My face from this city because of all their wickedness: 'Behold, I will bring to it health and healing, and I will heal them; and I will reveal to them an abundance of peace and truth.
>
> 'I will restore the fortunes of Judah and the fortunes of Israel and will rebuild them as they were at first. I will cleanse them from all their iniquity by which they have sinned against Me, and I will pardon all their iniquities by which they have sinned against Me and by which they have

transgressed against Me. It will be to Me a name of joy, praise and glory before all the nations of the earth which will hear of all the good that I do for them, and they will fear and tremble because of all the good and all the peace that I make for it.'

"Thus says the LORD, 'Yet again there will be heard in this place, of which you say, "It is a waste, without man and without beast," that is, in the cities of Judah and in the streets of Jerusalem that are desolate, without man and without inhabitant and without beast, the voice of joy and the voice of gladness, the voice of the bridegroom and the voice of the bride, the voice of those who say,

"Give thanks to the LORD of hosts,

For the LORD is good,

For His lovingkindness is everlasting"; and of those who bring a thank offering into the house of the LORD. For I will restore the fortunes of the land as they were at first,' says the LORD.

"Thus says the LORD of hosts, 'There will again be in this place which is waste, without man or beast, and in all its cities, a habitation of shepherds who rest their flocks. In the cities of the hill country, in the cities of the lowland, in the cities of the Negev, in the land of Benjamin, in the environs of Jerusalem and in the cities of Judah, the flocks will again pass under the hands of the one who numbers them,' says the LORD.

"*Behold, days are coming,' declares the LORD, 'when I will fulfill the good word which I have spoken concerning the house of Israel and the house of Judah. 'In those days and at that time I will cause* **a righteous Branch of David** *to spring forth; and He shall execute justice and righteousness on the earth. In those days Judah will be saved, and Jerusalem will dwell in safety; and this is the name by which she will be called: the LORD is our righteousness.*

"For thus says the LORD, 'David [*This is a Davidic Covenant promise by God*] shall never lack a man to sit on the throne of the house of Israel; and the Levitical priests shall never lack a man before Me to offer burnt offerings, to burn grain offerings and to prepare sacrifices continually'" [*Another holy promise of God for the Levitical priesthood; more about this in the upcoming chapters of this book*].

The word of the LORD came to Jeremiah, saying, "Thus says the LORD, 'If you can break My covenant for the day and My covenant for

THE KING AND HIS GLORY

the night, so that day and night will not be at their appointed time, then My covenant may also be broken with David My servant so that he will not have a son to reign on his throne, and with the Levitical priests, My ministers. As the host of heaven cannot be counted and the sand of the sea cannot be measured, so I will multiply the descendants of David My servant and the Levites who minister to Me.'"

There is much, much more about these last verses and Messianic connectives later in Jeremiah, but we will have to leave that for your personal or group study. People would be hard-pressed to claim biblical clarity without believing "a righteous Branch of David" will return and reign in Jerusalem.

Fifth of Eight Night Visions in Zechariah 4:1–4: A Golden Lampstand and Two Olive Trees

Then the angel who was speaking with me returned, and roused me as a man who is awakened from his sleep. And he said to me, "What do you see?" And I said, "I see, and behold, a lampstand all of gold with its bowl on the top of it, and its seven lamps on it with seven spouts belonging to each of the lamps which are on the top of it; also two olive trees by it, one on the right side of the bowl and the other on its left side."

Then I answered and said to the angel who was speaking with me saying, "What are these, my lord?" So the angel who was speaking with me answered and said to me, "Do you not know what these are?" And I said, "No, my lord."

We do not have the time or room in this book to go into any details disclosed in Zechariah 4:6–14:

Then he answered and said to me, "This is the word of the LORD to Zerubbabel saying, 'Not by might nor by power, but by My Spirit,' says the LORD of hosts. What are you, O great mountain? Before Zerubbabel you will become a plain; and he will bring forth the top stone with shouts of "Grace, grace to it!"'

Also the word of the LORD came to me saying, "The hands of Zerubbabel have laid the foundation of this house, and his hands will finish it. Then you will know that the LORD of hosts has sent me to you.

"For who has despised the day of small things? But these seven will be glad when they see the plumb line in the hand of Zerubbabel—these are the eyes of the LORD which range to and fro throughout the earth."

Then I answered and said to him, "What are these two olive trees on the right of the lampstand and on its left?" And I answered the second time and said to him, "What are the two olive branches which are beside the two golden pipes, which empty the golden oil from themselves?" So he answered me saying, "Do you not know what these are?" And I said, "No, my lord."

Then he said, "These are the two anointed ones, who are standing by the Lord of the whole earth."

For time's sake, just note *the Sixth of Eight Night Visions in Zechariah 5:1–4*: The Flying Scroll; *the Seventh of Eight Night Visions in Zechariah 5:5–11*: The Vision of the Woman in an Ephah [*bushel basket*], and *Eighth of Eight Night Visions in Zechariah 6:1–8*: Four Chariots.

Zechariah 6:9–15 is an important appendix in the first 6 chapters of Zechariah and how Zechariah 6 concludes the eight night visions. The appendix shows the coronation [in a vision] of Joshua the High Priest, and a promise and designation of the Branch, a title that God has already used elsewhere in Scripture with verses 6:12–13 highlighted below—but it also gives another Messianic promise that we have not seen elsewhere in our study:

The word of the LORD also came to me saying,

"Take an offering from the exiles, from Heldai, Tobijah, and Jedaiah; and you go the same day and enter the house of Josiah the son of Zephaniah, where they have arrived from Babylon. And take silver and gold, make an ornate crown, and set it on the head of Joshua the son of Jehozadak, the high priest.

"Then say to him, 'Thus says the LORD of hosts, "***Behold, a man whose name is Branch***, for He will branch out from where He is; and He will build the temple of the LORD.

"Yes, it is He who will build the temple of the LORD, and He who will bear the honor and sit and rule on His throne. ***Thus, He will be a***

priest on His throne, and the counsel of peace will be between the two offices."'

"Now the crown will become a reminder in the temple of the LORD to Helem, Tobijah, Jedaiah, and Hen the son of Zephaniah. And those who are far off will come and build the temple of the LORD." Then you will know that the LORD of hosts has sent me to you. And it will take place, if you completely obey the LORD your God.

Everything about this section may seem incredible or unbelievable—in the literal sense, by many scoffers. Here are some items to consider: (1) This cannot refer to the present or pending Temple at that time, because God has previously promised the rebuilding of the Temple to someone else after the exiles returned, stating in Zechariah 4:9: "The hands of Zerubbabel have laid the foundation of this house, and his hands will finish it. Then you will know that the LORD of hosts has sent me to you." (2) Under the Mosaic Covenant, kings cannot enter into the Holy of Holies and priests cannot sit on thrones—particularly inside the Temple of Yahweh. And (3) critics of the Bible say there is no possible way for this part to be true, since it so plainly contradicts what has previously been promised in Scripture, so that it is impossible for Zechariah 6:13 to be taken as doctrinal truth: "Yes, it is He [***the One the previous verse describes as a Man whose name is Branch, Who has all of the "Branch attributes" that other Scripture passages reveal***] Who will build the temple of the LORD, and He Who will bear the honor and sit and rule on His throne. ***Thus, He will be a priest on His throne, and the counsel of peace will be between the two offices.***"'

Some continue to argue that it cannot be true because this has never happened in history. *That is exactly the point; it remains an unfulfilled Messianic promise that has not yet been fulfilled but will be awaiting the future return and reign of the King/Messiah Jesus*—which definitely has not been fulfilled yet. We can cower in the corner with them and shiver and say, "Oh, no! God never thought about that, and there is no answer, so the Bible has errors and God—if He exists at all—is totally untrustworthy!" Or we can see the only answers that fit, as we follow the biblical trails, as I do here in *The King and His Glory*. Every part of what many call lies or errors in the last part of

Zechariah 6 will be plainly answered from the Bible in the upcoming chapters of this book.

I often go to the last part of Isaiah 25:1: "Plans formed long ago with perfect faithfulness." Obviously, we have not seen all the prophecies fulfilled—nor even seen yet all the pertinent related prophecies pertaining only to the King and His true Glory that the Bible attributes to Him.

SUMMARY AND CONCLUSION

In this chapter we learned, among other things (1) one of the major roles of Zechariah was to encourage the returning Jewish exiles from Babylon that God had not forgotten about them nor any of the multiplicity of promises that would affect them; (2) We have seen that centuries before, in Isaiah 44–45, it was God Himself—Who had first said Jerusalem would be rebuilt— Who foretold the name of King Cyrus, about 150 years before God raised up the Gentile king to a position of world prominence; (3) God Himself was the one Who already had declared that it would be Cyrus who would give the decree for the Jews to return to their homeland. Before Cyrus appears in the biblical text (Isa. 44:28), God declares in Isaiah 44:24–26 that Jerusalem is to be rebuilt. (4) Simply stated, without God doing it, there would be no Cyrus, and no return from the Babylonian exile. As is so often the case, God used humans to carry out part of His plan. (5) When Cyrus issued the decree for the Jews to return home from exile, it was because God put all the right pieces in place—including Cyrus himself. (6) Both 2 Chron 36:22 and Ezra 1:1 show something of the spiritual realities behind the world events, writing, "Now in the first year of Cyrus king of Persia, in order to fulfill the word of the LORD by the mouth of Jeremiah, the LORD stirred up the spirit of Cyrus king of Persia, so that he sent a proclamation throughout all his kingdom, and also put it in writing, saying ..." (Ezra 1:1). (7) Ezra 2:64–65 shows that approximately 50,000 returned from Babylon to the land from where they were exiled, and they did not come back empty-handed. Zechariah was among the exiles who returned to his true homeland.

We also noted: (8) The Book of Zechariah begins with a declaration and invitation and an evaluation of the truthfulness of God's Word (Zech 1:1–6): twice God declares that *He* was the One who sent national Israel into exile. When angel messengers patrol the earth, Jerusalem plays a significant part in the conversation between the angelic messengers and God. (9) God uses "soothing words" in Zechariah 1:13–14 and answers with His holy jealousy for Jerusalem and Zion: "And the LORD answered the angel who was speaking with me with gracious words, comforting words. So the angel who was speaking with me said to me, "Proclaim, saying, 'Thus says the LORD of hosts, "I am exceedingly jealous for Jerusalem and Zion."'" (10) Not only did the nations do what Yahweh raised them up to do for Him by destroying Jerusalem and the Temple of the LORD, they went beyond what He wanted, so that Genesis 12:3, "I will curse the ones who curse you" weighed on them:

> "But I am very angry with the nations who are at ease; for while I was only a little angry, they furthered the disaster." Therefore, thus says the LORD, "I will return to Jerusalem with compassion; My house will be built in it," declares the LORD of hosts, "and a measuring line will be stretched over Jerusalem."'
>
> "Again, proclaim, saying, 'Thus says the LORD of hosts, "My cities will again overflow with prosperity, and the LORD will again comfort Zion and again choose Jerusalem"'" (Zechariah 1:15–17).

(11) Moving ahead to chapter 3, these are the opening lines of Zechariah 3:1–2:

> Then he showed me Joshua the high priest standing before the angel of the LORD, and Satan standing at his right hand to accuse him.
>
> And the LORD said to Satan, "The LORD rebuke you, Satan! Indeed, the LORD who has chosen Jerusalem rebuke you! Is this not a brand plucked from the fire?"

Three important items to note here are: (i) Satan's name is used three times in these verses, (ii) Satan is present in this portion, but God does not allow him to speak. God very much wanted Satan to know the disclosure of this particular divine revelation. (iii) This is the last time that Satan appears in the OT, and his name will not appear again until Matthew 4/Mark 1/Luke 4 with the 40-day temptation of Jesus the Messiah. (12) We remember that Zechariah 3:8–10 connects with the context of the opening verses of this incredibly important prophecy because it contains some Messianic truths that will become clearer in the New Testament. Zechariah 3:8–10:

> Now listen, Joshua the high priest, you and your friends who are sitting in front of you—indeed they are men who are a symbol, for behold, I am going to bring in My servant the Branch.
>
> For behold, the stone that I have set before Joshua; on one stone are seven eyes. Behold, I will engrave an inscription on it,' declares the LORD of hosts, 'and I will remove the iniquity of that land in one day.
>
> In that day,' declares the LORD of hosts, 'every one of you will invite his neighbor to sit under his vine and under his fig tree.'"

We further learned that (13) the wondrous truths of Zech 6:9–15 are an important appendix to the first 6 chapters of Zechariah and how Zechariah 6 concludes the eight night visions. The appendix shows the coronation [in a vision] of Joshua the High Priest, but (14) it is also a promise and designation of a previous One God has used already in other places in Scripture, with verses 6:12–13 highlighted below—but also another Messianic promise that we have not studied previously in our study:

> The word of the LORD also came to me saying,
>
> "Take an offering from the exiles, from Heldai, Tobijah, and Jedaiah; and you go the same day and enter the house of Josiah the son of Zephaniah, where they have arrived from Babylon. And take silver and gold, make an ornate crown, and set it on the head of Joshua the son of Jehozadak, the high priest.
>
> "Then say to him, 'Thus says the LORD of hosts, "***Behold, a man whose name is Branch***, for He will branch out from where He is; and He will build the temple of the LORD.
>
> "Yes, it is He who will build the temple of the LORD, and He who will bear the honor and sit and rule on His throne. ***Thus, He will be a priest on His throne, and the counsel of peace will be between the two offices***."'"
>
> "Now the crown will become a reminder in the temple of the LORD to Helem, Tobijah, Jedaiah, and Hen the son of Zephaniah. And those who are far off will come and build the temple of the LORD." Then you will

know that the LORD of hosts has sent me to you. And it will take place, if you completely obey the LORD your God.

Everything about this section may seem incredible or unbelievable—in the literal sense, by many scoffers—and here are some of the items to consider: (15) This cannot refer to the present or pending Temple at that time because God has previously promised the rebuilding of the Temple to someone else after the exiles returned, stating in Zechariah 4:9: "The hands of Zerubbabel have laid the foundation of this house, and his hands will finish it. Then you will know that the LORD of hosts has sent me to you." (16) Under the Mosaic Covenant, kings cannot enter into the Holy of Holies and priests cannot sit on thrones—particularly inside the Temple of Yahweh. And (17) critics of the Bible say there is no possible way for this part to be true, since it so plainly contradicts what has previously been promised in Scripture, so that it is impossible for Zechariah 6:13 to be taken as doctrinal truth: "Yes, it is He [*the One the previous verse describes as a Man whose name is Branch—with all the "Branch attributes" that other Scripture passages reveal*] Who will build the temple of the LORD, and He Who will bear the honor and sit and rule on His throne. *Thus, He will be a priest on His throne, and the counsel of peace will be between the two offices.*'" (18) This truth about the Messiah being both priest and king will play a major role in the remainder of our studies.

DEEPER WALK STUDY QUESTIONS

(1) List 5 historical/biblical background items to set the stage for the Book of Zechariah.

(2) Show ten ways biblically that God is concerned about Jerusalem in Zechariah 1–3. Give the verses and a brief explanation of the verses where needed. Write a one-sentence summary statement about God and Jerusalem from these three chapters.

(3) Why and what is the significance of Satan being present in Zechariah 3. Why was he there, where does he next show up in Scripture, and why is this important? Explain.

(4) Why is the Messianic prophecy of Zechariah 6:12–13 very important? How can this be accomplished under the Mosaic Covenant? Explain in detail and defend your answer with five biblical supports.

(5) Give 15 biblical truths and characteristics about "the Branch." You may choose to include any Isaiah or Jeremiah references where appropriate.

(6) Make up your own study question, answer it, and be able to give people five reasons why your question was important.

CHAPTER SEVEN

THE STUNNING MESSIANIC PROPHECIES OF PSALM 110

INTRODUCTION

We have taken many words that are true about God alone, words that originally applied only to Him, and have saturated the culture with them describing everything from yoyos to soaps, while loud sports announcers repeatedly holler "Awesome!" When it came time to write this introduction, I was trying to find the remaining, most relevant words that describe only Jesus Christ. It is not that words do not exist that convey some of the attributes and activities of God—they do exist. It is rather that the culture has been so saturated with highly attributive words that every word of such value has been used so much by modern culture that there is nothing left to use.

When I prayed about how to write this chapter and choose a descriptive word to use, maybe I don't move in the same circles in which this particular word is greatly over-used, but as you can see, the one word I chose for the title was "stunning."

Do Jesus Christ and "stunning" go together? They certainly do, as do many other words that best apply uniquely to the Trinity.

But "stunning"?

The enemies of Jesus surely thought so that one day about 2,000 years ago when Jesus had just a few days left to live.

SETTING THE TABLE BIBLICALLY

The two most-cited Psalms in the New Testament are Psalm 110 and Psalm 118. An example is when Jesus used them against the religious officials who hated Him with an enflamed hatred that became even hotter once they eventually understood, (1) what Jesus was claiming for Himself and the Father, and (2) how the religious leaders of that day were opposing God's Messiah, (3) in precise accordance and fulfillment of exactly what Psalm 118 promised—penned about 1,000 years before that day—as shown in Matthew 21:41–46:

> They said to Him, "He will bring those wretches [*who have killed the vineyard owner's son*] to a wretched end, and will rent out the vineyard to other vine-growers who will pay him the proceeds at the proper seasons."
>
> Jesus said to them, "Did you never read in the Scriptures [*in Psalm 118:22–23*]
> 'THE STONE WHICH THE BUILDERS REJECTED,
> THIS BECAME THE CHIEF CORNER [STONE];
> THIS CAME ABOUT FROM THE LORD,
> AND IT IS MARVELOUS IN OUR EYES'?
> "Therefore I say to you, the kingdom of God will be taken away from you and given to a people, producing the fruit of it. And he who falls on this stone will be broken to pieces; but on whomever it falls, it will scatter him like dust."
>
> When the chief priests and the Pharisees heard His parables, they understood that He was speaking about them. When they sought to seize Him, they feared the people, because they considered Him to be a prophet.

As we have seen already, Genesis 48:20 is the beginning of specific prophetic truths concerning each of the twelve tribes in the last days, and those truths continue in Genesis 49:1-28. The Lion from the tribe of Judah will eventually reign over all the earth, including the Gentiles (Gen 49:8–12). We also saw that two additional Messianic titles come from this same context: Genesis 49:24, "From the hands of the Mighty One of Jacob (From there is *the Shepherd*, **the Stone of Israel**)" It is vitally important that this is the same Stone mentioned in the Stone prophecy (Psalm 118:22–23) that

Jesus quoted in Matthew 21:42 when He publicly denounced and greatly humiliated and infuriated the religious leaders.

Later that same day, after answering various questions from the different groups who had wanted to make Him stumble by assuming that He could give no biblical answer, the section closes with Jesus going on the offensive against the Pharisees (Matt 22:41-46):

> Now while the Pharisees were gathered together, Jesus asked them a question: "What do you think about the Christ [Messiah], whose son is He?" They said to Him, "The son of David."
>
> He said to them, "Then how does David in the Spirit call Him 'Lord,' saying [*quoting from Psalm 110:1*],
>
> 'THE LORD [**LORD**] SAID TO MY LORD [**Lord**],
>
> "SIT AT MY RIGHT HAND,
>
> UNTIL I PUT YOUR ENEMIES BENEATH YOUR FEET"'?
>
> "If David then calls Him 'Lord,' how is He his son?"
>
> No one was able to answer Him a word, nor did anyone *dare* from that day on to ask Him another question.

Why would the previous brief encounter result in Matthew 22:46: "No one was able to answer Him a word, nor did anyone ***dare*** from that day on to ask Him another question"? One of the few usages of the word *dare* occurs later in one of the most amazing verses in the Bible—Jude 9—which we would know nothing of unless God disclosed a small peek behind the scenes spiritually, "But Michael the archangel, when he disputed with the devil and argued about the body of Moses, did not *dare* pronounce against him a railing judgment, but said, 'The LORD rebuke you!'" as we have seen/as we will see, Michael quoted from Zechariah 3:1-2, which is loaded with eternal significance.

How could Jesus answer His hostile foes with one prophetic Messianic verse and totally shut down their entire belief system? Beyond that, He did so in a way that even the mostly highly trained individuals—such as someone like Saul of Tarsus, who eventually became Saul the Christian, and finally became Paul the apostle—or the collective whole of the intelligentsia were fearful to ask Him any other thing! But why was that? The short-list answer: (1) David tells of two different Godhead members ("Yahweh said to Adonai"), (2) and this One, about 1,000 years before the birth of Jesus, is already alive in heaven and is sharing worship and all the components of heaven that we do not know yet know while on earth, while "we see in a mirror dimly," and (3) yes, the pre-incarnate Godhead member would become David's Son, as is required to be in the Davidic Covenant lineage, (4) but even before that, David had already worshiped the eternal, pre-existent One, (5) Who became obedient to the point of death, but Who one day will experience the coming exaltation described in verses familiar to many, Philippians 2:5–11:

> "Have this attitude in yourselves which **was** also in Christ Jesus [***KEY: was—not is;*** *all the truths from these passages have been fulfilled by the Messiah Jesus Christ in the Incarnation and will never again be true of Him in regard to those who oppose Him; see such passages as Revelation 1 or 19*] who, although **He existed in the form of God**, did not regard equality with God a thing to be grasped, but emptied Himself, taking the form of a bond-servant, and being made in the likeness of men. And being found in appearance as a man, He humbled Himself by becoming obedient to the point of death, even death on a cross.
>
> "Therefore also God highly exalted Him, and bestowed on Him the name which is above every name, that at the name of Jesus EVERY KNEE SHOULD [*WILL*] BOW, of those who are in heaven, and on earth, and under the earth, and that every tongue should confess that Jesus Christ is Lord, to the glory of God the Father."

A BRIEF LOOK AT PSALM 110 IN ITS ENTIRETY

Although two verses from this Psalm (abbreviated version: Ps 110:1: "The LORD says to my Lord / Sit at My right hand," and Ps 110:4: "You are a priest forever according to the order of Melchizedek"), are the verses people who study their Bible are familiar with. All 7 verses of this relatively short Psalm will be included in our studies. Here is the entire Holy-Spirit-inspired Psalm, written about 3,000 years ago, and it is just as true, just as inspired, just as binding today as it was on the day that the Holy Spirit used the human instrument King David to pen this beautiful doctrinal composition that is also filled with some previously revealed doctrinal gold from the Godhead. Look how loaded with truth Psalm 110 is:

A Psalm of David.
The LORD says to my Lord:
"Sit at My right hand,
Until I make Your enemies a footstool for Your feet."
The LORD will stretch forth Your strong scepter from Zion, saying,
"Rule in the midst of Your enemies."
Your people will volunteer freely in the day of Your power;
In holy array, from the womb of the dawn,
Your youth are to You as the dew.
The LORD has sworn and will not change His mind,
"You are a priest forever
According to the order of Melchizedek."
The LORD is at Your right hand;
He will shatter kings in the day of His wrath.
He will judge among the nations,
He will fill them with corpses,
He will shatter the chief men over a broad country.
He will drink from the brook by the wayside;
Therefore He will lift up His head.

KEY: Many Orthodox Jews and Christians rightly consider this to be written about the Messiah. More importantly, God does, also—although many Orthodox Jews have wildly varying interpretations of how the priesthood fits in with the obvious Kingship that God gives. Psalm 110:1 has only one answer about Who qualifies, and that is none other than the One Who would become flesh Who had existed from eternity past as a Godhead member.

NOTE ALSO: From the entirety of the Psalm, notice how many future tenses occur and the way the vast majority of these are used by marking/highlighting the number of times the word "will" is used (e.g. Psalm 110:5 uses such a future tense: "He will shatter kings in the day of His wrath").

Every verse in this Psalm, contains important doctrinal unveilings of truth given to us by God: (1) this psalm is about only one King—not the Davidic Covenant lineage, although the One who will fulfill these prophecies will be—and must be—a Davidic Covenant heir (see Matt 1:1); (2) Who after He has conquered all His opponents—both spiritual foes and satanic foes—will have a worldwide reign; (3) consequently, most of the promises when first composed and even up to the present time use future tenses, and still have yet to be fulfilled; however (4) Psalm 110:4 speaks of another Priest—and another priesthood—(5) which is not based on the Mosaic Covenant, which was functioning at the time when Psalm 110 was composed, and during the time of Jesus' Incarnation (6) but one concerning which the LORD has sworn that this One, when once He begins His role, will be a Priest forever. These verses are so important, that (8) Psalm 110 and Psalm 118 are the most-quoted OT verses in the NT—some scholars hold that they are equally cited in usage; (9) and remember how Jesus with one verse from Psalm 110 shut down the entirely off-base theological system of the Pharisees.

KEY: All of Psalm 110 is in reference to only one future Davidic Covenant Heir—Who already existed in heaven, so He must be from eternity past. So Whoever He is—and if you are saved you may already know this—He must be both Priest and King.

Psalm 110 has two distinct topics (1) the kingship, and (2) a different priesthood. Since Jesus started with Kingship in His Matthew 22:41–46 encounter—which we have already seen—we will mark other brief but beautiful truths as well. The second part will deal with the priesthood.

HOW JESUS USED THE KINGSHIP PORTION OF PSALM 110 AND WHY IT IS STILL IRREPLACEABLE DOCTRINE

In Matthew 22:41–46, there is no doubt that Jesus refers to the Holy Spirit in verse 43: "He said to them, "Then how does David *in the Spirit* call Him 'Lord,' saying,…" and the shorter version in the parallel passage in Mark 12:35–37 confirms this for us:

> And Jesus answering began to say, as He taught in the temple, "How is it that the scribes say that the Christ is the son of David?
> "David himself said *in the Holy Spirit*,
> 'THE LORD SAID TO MY LORD,
> "SIT AT MY RIGHT HAND,
> UNTIL I PUT THINE ENEMIES BENEATH THY FEET."'
> "David himself calls Him 'Lord'; and so in what sense is He his son?"
> And the great crowd enjoyed listening to Him.

The biblical logic that God has set forth in these verses in Matthew and Mark erupts into incredible, cascading truths about God and His Messiah and even beyond that: (1) I and many other Bible believers accept this as David's Son and David's Lord—which is true and remains a crucial doctrinal part and could accurately be said to be the main point; (2) the Holy Spirit is implied in this account in Matthew, but Mark's account makes it more precise and without question [Mark 12:36 "David himself said *in the Holy Spirit*], (3) taking both passages together with the opening of how Psalm 110:1 states it [not the Greek NT] "The LORD says to my Lord." (4) Not only does it have/require the pre-incarnate Second Member of the Godhead to be David's Lord 1,000 years before the Son is born (so He fulfills both parts as David's Son yet David's Lord), using Psalm 110:1 as biblical proof for this; (5) but Psalm 110:1 and Mark 12:36 give us all three members of the Trinity in this account, given by divine revelation from the Holy Spirit:

—The LORD" **God the Father**
—"said to "my Lord" **God the Son**
—"David himself said in the Holy Spirit" (Mark 12:36)
   God the Holy Spirit

(6) This unity of Father, Son and Holy Spirit will not only eventually be at the end of the Gospel of Matthew, but (7) these verses become the exact basis for the Great Commission (Matt 28:18–20), and all the members of the Godhead are equal as a unit, "baptizing them in the name" [singular—not names]; stressing the collective unity of the three-member Godhead.

THE FOURTH APPOINTED TIME OF YAHWEH (PENTECOST) AND THE START OF THE CHURCH IN ACTS 2

It is wonderfully fitting for the pouring out of the Holy Spirit on the fourth Appointed Time of Yahweh that Psalm 110 would play a vital role in Peter's first sermon. You can read the entire chapter on your own. We will limit ourselves to Acts 2:29–36:

> "Brethren, I may confidently say to you regarding the patriarch David that he both died and was buried, and his tomb is with us to this day.
> "And so, because he was a prophet and knew that GOD HAD SWORN TO HIM WITH AN OATH TO SEAT one OF HIS DESCENDANTS ON HIS THRONE, he looked ahead and spoke of the resurrection of the Christ, that HE WAS NEITHER ABANDONED TO HADES, NOR DID His flesh SUFFER DECAY.
> "This Jesus God raised up again, to which we are all witnesses.
> "Therefore having been exalted to the right hand of God [*the Ascension*], and having received from the Father the promise of the Holy Spirit, He has poured forth this which you both see and hear [Luke 24:49: *"And behold, I am sending forth the promise of My Father upon you; but you are to stay in the city until you are clothed with power from on high;"* and Acts 1:4–5:

"And gathering them together, He commanded them not to leave Jerusalem, but to wait for what the Father had promised, "Which, " He said, "you heard of from Me; for John baptized with water, but you shall be baptized with the Holy Spirit not many days from now;" and Acts 1:7–8: "He said to them, 'It is not for you to know times or epochs which the Father has fixed by His own authority; but you shall receive power when the Holy Spirit has come upon you; and you shall be My witnesses both in Jerusalem, and in all Judea and Samaria, and even to the remotest part of the earth.'"]

"For it was not David who ascended into heaven, but he himself says:
'THE LORD SAID TO MY LORD,
"SIT AT MY RIGHT HAND,
UNTIL I MAKE YOUR ENEMIES A FOOTSTOOL FOR YOUR FEET.'"'

"Therefore let all the house of Israel know for certain that God has made Him both Lord and Christ—this Jesus whom you crucified."

This connects Psalm 110:4 to the priestly ministry that Jesus started *only* after His Ascension to the right hand of God [***accepted work***]. And we remember that it was Jesus, just days before His crucifixion, Who attributed this same verse, Psalm 110:4, to Himself as being David's Lord [***in eternity past***], and also as being David's son [***the Davidic Covenant heir***]—all in complete harmony with the entirety of Psalm 110.

CHAPTER 1 OF HEBREWS CONTAINS MUCH OF WHAT WE HAVE ALREADY STUDIED IN OUR BOOK

The Book of Hebrews was written to professing Hebrew Christians. It is not an evangelistic message to the Hebrew people to come and meet their unknown God. It is for one or more churches of professing Jewish believers; as with most churches, some are truly saved, and others would claim to be saved although they never were. Others were on the brink of withdrawing, abandoning Jesus Christ, and renouncing Him and His claims as Savior and King and returning to Judaism. They had not done so yet when the Book of Hebrews was written.

Hebrews 1 could have been written as a one-chapter epistle. We have already studied much of it, but perhaps we can now read the book with more biblical understanding of Who the Messiah is and what He will do in the future.

HEBREWS 1:1–4

Heb. 1:1 God, after He spoke long ago to the fathers in the prophets in many portions and in many ways,

Heb. 1:2 in these last days has spoken to us *in His Son* [*Remember the Matt 22 questions about whose Son the Messiah is*], whom He appointed heir of all things, **through whom also He made the world**. [*The Messiah must be a Godhead member before creation and at the Creation to create all things*].

Heb. 1:3 And He is the radiance of His glory and **the exact representation of His nature** [*Phil 2*] and **upholds all things by the word of His power**. [*These are attributes of God, and the means by which the Godhead members chose to radiate the Glory of God is by Jesus Messiah/Second Member of the Godhead*].

When He had made purification of sins [*completed work*], **He sat down at the right hand of the Majesty on high**; [*accepted work—and requires an ascension to the right hand of God. Remember the Matt 22 background and Jesus' questions. The Lord said to my Lord, "Sit at My right hand …"*]

Heb. 1:4 having become much better than the angels, as He has inherited a more excellent name than they.

HEBREWS 1:5–8

Hebrews 1:5–8 continues primarily with the verses about the already-ascended Jesus who will return to earth at His Second Coming and will rule all the nations:

Hebrews 1:5 For to which of the angels did He ever say,
    "YOU ARE MY SON,

TODAY I HAVE BEGOTTEN YOU"? [*Psalm 2:7*]

And again,

"I WILL BE A **FATHER TO HIM**
AND HE SHALL BE **A SON TO ME**"? [*2 Sam 7—the OT chapter that first reveals details about the Davidic Covenant*]

Hebrews 1:6 And when **He again brings the first-born into the world**, He says, [Second Coming material from Ps 89:27: "I also shall make him *My* firstborn, / The highest of the kings of the earth."]

"AND LET ALL THE ANGELS OF GOD WORSHIP HIM."

[*Only 2 options: this is either/ 100% lies and blasphemies or 100% truth for angels to worship the Second Member of the Godhead and of the Davidic Covenant.*]

Hebrews 1:7 And of the angels He says,
"WHO MAKES HIS ANGELS WINDS,
AND HIS MINISTERS A FLAME OF FIRE."

Hebrews 1:8 But of the Son He says, [*Remember again: the two questions by Jesus in Matthew 22 using Ps. 110:1 requiring a Godhead Member, as it does here*]

**"YOUR THRONE, O GOD, IS FOREVER AND EVER,
AND THE RIGHTEOUS SCEPTER IS THE SCEPTER OF HIS
KINGDOM.** [*Davidic Covenant/Goes all the way back to Gen 49:1, 28, 49:8–12 The Lion from the tribe of Judah, and His reign is to be everlasting*]

HEBREWS 1:9–12

Hebrews 1:9 "YOU HAVED LOVED RIGHTEOUSNESS AND HATED LAWLESSNESS;
THEREFORE **GOD, YOUR GOD, HAS ANOINTED YOU**
[*Godhead and Messiah, the Anointed One*]**.**
WITH THE OIL OF GLADNESS ABOVE THY COMPANIONS."

Hebrews 1:10

And, "**YOU, LORD, IN THE BEGINNING DID LAY THE FOUNDATION OF THE EARTH**, [*Eternality and attributes of the Creator God*]. **AND THE HEAVENS ARE THE WORKS OF YOUR HANDS** [*Jesus as the Creator Godhead Member of even the heavens*]

Hebrews 1:11

THEY WILL PERISH, BUT THOU REMAINEST;
AND THEY ALL WILL BECOME OLD AS A GARMENT,

Hebrews 1:12

AND AS A MANTLE THOU WILT ROLL THEM UP;
AS A GARMENT THEY WILL ALSO BE CHANGED.
**BUT YOU ARE THE SAME,
AND YOUR YEARS WILL NOT COME TO AN END**."
[*Eternality/Godhead Member*]

Hebrews 1:13

But to which of the angels has He ever said,
"SIT AT MY RIGHT HAND [*completed work*],
UNTIL I MAKE THINE ENEMIES
A FOOTSTOOL FOR THY FEET"? [*At His Second Coming to Earth*]

REMEMBER: *This is the same verse Jesus used in Matthew 22 where He answered by using Psalm 110:1 as the biblical base*; Yahweh said this to another Godhead member named Adonai in the Hebrew of Psalm 110:1, so it ***must*** be God talking to someone other than Himself but Who is still part of the Godhead.

SIMIPLY PUT: Jesus is David's Lord before He is David's Son, but that is just the beginning of Godhead qualifications. Hebrews 1 and the remaining chapters of Hebrews are laden with **many** other attributes and/or activities of God, including—among others—creating the heavens and the earth, eternality in past and future, His special Son relationship with God the Father, being worshiped by the angels, His Ascension where He sat down [*completed work*] at the right hand of God [*accepted work*], being the One Who will one day rule the entire world, after He again enters the world at His Second Coming.

THE HIGH PRIEST VERSES IN HEBREWS

Psalm 110:4 refers to the Messianic Priest, who, when once He begins the priesthood—according to the same verse—will remain a Priest forever. Regarding this, under the Mosaic Covenant, however, the high priest was, (1) to be of Aaron's descendants, (2) just one man—**only one high priest at a time**—though there were many thousands of priests working at various duties, (3) susceptible to death; 4) when he died, replaced by the next qualified and specified "son of Aaron." Exodus 28:1–39 gives the original and highly ornate design for the garments for the high priest to wear, particularly on special occasions. Numbers 35:25–28 gives an example of when changing of the high priest would affect another part of Jewish life. For someone who had fled to one of the cities of refuge, there was a distinction between two times: "until the death of the high priest" and "after the death of the high priest." Note that each time, the designation is singular—"high priest," not "high priests."

> "And the congregation shall deliver the manslayer from the hand of the blood avenger, and the congregation shall restore him to his city of refuge to which he fled; *and he shall live in it until the death of the high priest who was anointed with the holy oil.*

But if the manslayer shall at any time go beyond the border of his city of refuge to which he may flee, and the blood avenger finds him outside the border of his city of refuge, and the blood avenger kills the manslayer, he shall not be guilty of blood because he should have remained in his city of refuge *until the death of the high priest. But after the death of the high priest the manslayer shall return to the land of his possession.*

JESUS CHRIST AS OUR HIGH PRIEST

Psalm 110:4 gave the initial—but incomplete—description of the Lord Jesus Christ as a Priest forever. It is not until in the book of Hebrews that God reveals that at present, Jesus is our High Priest in heaven. We find many other wonderful characteristics of Him, such as Hebrews 2:17: "Therefore, He had to be made like His brethren in all things, that He might become *a merciful and faithful high priest* in things pertaining to God, to make propitiation for the sins of the people." "Therefore, holy brethren, partakers of a heavenly calling, *consider Jesus, the Apostle and High Priest of our confession*" (Heb 3:1). Hebrews 4:14–15 offers this wonderful description, "*Since then we have a great high priest who has passed through the heavens, Jesus the Son of God,* let us hold fast our confession. For we do not have a high priest who cannot sympathize with our weaknesses, but One who has been tempted in all things as we are, yet without sin."

Explaining that Jesus Christ is our High Priest is a major section of the book of Hebrews. Hebrews 5:1–6 gives much of the logic that the Holy Spirit intends:

> For every high priest taken from among men is appointed on behalf of men in things pertaining to God, in order to offer both gifts and sacrifices for sins; he can deal gently with the ignorant and misguided, since he himself also is beset with weakness; and because of it he is obligated to offer sacrifices for sins, as for the people, so also for himself. And no one takes the honor to himself, but receives it when he is called by God, even as Aaron was.
>
> So also Christ did not glorify Himself so as to become a high priest, but He who said to Him,

"YOU ARE MY SON,
TODAY I HAVE BEGOTTEN YOU";
[2 Sam 7/Davidic Covenant Promises];

Just as He says also in another passage, [Remember: Jesus used the opening part of Psalm 110:1 in Matthew 22; here He uses the last part of that verse]:

"YOU ARE A PRIEST **FOREVER**
ACCORDING TO THE ORDER OF MELCHIZEDEK."

KEY: The promise from God was that whenever this Promised One—we find out in the Book of Hebrews that the Lord Jesus Christ was the One that the Godhead intended all the time, it is just not called being a priest until Psalm 110—begins this aspect of His ministry, He will remain forever. There will *never* be another high priest that God accepts other than Jesus our Lord.

KEY: The One who is described in Psalm 110:1 must also be the One described in Psalm 110:4. How do we know? Zechariah 6:12–13 demands and prophesies:

"Then say to him, 'Thus says the LORD of hosts, "Behold, a Man whose name is Branch, for He will branch out from where He is; and He will build the temple of the LORD.

"Yes, it is He who will build the temple of the LORD, and He who will bear the honor and sit and rule on His throne. Thus, He will be a priest on His throne, and the counsel of peace will be between the two offices.'"

The Author/author of Hebrews reasons further biblically:

In the days of His flesh, He offered up both prayers and supplications with loud crying and tears to the One able to save Him from death, and He was heard because of His piety. Although He was a Son, He learned obedience from the things which He suffered. And having been made perfect, He became to all those who obey Him the source of eternal salvation, **being designated by God as a high priest** according to the order of Melchizedek (Heb 5:7–10).

We are limited in our study of Hebrews in the remainder of this chapter, and although the Psalm 110:4 promise isn't given here, Hebrews concentrates on the high priesthood—and remember, God accepts only *one* high priest at a time. There were thousands of active priests, but only one high priest at a time. We will allow some of the priesthood verses to speak for themselves, such as in Hebrews 6:16–7:2:

For men swear by one greater than themselves, and with them an oath given as confirmation is an end of every dispute. In the same way God, desiring even more to show to the heirs of the promise the unchangeableness of His purpose, interposed with an oath, in order that by two unchangeable things, in which it is impossible for God to lie, we may have strong encouragement, we who have fled for refuge in laying hold of the hope set before us. This hope we have as an anchor of the soul, a hope both sure and steadfast and one which enters within the veil, where Jesus has entered as a forerunner for us, having become a high priest forever according to the order of Melchizedek.

For this Melchizedek, king of Salem, priest of the Most High God, who met Abraham as he was returning from the slaughter of the kings and blessed him, to whom also Abraham apportioned a tenth part of all the spoils, was first of all, by the translation of his name, **king of righteousness**, and **then also king of Salem, which is king of peace.**

KEY: There was no acceptable way for God to have anyone as both king and priest under the Mosaic Covenant, and this designation would have been considered a high-handed sin before God. Being from the tribe of Levi, priests were not kings; being from the tribe of Judah, kings were not priests. God had already figured out the answer long ago.

The Book of Hebrews Uses God's Holy Logic to Show That the Biblical Necessity of Changing the Priesthood Also Requires Changing the Covenant [8]

Hebrews 9:1–4 shows what those who know their Old Testament know: the Mosaic Covenant is the basis for the tabernacle first and the temple later:

> Now even the first covenant [*in this context, the Mosaic Covenant*] had regulations of divine worship and the earthly sanctuary. For there was a tabernacle prepared, the outer one, in which were the lampstand and the table and the sacred bread; this is called the holy place. Behind the second veil there was a tabernacle which is called the Holy of Holies, having a golden altar of incense and the ark of the covenant covered on all sides with gold, in which was a golden jar holding the manna, and Aaron's rod which budded, and the tables of the [*Mosaic*] Covenant.

However, it was not just the outer structure for which the design was commanded, but also there were requirements for the priesthood and its order, with what was called the Levitical priesthood that must come by Aaron's descendants. Numbers 3:10 not only specifies these requirements but also demonstrates God's seriousness about them and about anyone who would attempt to fraudulently attain the priesthood who was not from God's designated order under the Mosaic Covenant: "So you shall appoint Aaron and his sons that they may keep their priesthood, but the layman who comes

---

8 Adapted from Greg Harris, *The Bible Expositor's Handbook (OT/NT)* Chapter 28, "Twelve Things Most People Do Not Know about the book of Hebrews," pp. 524–27. Used by permission. See the remainder of the chapter from *The Bible Expositor's Handbook (OT/NT)* for much more information that is important and relevant to your study of Hebrews.

near shall be put to death." Not long afterward, during Korah's rebellion (Numbers 16), Yahweh showed Himself true to His own Word again by punishing 250 sinners who presented themselves as priests though they did not qualify, as seen in Num 16:35–40:

> Fire also came out from the LORD and consumed the 250 men who were presenting the incense.

> Then the LORD spoke to Moses: "Tell Eleazar son of Aaron the priest to remove the firepans from the burning debris, because they are holy, and scatter the fire far away. As for the firepans of those who sinned at the cost of their own lives, make them into hammered sheets as plating for the altar, for they presented them before the LORD, and the firepans are holy. They will be a sign to the Israelites."

> So the priest Eleazar took the bronze firepans that those who were burned had presented, and they were hammered into plating for the altar, just as the LORD commanded him through Moses. It was to be a reminder for the Israelites that no unauthorized person outside the lineage of Aaron should approach to offer incense before the LORD and become like Korah and his followers. (CSB)

Numbers 18:7, in which God was reaffirming Aaron and his descendants for the priesthood under the Mosaic Covenant, states, "But you and your sons with you shall attend to your priesthood for everything concerning the altar and inside the veil, and you are to perform service. I am giving you the priesthood as a bestowed service, but the outsider who comes near shall be put to death."

As the author/Author of Hebrews has said, so it would be here: "time does not permit me to speak" in any detail about the priesthood of Melchizedek, as seen in Heb 7:11–14:

> Now if perfection [*completion*] was through the Levitical priesthood (for on the basis of it the people received the [*Mosaic Covenant*] Law), what further need was there for another priest to arise according to the order of Melchizedek, and not be designated according to the order of Aaron? For when the priesthood is changed, of necessity there takes place a change

of law also. For the one concerning whom these things are spoken belongs to another tribe, from which no one has officiated at the altar. For it is evident that our Lord was descended from Judah, a tribe with reference to which Moses spoke nothing concerning priests.

Note these crucial matters in this section. Initially, not only does the Old Testament reveal that another covenant would come at some undisclosed time in the future—the New Covenant—it also tells of another priesthood outside of Aaron and his descendants and beyond the parameters of the Mosaic Covenant. Secondly, this part is so important that I must emphasize it:

KEY: As long as the Mosaic Covenant functioned, you *must* have only Aaron and his descendants as priests. Hebrews 7:12 states, "For when the priesthood is changed, of necessity there takes place a change of law also." If the priesthood is changed, then the covenant from which it originates must be changed. And the reverse is true: change the covenant [the Mosaic Covenant], then the priesthood *must* change as well. So, with Jesus the covenant becomes the New Covenant, and the old priesthood of the Mosaic Covenant is eradicated.

Notice another important point. Many priests operated under the Mosaic Covenant, but there was only one high priest—who was originally Aaron—at a time. But under the New Covenant, a new High Priest serves, as Heb 4:14–16 initially explains:

Therefore, since we have a great high priest who has passed through the heavens, Jesus the Son of God, let us hold fast our confession. For we do not have a high priest who cannot sympathize with our weaknesses, but One who has been tempted in all things as we are, yet without sin. Therefore let us draw near with confidence to the throne of grace, so that we may receive mercy and find grace to help in time of need.

The concept of Jesus being our High Priest—that is, the High Priest of those who are saved—and the qualifying requirements He meets are beautifully developed in Heb 7:26–28:

> For it was fitting for us to have such a high priest, holy, innocent, undefiled, separated from sinners and exalted above the heavens; who does not need daily, like those high priests [*under the Mosaic Covenant*], to offer up sacrifices, first for His own sins and then for the sins of the people, because this He did once for all when He offered up Himself. For the Law [*the Mosaic Covenant*] appoints men as high priests who are weak, but the word of the oath [*which tells of the Melchizedekian priesthood*], which came after the [*Mosaic Covenant*] Law, appoints a Son, made perfect forever.

To emphasize this, the author/Author of Hebrews specifically calls our attention to the main point in Heb 8:1–2:

> Now the main point in what has been said is this: **we have** [*present tense*] **such a high priest,** who has taken His seat at the right hand of the throne of the Majesty in the heavens, a minister in the sanctuary and in the true tabernacle, which the Lord pitched, not man.

CRUCIAL CONCEPT TO USE: God permits only one high priest at a time. Key questions to ask the original audience for Hebrews also offer incredibly simple—but powerful—doctrinal truths. These connected evangelistic questions can be used with others, especially with those who think they are saved automatically and do not need to be born again:

- Who is your High Priest? (Mine is Jesus Messiah. He is yours, too, if you are saved.)
- What covenant does He minister under? (the New Covenant)
- When did that begin for you? (at the moment I received Him by faith, on the reception of the finished work that He did for my salvation)

The Book of Hebrews Logically Tells Us That Jesus Would Have Sinned If He Had Offered a Sacrifice in Either the Holy Place or the Holy of Holies[9]

This may initially seem like a radical question: Are there things that God cannot do? Yes, there are—and we are eternally grateful for that. For instance, God cannot lie. God cannot sin. God cannot be defeated by evil. The things that God cannot do are for our good, and the Bible substantiates these answers to the question.

During His incarnation, Jesus Christ was God in the flesh; He was born of a woman, born under the Mosaic Covenant (Gal 4:4). With Jesus being from the tribe of Judah and from the direct lineage of David—and from what we have seen in our verses from Numbers about who could perform any of the priestly functions—consider the great-great ... grandfather of Jesus, King Uzziah. After a list of acts of faithfulness that the Davidic Covenant King Uzziah did (2 Chr 26:1–15) comes this sad and sobering account from 2 Chronicles 26:16–21:

> But when he became strong, his heart was so proud that he acted corruptly, and he was unfaithful to the LORD his God, for he entered the temple of the LORD to burn incense on the altar of incense. Then Azariah the priest entered after him and with him eighty priests of the LORD, valiant men. They opposed Uzziah the king and said to him, "It is not for you, Uzziah, to burn incense to the LORD, but for the priests, the sons of Aaron who are consecrated to burn incense. Get out of the sanctuary, for you have been unfaithful and will have no honor from the LORD God." But Uzziah, with a censer in his hand for burning incense, was enraged; and while he was enraged with the priests, the leprosy broke out on his forehead before the priests in the house of the LORD, beside the altar of incense. Azariah the chief priest and all the priests looked at him, and behold, he was leprous on his forehead; and they hurried him out of there, and he himself also hastened to get out because the LORD had smitten him. King Uzziah was

---

9 Greg Harris, *The Bible Expositor's Handbook (OT/NT)* Chapter 28, "Twelve Things Most People Do Not Know about the book of Hebrews," pp. 527–29. Used by permission. See the remainder of the chapter from *The Bible Expositor's Handbook (OT/NT)* for much more on the biblical importance and relevance than we could cover in this chapter.

a leper to the day of his death; and he lived in a separate house, being a leper, for he was cut off from the house of the LORD. And Jotham his son was over the king's house judging the people of the land.

In giving the royal lineage of the descendants of Jesus, Matt 1:8–9 shows King Uzziah as being one of the forefathers of Jesus: "Asa was the father of Jehoshaphat, Jehoshaphat the father of Joram, and Joram the father of Uzziah. Uzziah was the father of Jotham, Jotham the father of Ahaz, and Ahaz the father of Hezekiah." Jesus was born and lived just as much under the Mosaic Covenant as did his Davidic Covenant ancestor, King Uzziah.

So, in the passage we have already seen, look at God's logic in Heb 7:11–14:

> If perfection [*that is, completion*] came through the Levitical priesthood (for on the basis of it the people received the law), what further need was there for another priest to appear, said to be according to the order of Melchizedek and not according to the order of Aaron? For when there is a change of the priesthood, there must be a change of law as well. For the One these things are spoken about belonged to a different tribe. No one from it has served at the altar. Now it is evident that our Lord came from Judah, and Moses said nothing about that tribe concerning priests. (HCSB)

With this, add Heb 8:4: "Now if He were on earth, He would not be a priest at all, since there are those who offer the gifts according to the [*Mosaic Covenant*] Law".

Under these circumstances of the law, if Jesus had offered a sacrifice, even as His direct ancestor Uzziah had, Jesus would have been just as sinful. If Jesus had offered a sacrifice, He would not have been able to have answered His critics as He did in John 8:42–46:

> Jesus said to them, "If God were your Father, you would love me, because I came from God and I am here. For I didn't come on my own, but he sent me. Why don't you understand what I say? Because you cannot listen to my word. You are of your father the devil, and you want to carry out your father's desires. He was a murderer from the beginning and does not stand in the truth, because there is no truth in him. When he tells a lie, he speaks from his own nature, because he is a liar and the father of liars. Yet

because I tell the truth, you do not believe me. Who among you can convict me of sin? If I am telling the truth, why don't you believe me?" (CSB)

If Jesus had done what His ancestor Uzziah had done, His critics would have pointed that out before or during His trial.

And even more tragic—horribly and eternally so for us—Jesus no longer would have been qualified to fit the description in 1 Pet 1:17–19:

> If you address as Father the One who impartially judges according to each one's work, conduct yourselves in fear during the time of your stay on earth; knowing that you were not redeemed with perishable things like silver or gold from your futile way of life inherited from your forefathers, but with precious blood, as of a lamb unblemished and spotless, the blood of Christ.

He would have been blemished; He would not have been spotless—and we would have no one to shed His blood for us. But instead He was spotless; He did shed His blood for us; and we graciously thank God for Him. "For He was foreknown before the foundation of the world, but has appeared in these last times for the sake of [*us*]" (1 Pet 1:20).

HEBREWS 13:7–15; THE LAST USE OF "HIGH PRIEST" IN HEBREWS AND AN EXHORTATION TO COUNT THE COST AND TO FOLLOW JESUS CHRIST

> "Remember those who led you, who spoke the word of God to you; and considering the result of their conduct, imitate their faith. Jesus Christ is the same yesterday and today, yes and forever. Do not be carried away by varied and strange teachings; for it is good for the heart to be strengthened by grace, not by foods, through which those who were thus occupied were not benefited.
>
> We have an altar, from which those who serve the tabernacle have no right to eat. For the bodies of those animals whose blood is brought into the holy place by the high priest as an offering for sin, are burned outside

the camp. Therefore Jesus also, that He might sanctify the people through His own blood, suffered outside the gate.

Hence, let us go out to Him outside the camp, bearing His reproach. For here we do not have a lasting city, but we are seeking the city which is to come. Through Him then, let us continually offer up a sacrifice of praise to God, that is, the fruit of lips that give thanks to His name."

SUMMARY AND CONCLUSION

Among other things in this chapter we learned: (1) Psalms 118 and 110 are the two most-quoted Psalms in the New Testament and both are repeatedly used with Jesus' last week on earth; (2) The one usage of Psalm 110 in the Matthew 22 account made such an impact on His enemies—not His disciples, such as Matthew 24:1–2—that no one dared to ask Him a question after that. (3) Part of the answers are: (i) David tells of two different Godhead members ("Yahweh said to Adonai"), (ii) and this One, about 1,000 years before the birth of Jesus, is already alive in heaven and is sharing worship and all the "we see in a mirror dimly" components of heaven that we do not yet know while on earth, and (iii) yes, David's pre-incarnate Godhead member (Lord) would become David's Son, so is required to be in the Davidic Covenant lineage, (iv) but even before that, David had already worshiped the One Who is from eternity past, (v) Who became obedient to the point of His pending sacrificial death for the sins of the world.

(4) Although two verses from this Psalm (abbreviated version: Ps 110:1: "The LORD says to my Lord/Sit at My right hand," and Ps 110:4: "You are a priest forever according to the order of Melchizedek"), are the verses people who study their Bible are familiar with, (5) the entirety of this relatively short—7 verses—Psalm 110 is very important doctrinal truth. (6) Every verse in this psalm contains incredibly important doctrinal unveiling of truth given to us by God: (i) this psalm is about only one King—not the Davidic Covenant lineage, although the One who will fulfill these prophecies will be—and must be—a Davidic Covenant heir (see Matthew 1:1); (ii) Who after He has conquered all His opponents—both spiritual foes and satanic foes—will have a worldwide reign; (iii) consequently, most of the

promises when first composed and even up to the present time use future tenses, and still have yet to be fulfilled.

While the above doctrinal truths are foundational truths about the Messiah that are tremendously important biblically, (7) Psalm 110:4 (i) speaks of another priest—and another priesthood—(ii) which is not based on the Mosaic Covenant, (iii) but one concerning which the LORD has sworn that this One, when once He begins His role, will be a priest forever; and (8) the Bible shows how Jesus with one verse from Psalm 110 shut down an entirely off-base theological system of the Pharisees. (9) The only answer that makes sense so all of the above doctrinal truths—and many, many more—harmonize demands that the Messiah be a Godhead Member. In fact, (10) the Matthew 22:41–46 account when compared with Mark 12:36 ["David himself said *in the Holy Spirit*] gives us all three members of the Trinity in this account. (10) This unity of Father, Son and Holy Spirit will not only eventually be at the end of the Gospel of Matthew, these verses will also become the exact basis for the Great Commission (Matthew 28:18–20).

(11) It is especially fitting for the pouring out of the Holy Spirit on the fourth Appointed Time of Yahweh that Psalm 110 would play a vital role in Peter's first sermon. I'll limit the quotation to Acts 2:32–37:

> "This Jesus God raised up again, to which we are all witnesses.
> "Therefore having been exalted to the right hand of God [*the Ascension*], and having received from the Father the promise of the Holy Spirit, He has poured forth this which you both see and hear.
> "For it was not David who ascended into heaven, but he himself says:
> 'THE LORD SAID TO MY LORD,
> "SIT AT MY RIGHT HAND,
> UNTIL I MAKE YOUR ENEMIES A FOOTSTOOL FOR YOUR FEET.'"
> "Therefore let all the house of Israel know for certain that God has made Him both Lord and Christ—this Jesus whom you crucified."

Again, how appropriate for the pouring out of the Holy Spirit on the fourth Appointed Time of Yahweh that Psalm 110 would play a vital role in Peter's first sermon!

We saw that (12) Hebrews 1 contains many of the same truths we have already studied so far, and (13) even if we just limited ourselves to Hebrews 1:13, it would be worthwhile:

"THE LORD SAID TO MY LORD, SIT AT MY RIGHT HAND
[*completed work*],
UNTIL I MAKE THINE ENEMIES
A FOOTSTOOL FOR THY FEET"? [*At His Second Coming to Earth*]

Also important to know is (14) This is *the same verse* Jesus used in Matthew 22 where He answered by using Psalm 110:1 as His biblical source.

We further saw, (15) Psalm 110:4 gave the initial—but incomplete—description of the Lord Jesus Christ as a Priest forever. It is not until in the book of Hebrews that God reveals that Jesus is our High Priest in heaven, for the present time. We find many other wonderful characteristics of Him, such as Hebrews 2:17: "Therefore, He had to be made like His brethren in all things, that He might become *a merciful and faithful high priest* in things pertaining to God, to make propitiation for the sins of the people." "Therefore, holy brethren, partakers of a heavenly calling, *consider Jesus, the Apostle and High Priest of our confession*" (Heb 3:1). Hebrews 4:14–15 offers this wonderful description, *"Since then we have a great high priest who has passed through the heavens,* Jesus the Son of God, let us hold fast our confession. For we do not have a high priest who cannot sympathize with our weaknesses, but One who has been tempted in all things as we are, yet without sin." (16) It is crucial to our biblical understanding that present tenses were and are used when referring to the High Priest; this is not unfulfilled prophecy but rather the present reality of an aspect of our Savior's word.

Looking ahead to the Second Coming of our Lord Jesus Christ, we saw this foundational truth: (17) the One who is described in Psalm 110:1 must also be the One described in Psalm 110:4, because Zechariah 6:12–13 demands and prophesies:

"Then say to him, 'Thus says the LORD of hosts, "Behold, a Man whose name is Branch, for He will branch out from where He is; and He will build the temple of the LORD.

"Yes, it is He who will build the temple of the LORD, and He who will bear the honor and sit and rule on His throne. Thus, He will be a priest on His throne, and the counsel of peace will be between the two offices.'"

And make sure we also add this crucial truth: (18) There was no acceptable way for God to have anyone as both king and priest under the Mosaic Covenant, and this designation would have been considered a tribe high-handed sin before God. (19) Being from the tribe of Levi, priests were not kings; being from the of Judah, kings were not priests. God had already figured out the answer long ago. (20) As long as the Mosaic Covenant functioned, there *must* be only Aaron and his descendants as priests. Hebrews 7:12 states, "For when the priesthood is changed, of necessity there takes place a change of law also." If the priesthood is changed, then the covenant from which it originates must be changed. And the reverse is true: change the covenant [the Mosaic Covenant], then the priesthood *must* change as well. So, with Jesus the covenant becomes the New Covenant, and the old priesthood of the Mosaic Covenant is eradicated.

(21) A crucial doctrine to understand is that God allows only one High Priest at a time. We have seen from several verses that Jesus has already ascended to the right hand of God the Father and has already become our—if you are saved—High Priest, and (22) once started in this role, He will never be replaced by anyone. However, (23) during His incarnation, Jesus Christ was God in the flesh; He was born of a woman, born under the Mosaic Covenant (Gal 4:4). With Jesus being from the tribe of Judah and from the direct lineage of David—and from what we have seen from Numbers about who could perform any of the priestly functions—consider the great-great ... grandfather of Jesus, King Uzziah.

DEEPER WALK STUDY QUESTIONS

(1) Show from Scripture how Matthew (and others) used Psalm 118 and 110 in presenting the story of Jesus. List five lessons from each Psalm.

(2) Name 5 reasons why Jesus' answer using Psalm 110:1 shattered the belief system of the religious leaders to such a degree that no one [of

His enemies; not His disciples; e.g. Matt. 24] dared to ask Him a question. Be specific.

(3) Write 10 doctrinal truths from Psalm 110 and briefly explain how each of the doctrinal truths is important. Be specific.

(4) Why is the way that Jesus used Psalm 118 in Matthew 22:43 when compared to the Mark 12:36 make it important? What is the main point here? Give 5 biblical reasons why this is important. Be specific.

(5) Why is what Peter preached in Acts 2:29–36 very important for understanding God's bigger plan? Give 10 doctrinal truths, and do not neglect having one of them as one of the seven "Appointed Times of Yahweh," and tell specifically why that is important.

(6) Name 20 doctrinal truths from the passages in Hebrews (they can be short or long), but save Hebrews 1:13 for a different part. Name 5 foundational doctrinal truths found there, and conclude with a summary statement of why Hebrews 1:13 is crucial for understanding both God Himself and His Word.

(7) From the High Priest verses about Jesus in the book of Hebrews, describe and support biblically 20 important doctrinal truths and/or specific characteristics of the work now being done by our High Priest Jesus.

(8) From Hebrews and other books and chapters of the Bible, develop 12 biblical truths that show that Jesus would have sinned if He had entered into the Holy of Holies during His incarnation. Why is this so, and be specific with your answers?

(9) Make up your own study question, answer it, and be able to give people five reasons why your question was important.

CHAPTER EIGHT

MERRY CHRISTMAS, ADAM AND EVE!

INTRODUCTION

Many Christians and non-Christians alike observe Christmas, with hostility toward this holiday mounting each year. If for no other reason, many observe it for family customs such as the exchanging of gifts, holiday food, and on the list goes. While the birth of Jesus the Messiah certainly is tremendously important and an irreplaceable part of God's eternal plan and with His foreknowledge (Acts 2:22–23), nothing changed at that point— (1) the Temple veil separating the Holy of Holies was not torn in half at our Savior's birth, (2) the Mosaic Covenant did not end at the birth of Jesus, with Galatians 4:4–5 explaining,

> But when the fullness of the time came, God sent forth His Son, born of a woman, born under the Law [*the Mosaic Covenant*], so that He might redeem those who were under the Law, that we might receive the adoption as sons.

Finally, (3) nothing else changed other than this was the first day of the entirely sinless life in order for Jesus to qualify as the spotless Lamb of God, who was qualified to take away sin, as shown in 1 Peter 1:17–21:

> And if you address as Father the One who impartially judges according to each man's work, conduct yourselves in fear during the time of your stay upon earth; knowing that you were not redeemed with perishable things like silver or gold from your futile way of life inherited from your forefathers, but with precious blood, as of a lamb unblemished and

spotless, the blood of Christ. For He was foreknown before the foundation of the world, but has appeared in these last times for the sake of you who through Him are believers in God, who raised Him from the dead and gave Him glory, so that your faith and hope are in God.

And then later in the same epistle, in 1 Peter 2:21–25:

For you have been called for this purpose, since Christ also suffered for you, leaving you an example for you to follow in His steps, WHO COMMITTED NO SIN, NOR WAS ANY DECEIT FOUND IN HIS MOUTH; and while being reviled, He did not revile in return; while suffering, He uttered no threats, but kept entrusting Himself to Him who judges righteously; and He Himself bore our sins in His body on the cross, that we might die to sin and live to righteousness; for by His wounds you were healed. For you were continually straying like sheep, but now you have returned to the Shepherd and Guardian of your souls.

But that is very far along in the story. We need to back up in our study.

From The Stone and the Glory of Israel, *Chapter Eleven: "The Return," (pp. 189–93)*[10]

They have come there alone—a country man and his country wife, now with their newborn boy: a Son partly theirs, partly not. Unto them a Child is born; unto them a Son is given—but given even more unto the world. Even at His early stage, they would learn that their Son was theirs; they would learn in an ever-expanding way that He was also God's—as well as God's gift to the world. Mary and Joseph would grow in their understanding of this by the various ones they encountered who in some way had expected the arrival of this Promised One.

The first to arrive were the shepherds from Bethlehem (Luke 2:8–16). Having found the parents and baby just as the angel had said, these recipients of the Word excitedly would have told of their angelic encounter—and yet at the same time, due to their lowly status in life and the custom of

---

10   From Greg Harris, *The Stone and the Glory of Israel: An Invitation for the Jewish People to Meet Their Messiah* (The Woodlands, TX: Kress Biblical Resources, 2016). Used by permission.

the day, likely would have apologized for the intrusion on one who had just given birth. Joseph and Mary listened. Each had heard similar words from a similar source. Each could have looked into the other's eyes, remembering the time months before when each had a revelatory episode with God's messenger angels. Did Joseph reveal this to the shepherds, or did he merely nod understandingly? The shepherds had no need to try to persuade the couple of the truthfulness of their testimony. Joseph knew the reliability of their account. He would have very few—if any—questions for the shepherds, as one whose spiritual experience so similarly resembled their own.

Eventually, in the reverence of the moment, there would be nothing else to say. Worshipful silence and wonder in the presence of God is always appropriate. Besides, these seekers did not come to discuss angelology—they came to behold their King. Somewhat similar to Jacob's dream of the ladder that reached to heaven, these shepherds likewise received progressive divine revelation that they would ponder for the rest of their lives: an angel, glory, angels—God. And it changed them eternally. Huddled around the One whom the prophets had foretold, what words could be added in the presence of the Promised Child—God Incarnate born as a baby? As Paul would later write in Romans 8:26, deep-heart expressions before God so often clumsily trip over any attempt at words.

Mary probably would not have said much—if anything. Out of innate modesty, out of recuperation from the arduous travel and then the labor, out of the norms of her culture, she would have deferred any discourse to her God-given soul mate with her. Besides, Mary was a heart-ponderer (Luke 2:19), as she would be all of her life. Heart-ponderers rarely engage strangers about their treasures stored within their souls' confines. But she would eventually. Decades later, Mary would confide to a kindred spirit, the gentle Gentile Dr. Luke, who would end his chapter in poetic description: "and His mother treasured all these things in her heart" (Luke 2:51). A gentle teacher of her Son she would be; a gentle disciple of her Savior she would become.

Her Baby was "born of a woman, born under the Law" (Gal. 4:4), and the Law had much to say about mothers and their newborns. In keeping with the God-ordained procedure, a little over a week would elapse before this One would receive His divinely-revealed name that is both a description and a promise, as the angel had declared nine months earlier in Matthew 1:21: "and you shall name Him Jesus, for it is He who will save His people from their sins." Luke 2:21 records accordingly, "And when eight days had passed, before His circumcision, His name was then called Jesus, the name given by the angel before He was conceived in the womb."

Luke added other revealing aspects of what the Law required. In Luke 2:22 he wrote, "And when the days for their purification according to the Law of Moses were completed, they brought Him up to Jerusalem to present Him to the Lord."

What a sight this young couple and Child must have been, and yet how they must have blended in completely with the masses who surrounded them. Like anything else concerning God's truth, if you apprehended the significance of the revelation, this event was earthshaking. If you did not, they were merely another couple from the country who were lost in the whirring busyness of the big city. Hailing from tiny Nazareth in Galilee, Joseph and Mary probably never would have felt at home in the bustle of Jerusalem. Besides, parents of their first newborn rarely marvel at their physical trappings, wherever they are. It usually takes a lot of effort to remove their eyes from this miracle of life. Protecting, fearing failure as parents, sensing far too much activity and noise surrounding them that was not good for a baby, God's couple would, nonetheless, obey His word and proceed to the Temple precincts as required by the Law.

Such designated ceremonies for firstborns had occurred for over fourteen hundred years. Leviticus 12:1–7 describes the procedure Mary and Joseph would follow:

> Then the LORD spoke to Moses, saying, "Speak to the sons of Israel, saying: 'When a woman gives birth and bears a male child, then she shall be unclean for seven days, as in the days of her menstruation she shall be unclean.
>
> 'On the eighth day the flesh of his foreskin shall be circumcised.
>
> 'Then she shall remain in the blood of her purification for thirty-three days; she shall not touch any consecrated thing, nor enter the sanctuary until the days of her purification are completed. But if she bears a female child, then she shall be unclean for two weeks, as in her menstruation; and she shall remain in the blood of her purification for sixty-six days.

'When the days of her purification are completed, for a son or for a daughter, she shall bring to the priest at the doorway of the tent of meeting a one year old lamb for a burnt offering and a young pigeon or a turtledove for a sin offering. Then he shall offer it before the LORD and make atonement for her, and she shall be cleansed from the flow of her blood. This is the law for her who bears a child, whether a male or a female.'"

The following verse adds a touch of grace for the poor—including Mary and Joseph—and what they were to offer:

"But if she cannot afford a lamb, then she shall take two turtledoves or two young pigeons, the one for a burnt offering and the other for a sin offering; and the priest shall make atonement for her, and she will be clean" (Lev. 12:8).

Luke 2:24 states that Mary came "to offer a sacrifice according to what was said in the Law of the Lord, 'A pair of turtledoves or two young pigeons.'" This shows, among other things, that the divinely-chosen couple was poor—very poor. The wise men would come eventually and bring their costly gifts, but that would be many days after Jesus was born. The poverty that would follow the humble Servant of Yahweh His entire life (2 Cor. 8:9) began with His earthly caretakers.

God could have written—and actually did write scattered throughout His unfolding Word: "But if she cannot afford a lamb for a burnt offering (Lev. 12:8) … God will provide for Himself the lamb for the burnt offering" (Gen. 22:8). On Moriah, where "Abraham called that place The LORD Will Provide, as it is said to this day, 'In the mount of the LORD it will be provided'" (Gen. 22:14). Moriah—the place to see God. Moriah—the place where God will appear. Moriah—where the present Temple stood. Moriah—where the Baby Jesus was presented before His Father. Mary, too poor to afford a lamb for the burnt offering, brings the Lamb of God whom God Himself had provided into His very own Temple where God had chosen for His name to dwell there forever.

(End of The Stone and the Glory of Israel *portion)*

**From The Stone and the Glory of Israel, *Chapter Eleven:*
"The Return," (pp. 193–95):[11]**

He comes alone. No masses accompany him. Neither does a group such
as the shepherds of Bethlehem join him. In the midst of an apostate high
priesthood and a nation not yet prepared by the Forerunner, he still comes.
He, however, needs no preparation. He is Simeon, a man "righteous and
devout, looking for the consolation of Israel" (Luke 2:25). He arrives early,
waiting, and anticipating what he knows will surely follow. In the midst of
the thousands associated with the hectic Temple activities and rituals, there
is One who will come—and he knows this deep within his soul.

The couple entered the Temple, dressed in humble garb of their eco-
nomic status. Nothing about them called any attention to themselves whatsoever—not even the Baby in her arms. Hundreds of parents; hundreds
of babies. Nothing different about these, unless you had been told who He
was—and Simeon had.

Simeon did not seek the high priest; he awaited the Messiah. He would
not have marveled at the dazzling attire of the high priest; he longed for
One—and he knew Him when he saw Him. Approaching the puzzled couple, he took the baby Jesus into his arms (Luke 2:28). Although not understanding the full import of what was happening, something about this old
man must have given Mary peace that this stranger was a friend. She did
not resist placing Him in Simeon's arms.

Looking down into the face of the Baby, Simeon immediately knew He
was the One. Accordingly he blessed God, stating:

> "Now Lord, You are releasing Your bond-servant to depart in peace,
> according to Your word; for my eyes have seen Your salvation, which You
> have prepared in the presence of all peoples, a light of revelation to the
> Gentiles, and the glory of Your people Israel" (Luke 2:29-32).

After Simeon's proclamation concerning Jesus, Luke added in the next
verse, "And His father and mother were amazed at the things which were
being said about Him" (Luke 2:33). Yet we generally take this the wrong way.

11 Adapted from Greg Harris, *The Stone and the Glory of Israel: An Invitation for the Jewish People to Meet Their Messiah.*
Used by permission.

Mary and Joseph were not amazed at what Simeon said—they marveled at how accurate and how similar it was to what the angels long before had informed them. Everything that they heard from Simeon they had heard either from their own encounter with the angels, or from John the Baptist's parents, Elizabeth and Zacharias, especially as Mary had stayed three months with her relative Elizabeth (Luke 1:56). With joyful delight Elizabeth would disclose to Mary the angel's revelation to Zacharias concerning his child that she herself carried—as well as about the One that Mary would bear. Mary's baby had a God-ordained forerunner given Him (Luke 1:17). Mary *knew* her baby was God's Son; she did not fully understand, but she knew it to her core. Gabriel's discourse with her in Luke 1:31–35 disclosed deep wells of theology we still do not grasp in their entirety:

> "And behold, you will conceive in your womb and bear a son, and you shall name Him Jesus. He will be great and will be called the Son of the Most High; and the Lord God will give Him the throne of His father David; and He will reign over the house of Jacob forever, and His kingdom will have no end."
>
> Mary said to the angel, "How can this be, since I am a virgin?"
>
> The angel answered and said to her, "The Holy Spirit will come upon you, and the power of the Most High will overshadow you; and for that reason the holy Child shall be called the Son of God."

Joseph, too, had his own divinely-sent messenger who identified the Child who would be born and His saving mission:

> "Joseph, son of David, do not be afraid to take Mary as your wife; for the Child who has been conceived in her is of the Holy Spirit.
>
> "She will bear a Son; and you shall call His name Jesus, for He will save His people from their sins" (Matt. 1:20–21).

When John (the Baptist) was born, Zacharias, under the power of the Holy Spirit, described a major aspect of the Forerunner's ministry: "To give to His people the knowledge of salvation by the forgiveness of their sins" (Luke 1:77).

So when Simeon declared that he had witnessed God's salvation, "a light of revelation to the Gentiles, and the glory of Your people Israel," this was not new revelation—this was new affirmation. Not that Mary and Joseph needed personal assurance, but it no doubt crossed their minds as to how many others also knew the true identity of their Child.

Their amazement was not about the content of Simeon's statement as much as it was about how this stranger had access to these truths. If Mary and Joseph said anything, it would not have been, "What do you mean?" Instead, it would be more along the lines of, "How do you know this?" or "Who told you these things?"

Why, God did, of course.

In the midst of a high priesthood that did not believe in the spiritual world, God sent one as a prophetic witness in the midst of spiritual darkness. It is not a random occurrence that in three successive verses Luke penned a reference to the Holy Spirit of God. Concerning Simeon, "the Holy Spirit was upon him" (Luke 2:25). "And it had been revealed to him by the Holy Spirit that he would not see death before he had seen the Lord's Christ" (Luke 2:26). For one who walked so closely with God, it should not be surprising that his rendezvous would likewise come from God's leading: "And he came in the Spirit into the Temple" (Luke 2:27). And so Simeon, by the Spirit, identified the same One whom John the Baptist had identified even while in his mother's womb.

What Simeon disclosed was actually more than what the shepherds had understood. They were told about the birth—of the promised Messiah, their Savior, the Lord, and went to see Him. Simeon knew that more was needed: God's Salvation; God's Light; God's Glory. Appropriately, Simeon identified that the Light and the Glory had returned—briefly—to the Temple of God where God's special presence had not resided for over six hundred years.

However, it would not be the last time. God had much, much more glory to disclose in His own house—and ultimately to the world.

(End of *The Stone and the Glory of Israel* portion)

ADAM'S PERSPECTIVE
FROM A SINNER'S VANTAGE POINT

We pick up a story very familiar for many of us, on Christmas Eve night. Adam's different vantage point that he so sadly knew so well so quickly.

From The Darkness and the Glory, *Chapter Eight:* "The Exchange," (pp. 155–57):[12]

The utter tragedy of man's fall in Genesis 3 erupts against the divine creation glories of Genesis 1–2. Only two relatively short chapters in the Bible present the world and its inhabitants at peace with itself and its Creator; the severity of man's fall follows shortly thereafter. Everything—and everyone—changed. Imperfection replaced perfection; purity transformed instantly into defilement. Sin. Crime. Disease. Death. War—all active components of a world helplessly degraded by the savage ramifications of man's sin. Even beyond these tragic reverberations, the most severe change was the wedge sin drove in between the Creator and His creatures. No longer could God and His image-bearing children enjoy walks in the cool of His garden. Sin separated—as sin still separates. God responded to the Fall in keeping with His holiness. After decreeing His verdict against mankind, the earth, and Satan in Genesis 3, God expelled the first couple from His Garden, and in a sense, away from His presence.

What thoughts Adam must have pondered that first night in his newly fallen domain. How quickly his world—and he himself—had changed. How much he had given up—and given over—to the Enemy. We of the human realm do not experientially know perfection with others, with our world, or even within our own selves. All we have ever known is sin's contamination, being conceived and born into a state of sin (Ps. 51:5; Eph. 2:1–3).

Adam knew. He knew firsthand what he had once possessed. Even more he knew what he had been: sinless, undefiled, holy. For the remainder of his days on earth Adam would always have a base of comparison restricted only to himself and Eve. Adam once enjoyed the perfect union

---

12 Greg Harris, *The Darkness and the Glory: His Cup and the Glory from Gethsemane to the Ascension* (The Woodlands, TX: Kress Biblical Resources, 2008). Used by Permission.

with his God-given bone-of-his-bone wife. Together the two cohabited an environment that contained no trace of sin's death-filled effects. Yet even beyond these blessings—and harmonizing with Jesus' statement thousands of years later that man does not live by bread alone, but by every word that proceeds from the mouth of God—Adam once basked in radiant fellowship with his Father and Creator, a pristine union unrestrained by sin. His other blessings, such as Eve and his environment, were mostly external and temporary. Adam's relationship with God, as Scripture would repeatedly disclose throughout the unfolding of God's revelation, emerges from the inside out—and is eternal.

In the engulfing darkness of the first night away from Eden, a depleted Adam brooded over his plight. If Eve sat by him physically, it would still be as though she never existed. Inner core searchings of this magnitude required sifting through Adam's own heart before considering input from another. An enemy had struck, a devastator had plundered, and together the first man and woman stepped away from God and into the non-retractable arena of sin. While Adam and Eve shared the responsibilities of a married couple, the burden of a fallen world's plight resided uniquely on Adam. Although Eve had first entered into this new realm of disobedience, deep inside Adam knew he was where he was by his own choice, as a consequence of his own actions. No one had deceived him; of his own free will he had chosen the creature over the Creator (Rom. 1:25). The previously prophesied death resulted just as God had promised, spiritually at this point, with the physical death to follow at some undisclosed time in the future. Now Adam sat in darkness; perhaps a fire or some torch struggled to illuminate his newly darkened world. Yet everywhere fallen man looked—other than at the meager first glimmers of the Light—he saw only darkness. Hope had become a distant memory, not so much in time, but in grasp.

Adam now existed in the midst of a curse that marred every good thing he had once experienced and possessed. The very ground on which he sat, as well as every aspect of God's physical creation, already began to sprout the contaminated fruit of his sin. His marriage immediately changed forever, never returning to the perfect relationship God had originally intended in Genesis 2. Hardship, toil, worry, and grief would likewise mark Adam all the days of his life, haunting him in varying degrees, as it continues to do so with his collective progeny today. Every day would bring forth new evidences of his fallen condition: some mild, others severe. Adam would eventually learn a new depth of sorrow as his first son Cain murdered his second son Abel, with even this crime ultimately traced back to the effects of his own disobedience to God. Many know the mammoth weight one carries for the consequences of their own sins; a deeper misery resides within those whose sins ensnare the ones they love—and Adam experienced this darkness before anyone else did. He also carried the weightier burden of having no past experience or example of others from which to learn, or from which to see God's divine working to bring about good even out of the residual embers of tragic sins.

After Adam lived nine hundred and thirty years (Gen. 5:5), experiencing both the joys and hardships of life, he would die physically, as he had initially died spiritually the moment he transgressed against God. This once majestic being, one-half of the pinnacle of God's creation, a component of the handiwork God Himself had pronounced "very good" (Gen. 1:31), ultimately returned to the dust from which God had created him (Gen. 3:19). Yet before this promised end, no matter how good any segment of Adam's life was, he still never retrieved what he once possessed in the Garden. Some people dream—Adam *remembered*. His fallen condition remained a thorn too deeply embedded within his soul for him ever to remove by his own strength or efforts as he sat amidst a new realm of darkness.

(End of The Darkness and the Glory portion)

More of the story unfolds with the life of the One who would crush the head of the devil. We will return to these pivotal truths further in the book. It will be thousands of years before One born of woman would crush the head of the serpent Satan, and eventually return in God's Glory to take back what is His.

ADAM, SETH, ENOSH

Does God offer any help in such a destitute situation, especially for people of Zechariah's time—and beyond? God most certainly does, and He does so in verses that most people would not associate with Christmas—nor with usage at any time of the year. Most Christians do not know that (1) the Book of Chronicles is one book (not two) in the Hebrew Bible, which leads us to a more important point, (2) Chronicles is the last book in the Hebrew Bible, and without author or date stated in the book, most Bible-believing scholars put Chronicles somewhere in time after 450 BC and attribute to Ezra its authorship, based on verses such as Ezra 7:1–6:

> Now after these things, in the reign of Artaxerxes king of Persia, there went up Ezra son of Seraiah, son of Azariah, son of Hilkiah, son of Shallum, son of Zadok, son of Ahitub, son of Amariah, son of Azariah, son of Meraioth, son of Zerahiah, son of Uzzi, son of Bukki, son of Abishua, son of Phinehas, son of Eleazar, son of Aaron the chief priest.
>
> This Ezra went up from Babylon, and he was a scribe skilled in the law of Moses, which the LORD God of Israel had given; and the king granted him all he requested because the hand of the LORD his God was upon him.

So how—with so many different things that had happened, both good and bad—would God the Holy Spirit begin the Chronicles? First Chronicles 1:1 offers this beautiful reminder that may not make sense right away, but will soon; "Adam, Seth, Enosh."

Many people—even in the days of Jesus' Incarnation up to present time—want to talk about prophecy and world events. Other people—especially those who are not walking in covenant obedience to God, would often rather talk about different subjects, but that's not God's preference. The Holy Spirit takes us back to the core problem and eventually to the only solution that God gives for its remedy. Remember that the Fall is revealed in Genesis 3. Genesis 5:1–6 tells us more about Adam and his family:

> This is the book of the generations of Adam. In the day when God created man, He made him in the likeness of God. He created them male and female, and He blessed them and named them Man in the day when they were created.
>
> When Adam had lived one hundred and thirty years, he became the father of a son in his own likeness, according to his image, and named him

Seth. Then the days of Adam after he became the father of Seth were eight hundred years, and he had other sons and daughters.

So all the days that Adam lived were nine hundred and thirty years, and he died.

And Seth lived one hundred and five years, and became the father of Enosh.

As we have seen on other occasions, here was God's original plan and offer, in Genesis 1:26–28:

> Then God said, "Let Us make man in Our image, according to Our likeness; and let them rule over the fish of the sea and over the birds of the sky and over the cattle and over all the earth, and over every creeping thing that creeps on the earth."
>
> And God created man in His own image, in the image of God He created him; male and female He created them.
>
> And God blessed them; and God said to them, "Be fruitful and multiply, and fill the earth, and subdue it; and rule over the fish of the sea and over the birds of the sky, and over every living thing that moves on the earth."

Sin kills; it always kills. Sin separates; it always separates. Genesis 1 refers to that brief time prior to the Fall of Man. Genesis 3 tells of the Fall *and* the consequential judgment that followed for Adam and subsequent males, Eve and subsequent females:

> Then the LORD God said to the woman, "What is this you have done?"
> And the woman said, "The serpent deceived me, and I ate."
> And the LORD God said to the serpent,
> "Because you have done this,
> Cursed are you more than all cattle,
> And more than every beast of the field;
> On your belly shall you go,
> And dust shall you eat
> All the days of your life;
> And I will put enmity
> Between you and the woman,

And between your seed and her seed;
He shall bruise you on the head,
And you shall bruise him on the heel."

The judgment of the physical serpent is included above. It is not until later on that we find out that there was a spiritual serpent who used the physical one to lie and tempt Eve, and quickly ensnared Adam, as seen in John 8:44, "You are of your father the devil, and you want to do the desires of your father. He was a murderer from the beginning, and does not stand in the truth, because there is no truth in him. Whenever he speaks a lie, he speaks from his own nature; for he is a liar, and the father of lies."

In 2 Corinthians 11:1–3 Paul wrote:

> I wish that you would bear with me in a little foolishness; but indeed you are bearing with me. For I am jealous for you with a godly jealousy; for I betrothed you to one husband, that to Christ I might present you as a pure virgin.
>
> But I am afraid, lest as the serpent deceived Eve by his craftiness, your minds should be led astray from the simplicity and purity of devotion to Christ.

Second Corinthians 11:13–15 reveals the true source of false apostles, as well as some of the means that they—and Satan—still use to this day to deceive many people:

> For such men are false apostles, deceitful workers, disguising themselves as apostles of Christ. And no wonder, for even Satan disguises himself as an angel of light.
>
> Therefore it is not surprising if his servants also disguise themselves as servants of righteousness; whose end shall be according to their deeds.

And just in case there is any doubt left about who the true enemy is, Revelation 12:9 tells of a future time when the archangel Michael and his angels will be waging war in heaven—which very well may happen soon— and when Satan, with his four-fold designation, is thrown to earth.

> And the great dragon was thrown down, the serpent of old [*which places him directly in the Genesis 3 account—he used the physical serpent as a mouth piece*]

who is called the devil and Satan, who deceives the whole world; he was thrown down to the earth, and his angels were thrown down with him.

To lead into some connective verses, it may be helpful to return briefly to Genesis 5:1–6:

This is the book of the generations of Adam. In the day when God created man, He made him in the likeness of God. He created them male and female, and He blessed them and named them Man in the day when they were created. [*This was God's original design and doing, as we saw in Genesis 1:26–27, and perfect in every way*].

When Adam had lived one hundred and thirty years, he became the father of a son in his own likeness, according to his image, and named him Seth. Then the days of Adam after he became the father of Seth were eight hundred years, and he had other sons and daughters.

So all the days that Adam lived were nine hundred and thirty years, and he died.

And Seth lived one hundred and five years, and became the father of Enosh.

Notice that it is recorded: "When Adam had lived one hundred and thirty years, he [*Adam*] became the father of a son in his own [*fallen*] likeness, according to his [*fallen*] image, and named him Seth"—because this description is made after the sin, Fall, and punishment God meted out in Genesis 3.

It is obvious in this account and others that we as fallen humanity retained a certain aspect of being made in God's image, even after the sin of Genesis 3, but not like it originally was in Genesis 1:26–27. Right after the Flood, Genesis 9:6 bears witness of the following truth:

"Whoever sheds man's blood,
By man his blood shall be shed,
For in the image of God
He made man.

James 3:7–10 in the New Testament adds this account:

> For every species of beasts and birds, of reptiles and creatures of the sea, is tamed, and has been tamed by the human race. But no one can tame the tongue; it is a restless evil and full of deadly poison. With it we bless our Lord and Father; *and with it we curse men, who have been made in the likeness of God*; from the same mouth come both blessing and cursing. My brethren, these things ought not to be this way.

In a summary of a few items in Genesis, before moving on, we should note these foundational doctrinal truths: (1) The genealogy is not intended as a genealogy of all creation, nor even of Adam's entire family; Cain and Abel both are omitted from this account of Adam's lineage; (2) with one major exception—Enoch (Gen. 5:21–24), all throughout the Genesis account will be the phrase found in Genesis 5:5 "So all the days that Adam lived were nine hundred and thirty years, *and he died*"—sin kills; it always kills. Sin separates; it always separates; and (3) Genesis becomes part of the lineage of the promised One who will eventually crush the head of the serpent.

So on our way to Luke 3, take a quick peek at Matthew 1. The Gospel is delineated to show from Jesus' actions, with Old Testament prophecies to fulfill or prophecies yet to fulfill at His Second Coming, that Jesus is the only One who uniquely qualifies [present tense] to rule and reign as the King of the Jews and also to have His worldwide reign. In this Scripture we have a reminder of the base need of Adam, Seth and Enosh—and all their progeny who ever will be born—that God had by no means forgotten His people. Matthew 1:18–21:

> Now the birth of Jesus Christ was as follows. When His mother Mary had been betrothed to Joseph, before they came together she was found to be with child by the Holy Spirit.
>
> And Joseph her husband, being a righteous man, and not wanting to disgrace her, desired to put her away secretly. But when he had considered this, behold, an angel of the Lord appeared to him in a dream, saying, "Joseph, son of David, do not be afraid to take Mary as your wife; for that which has been conceived in her is of the Holy Spirit.

"And she will bear a Son; and you shall call His name Jesus, *for it is He who will save His people from their sins*."

Luke is a Gospel that shows much of the humanity of Jesus from His birth through the Crucifixion, and gives many personal details in Luke 1:26–35 that we do not find in the other Gospels. And we saw that Matthew was primarily about the king requirments for the Messiah, and yet in chapter 1 is the statement that He will save His people from their sins. And in this book of Luke, with so much focus on the humanity of Jesus during His Incarnation—just as in Matthew—it has in its opening chapter about the Davidic Covenant reign of the Messiah. So, to put it this way, it does not mean that the other Gospels omit such matters, it is only that Matthew 1, for instance, has the virgin birth account, and the forgiveness of sins for His people, as we saw. In Luke's Gospel, so much focus goes on the virgin birth pronouncement to Mary and its explanation from Gabriel. Many readers of the Bible over the centuries completely miss not just a Davidic Covenant pronouncement, but also His eternal reign, as seen in Luke 1:26–35:

> Now in the sixth month the angel Gabriel was sent from God to a city in Galilee, called Nazareth, to a virgin engaged to a man whose name was Joseph, of the descendants of David; and the virgin's name was Mary.
>
> And coming in, he said to her, "Hail, favored one! The Lord is with you."
>
> But she was greatly troubled at this statement, and kept pondering what kind of salutation this might be.
>
> And the angel said to her, "Do not be afraid, Mary; for you have found favor with God.
>
> "And behold, you will conceive in your womb, and bear a son, and you shall name Him Jesus. He will be great, and will be called the Son of the Most High; and the Lord God will give Him the throne of His father David; and He will reign over the house of Jacob forever; and His kingdom will have no end."
>
> And Mary said to the angel, "How can this be, since I am a virgin?"
>
> And the angel answered and said to her, "The Holy Spirit will come upon you, and the power of the Most High will overshadow you; *and for that reason the holy offspring shall be called the Son of God*."

One more tie in: Luke 3:21–24 contains His genealogy going backward, but noting that Jesus is the Father's Beloved Son:

> Now when all the people were baptized, Jesus was also baptized, and while He was praying, heaven was opened, and the Holy Spirit descended upon Him in bodily form like a dove, and a voice came out of heaven, "You are My beloved Son, in You I am well-pleased."
>
> When He began His ministry, Jesus Himself was about thirty years of age, being, as was supposed, the son of Joseph, the son of Eli, the son of Matthat, the son of Levi, the son of Melchi, the son of Jannai, the son of Joseph ...

We are just noting Luke 3:31: the son of Melea, the son of Menna, the son of Mattatha, the son of Nathan, the son of David ...

And as we come the end of the genealogy in Luke 3:36–38, we find many names that we should be familiar with, especially from the Genesis 5 genealogy:

> the son of Cainan, the son of Arphaxad, the son of Shem, the son of Noah, the son of Lamech, the son of Methuselah, the son of Enoch, the son of Jared, the son of Mahalaleel, the son of Cainan,

And in Luke 3:38, still in reverse order, the son of Enosh, the son of Seth, the son of Adam, the son of God—this is the same but reversed order of 2 Chronicles 1:1: "Adam, Seth, Enosh." Note also there are two Sons of God noted, Jesus and Adam. Note also that Luke 4 leads into the temptation of Jesus by Satan. Adam failed miserably with his encounter with Satan earlier in his life; the second Adam, the true—and holy and perfect Son of God goes into the battle arena to start the warfare that had failed, and He would come out of Luke's account of the encounter without any spot, blemish or failure, and God the Father could still say of God the Son, He is still His beloved Son, in Whom He was still well-pleased.

Merry Christmas, Adam and Eve!—For unto you is born this day in the city of David a Head Crusher Savior who is Christ the Lord.

Merry Christmas, Adam and Eve!—as Peter would say on the fourth Appointed Time of Yahweh, Pentecost, and the beginning of Jesus' Church, recorded in Acts 2:22–24:

"Men of Israel, listen to these words: Jesus the Nazarene, a man attested to you by God with miracles and wonders and signs which God performed through Him in your midst, just as you yourselves know—this Man, delivered up by the predetermined plan and foreknowledge of God, you nailed to a cross by the hands of godless men and put Him to death.

"And God raised Him up again, putting an end to the agony of death, since it was impossible for Him to be held in its power."

Merry Christmas, Adam and Eve!—as the Book of Philippians 2:6–11 would record thousands of years after your deaths, you have One related to you:

> who, although He existed in the form of God, did not regard equality with God a thing to be grasped, but emptied Himself, taking the form of a bond-servant, and being made in the likeness of men.

> And being found in appearance as a man, He humbled Himself by becoming obedient to the point of death, even death on a cross. Therefore also God highly exalted Him, and bestowed on Him the name which is above every name, that at the name of Jesus EVERY KNEE SHOULD BOW, of those who are in heaven, and on earth, and under the earth, and that every tongue should confess that Jesus Christ is Lord, to the glory of God the Father.

Merry Christmas, Adam and Eve!—as the Holy Angel of God revealed to a select teenage virgin, thousands of years removed from you, who was told by Gabriel, the high-ranking angel that:

> "the Holy Spirit will come upon you, and the power of the Most High will overshadow you; and for that reason the holy offspring shall be called ***the Son of God***."

Merry Christmas, Adam, Seth, Enosh!—and for all the Redeemed—present, past, future, for 1 John 3:6–8 reveals one other thing, one incredible and unchangeable promise from the Trinity:

No one who abides in Him sins; no one who sins has seen Him or knows Him. Little children, let no one deceive you; the one who practices righteousness is righteous, just as He is righteous; the one who practices sin is of the devil; for the devil has sinned from the beginning.

The Son of God appeared for this purpose, that He might destroy the works of the devil.

Amen!

Amen!

Amen!

SUMMARY AND CONCLUSION

Among other things in this chapter we learned: (1) Jesus was born under the Law (Mosaic Covenant; Gal. 4:4), and (2) Leviticus 12:1–7 gave very specific details about what a woman was supposed to do, which Mary and Joseph kept; (3) After Simeon's proclamation concerning Jesus, Luke added in the next verse, "And His father and mother were amazed at the things which were being said about Him" (Luke 2:33), and as we saw in the text, they marveled at how accurate and how similar it was to what the angels had informed them months earlier. (4) We also saw the short account of Adam being removed from Eden into darkness of that first night and how much he had handed over to an enemy that had been among them.

(5) Chronicles—one book in the Hebrew Bible, not two books, such as the English and other versions have—begins with "Adam, Seth, Enosh." While that may not have seemed important at that time, (6) "Adam, Seth, Enosh" takes us back to Genesis 5:1–6, where the genealogy begins briefly pre-fall, but is mostly post-fall. (7) However, after their sins, Adam and Eve know experientially that sin kills; it always kills; sin separates; it always separates. (8) Genesis 1 refers to that brief time prior to the Fall; Genesis 3 speaks of matters related to the Fall of Man *and* the consequential judgment that followed for Adam and subsequent males, Eve and subsequent females; (9) The judgment of the physical serpent is included with the Genesis 3 account. (10) It is not until later that we find out that there was a spiritual serpent who used the physical one to lie and tempt Eve, and quickly ensnared Adam, as seen in John 8:44, "You are of your father the devil,

and you want to do the desires of your father. He was a murderer from the beginning, and does not stand in the truth, because there is no truth in him. Whenever he speaks a lie, he speaks from his own nature; for he is a liar, and the father of lies."

(11) We also learned, just in case there is any doubt left about who the true enemy is, that Revelation 12:9 tells of a future time when Michael and his angels will be waging war in heaven—which very well may happen soon—and when Satan, who is identified with this fourfold designation, is thrown down to earth.

> And the great dragon was thrown down, the serpent of old [*which places him directly in the Genesis 3 account who used the physical serpent as a mouth piece*] who is called the devil and Satan, who deceives the whole world; he was thrown down to the earth, and his angels were thrown down with him.

(12) We saw further in Genesis 5 a few foundational doctrinal truths worth knowing: (i) The genealogy is not intended as a genealogy of all creation, nor even of Adam's entire family; Cain and Abel both are omitted from this account of Adam's lineage; (ii) With the exception of Enoch (Gen 5:21–24), all throughout the Genesis account will be these words found in Genesis 5:5 "So all the days that Adam lived were nine hundred and thirty years, *and he died*"—sin kills; sin always kills: sin separates; it always separates; and (iii) Genesis becomes part of the lineage of the promised One who will eventually crush the head of the serpent. (13) On our way to Luke 3 we noted briefly from Matthew 1:21 what the angel told Joseph in his dream about who his adopted Son would be: "And she will bear a Son; and you shall call His name Jesus, *for it is He who will save His people from their sins*." And earlier (chronologically) (14) this was told to the virgin Mary by Gabriel when he informed her about who the baby's Father would be, in Luke 1:35, "And the angel answered and said to her, 'The Holy Spirit will come upon you, and the power of the Most High will overshadow you; *and for that reason the holy offspring shall be called the Son of God.*'"

(15) After Luke 3:21 with the baptism of Jesus, God's Son, is a genealogy that goes all the way back (Luke 3:38) to: "the son of Enosh, the son of Seth, the son of Adam, the son of God." And then (16) we saw the importance of Jesus going into battle in Luke 4, because, after all, (17) from 1

John 3:8, "*The Son of God appeared for this purpose, that He might destroy the works of the devil.*"

DEEPER WALK STUDY QUESTIONS

(1) Show in Scripture the events related to the naming of Jesus, plus how the procedure gave clues about His parents' status.

(2) What did Simeon know? Be specific. How did he know this, and what information did he pass on to Mary and Joseph? Briefly tell what each item means.

(3) Name ten items after the Fall that would be different for the remainder of Adam's life and why this would be tragic to him.

(4) Tell ten facts about Ezra, 1 and 2 Chronicles, and why the writing of this book would be very encouraging.

(5) Tell five specific reasons why "Adam, Seth, Enosh" is important to know in the Old Testament.

(6) Tell five specific reasons why "Adam, Seth, Enosh" is important to know in the New Testament. Why would it matter whether they are included in the Luke account?

(7) Why did we go back in our study to Genesis 5:1–6? What does that account tell us, and what does it not tell us? Simply put, give five doctrinal truths from this account and support your answer biblically.

(8) Find fifteen doctrinal truths from John 8:44, 2 Corinthians 11:1–3, and 2 Corinthians 11:13–15. Be specific and make sure you support each part of your answer biblically.

(9) From the Matthew 1 and Luke 1 accounts, write down and support with Scripture ten doctrinal truths about the birth of Jesus and the work of Jesus. Be specific.

(10) Very specifically tell ten biblical reasons for why the baptism, genealogy, and the initial battle in Luke relates to the person and work of the Lord Jesus Christ.

(11) Summarize in 2 to 4 sentences the biblical importance of 1 John 3:6–8 and how the Trinity answered the problem.

(12) Make up your own study question, answer it, and be able to give people five reasons why your question was important.

CHAPTER NINE

A THEOLOGICAL WALK-THROUGH ZECHARIAH 7–8

INTRODUCTION

Just from the size of the Scripture covered, this will be a shorter chapter. Zechariah 7–8 are short transitional chapters that (1) bring us for a time into the real world of the people of Zechariah's time (2) before the remaining extraordinary truths that eventually transform into the final prophecies of the Book of Zechariah 9–14. Also, Zechariah 7–8 is a definitive break in that the eight night visions have occurred in Zechariah 1–6. Those reading the chapter in this book or just reading the Bible in Zechariah 7–8—if they have kept up with what we are doing by reading the text accurately—should clearly see that this is no forced break in the text. No one should miss that the night visions do not continue in chapters 7 and 8 of Zechariah. While the eight night visions of Zechariah 1–6 remain eternally important, at this time the Jewish people are (i) back in the land, but no Davidic lineage king reigns, (ii) in the times of the Gentiles, (iii) with much of Jerusalem still needing repairs. The question (Zech 7:1-3) that men ask Zechariah and the other prophets brings chapter 7 back to their present and sometimes to the hard life they were to live. We will see the question and two negative answers in chapter 7 and two positive answers in chapter 8.

THE HISTORICAL AND BIBLICAL
REALITIES OF ZECHARIAH 7

When I came to this chapter, it reminded me of the first two chapters in the Bible.

In Zechariah 7:1–7, the returned exiles of Jewish people ask Zechariah whether they should continue in the fast that the people had only done half-heartedly:

> Then it came about in the fourth year of King Darius, that the word of the LORD came to Zechariah on the fourth day of the ninth month, which is Chislev. Now the town of Bethel had sent Sharezer and Regemmelech and their men to seek the favor of the LORD, speaking to the priests who belong to the house of the LORD of hosts, and to the prophets saying, "Shall I weep in the fifth month and abstain, as I have done these many years?"
>
> Then the word of the LORD of hosts came to me saying, "Say to all the people of the land and to the priests, 'When you fasted and mourned in the fifth and seventh months these seventy years, was it actually for Me that you fasted? And when you eat and drink, do you not eat for yourselves and do you not drink for yourselves?
>
> Are not these the words which the LORD proclaimed by the former prophets, when Jerusalem was inhabited and prosperous with its cities around it, and the Negev and the foothills were inhabited?'"

God gives His answer to their question in Zechariah 7:8–14, as well as a holy assessment about national Israel's heart and their lack of obedience, with some overtones of James 1:27 ("This is pure and undefiled religion in the sight of our God and Father, to visit orphans and widows in their distress, and to keep oneself unstained by the world"):

> Then the word of the LORD came to Zechariah saying, "Thus has the LORD of hosts said, 'Dispense true justice, and practice kindness and compassion each to his brother; and do not oppress the widow or the orphan, the stranger or the poor; and do not devise evil in your hearts against one another.'

"But they refused to pay attention and turned a stubborn shoulder and stopped their ears from hearing. And they made their hearts like flint so that they could not hear the law and the words which the LORD of hosts had sent by His Spirit through the former prophets; therefore great wrath came from the LORD of hosts.

"And it came about that just as He called and they would not listen, so they called and I would not listen," says the LORD of hosts; "but I scattered them with a storm wind among all the nations whom they have not known. Thus the land is desolated behind them, so that no one went back and forth, for they made the pleasant land desolate."

Zechariah 7:12 best describes the spiritual status of the majority of the Jewish people with this condemning denouncement by God: "And *they* made *their hearts like flint* so that *they* could not hear the law and the words which the LORD of hosts had sent by His Spirit through the former prophets; therefore great wrath came from the LORD of hosts." That sad spiritual condition of the majority of the Jewish people was their own doing—not God's doing.

THE PROPHETIC
TRANSITION TO ZECHARIAH

When I began studying Zechariah 8, I was struck by how similar it is to Genesis 1–2. There is an entire chapter in *The Bible Expositor's Handbook (OT/NT)* that follows the biblical trail with much more information, especially in reference to God's speaking.[13] The question of what is or what is not God's Word has instigated an age-old theological battle going all the way back to creation. Genesis 1 contains eleven verses with some form of "And God said:"

3: "Then God said ..."
9: "Then God said ..."
11: "Then God said ..."

---

13 Adapted from Greg Harris, *The Bible Expositor's Handbook (OT/NT)* (Nashville: B & H Academic, 2020), Chapter 25: "The Word of God or the Word of Man?" Introduction, 433–55. Used by permission.

14: "Then God said ..."
20: "Then God said ..."
22: "God blessed them, saying ..."
24: "Then God said ..."
26: "Then God said ..."
28: "God said ..."
29: "Then God said ..."

Genesis 2 adds two more such references: "The Lord God commanded the man, saying" (v. 16), and "Then the Lord God said ..." (v. 18). Thus, thirteen times in the first two chapters of Genesis present God as actively speaking, and this context also sets forth the mighty nature of God's spoken word. The Bible presents Him as God alone, who has no need outside of Himself to validate His speech, with creation itself validating and bearing witness to the effectiveness of His Word.

Genesis 3:1 abruptly changes things in two tremendously significant ways. First, this is the first question recorded in Scripture ("Indeed, has God said?"), and second, it is also the first temptation recorded in the Bible from the one who will soon be disclosed as an archenemy of God and humankind. When Eve did not properly respond to this deceptive temptation by saying, "God has indeed said," the initial question digresses to a statement: "You surely will not die!" (Gen 3:4). When the first questioning of whether or not God has spoken is not properly responded to, the scene digresses to include a formal denial of the truthfulness of God's Word. Now, for the first time in Scripture two statements stand in total opposition to each other; both statements cannot be true, and if one of them is found to be a true statement, the remaining statement must be a lie. Both of the serpent's approaches cast into doubt the trustworthiness of God, first by the doubting of His Word and second, by doubting His character. In both cases, the evil words spoken frame the focus of the attack, and they ultimately undermine the integrity of the One who speaks.

(End of *The Bible Expositor's Handbook (OT/NT)* Introduction to Chapter 25. I highly recommend that you read the entire chapter, if you have not already done so.)

Look how Zechariah 8 differs from Zechariah 7 and notice also who is the true source of knowledge.

Zechariah 8:1–7:

8:1 "Then the word of the LORD of hosts came saying..."

8:2 "Thus says the LORD of hosts..."

8:3 "Thus says the LORD..."

8:4 "Thus says the LORD of hosts..."

8:6 "Thus says the LORD of hosts, 'If it is too difficult in the sight of the remnant of this people in those days, will it also be too difficult in My sight?' declares the LORD of hosts.

8:7 "Thus says the LORD of hosts, 'Behold, I am going to save My people from the land of the east and from the land of the west;

Zechariah 8:9–17:

8:9 "Thus says the LORD of hosts, 'Let your hands be strong. . .'"

8:11 "But now I will not treat the remnant of this people as in the former days,' declares the LORD of hosts.

8:14 "For thus says the LORD of hosts, 'Just as I purposed to do harm to you when your fathers provoked Me to wrath,' says the LORD of hosts, 'and I have not relented,

8:17 "Also let none of you devise evil in your heart against another, and do not love perjury; for all these are what I hate,' declares the LORD."

Zechariah 8:18–23:

8:18 "Then the word of the LORD of hosts came to me saying..."

8:19 "Thus says the LORD of hosts..."

8:20 "Thus says the LORD of hosts..."

8:23 "Thus says the LORD of hosts, 'In those days ten men from all the nations will grasp the garment of a Jew saying, 'Let us go with you, for we have heard that God is with you.'"

Simply put, **16 times** in Zechariah 8 there is some form of "Thus says the LORD."

BACK TO ZECHARIAH CHAPTER 8

God looks beyond the present situation with a promise in Zechariah 8:1–8 to tell of Zion/Jerusalem's future blessings that spring from the promise in Zechariah 8:3, "I will return to Zion and will dwell in the midst of Jerusalem." We see elsewhere how different things will be when Yahweh returns. We will let the text speak for itself. Here are the verses in their context beginning with Zechariah 8:1–17:

> Then the word of the LORD of hosts came saying, "Thus says the LORD of hosts, 'I am exceedingly jealous for Zion, yes, with great wrath I am jealous for her.'
>
> "Thus says the LORD, 'I will return to Zion and will dwell in the midst of Jerusalem. Then Jerusalem will be called the City of Truth, and the mountain of the LORD of hosts will be called the Holy Mountain.'
>
> "Thus says the LORD of hosts, 'Old men and old women will again sit in the streets of Jerusalem, each man with his staff in his hand because of age. And the streets of the city will be filled with boys and girls playing in its streets.'
>
> "Thus says the LORD of hosts, 'If it is too difficult in the sight of the remnant of this people in those days, will it also be too difficult in My sight?' declares the LORD of hosts.
>
> "Thus says the LORD of hosts, 'Behold, I am going to save My people from the land of the east and from the land of the west; and I will bring them back, and they will live in the midst of Jerusalem, and they will be My people and I will be their God in truth and righteousness.'
>
> "Thus says the LORD of hosts, 'Let your hands be strong, you who are listening in these days to these words from the mouth of the prophets, those who spoke in the day that the foundation of the house of the LORD of hosts was laid, to the end that the temple might be built.
>
> 'For before those days there was no wage for man or any wage for animal; and for him who went out or came in there was no peace

because of his enemies, and I set all men one against another. But now I will not treat the remnant of this people as in the former days,' declares the LORD of hosts.

'For there will be peace for the seed: the vine will yield its fruit, the land will yield its produce, and the heavens will give their dew; and I will cause the remnant of this people to inherit all these things. And it will come about that just as you were a curse among the nations, O house of Judah and house of Israel, so I will save you that you may become a blessing. Do not fear; let your hands be strong.'

"For thus says the LORD of hosts, 'Just as I purposed to do harm to you when your fathers provoked Me to wrath,' says the LORD of hosts, 'and I have not relented, so I have again purposed in these days to do good to Jerusalem and to the house of Judah. Do not fear!

'These are the things which you should do: speak the truth to one another; judge with truth and judgment for peace in your gates.

'Also let none of you devise evil in your heart against another, and do not love perjury; for all these are what I hate,' declares the LORD."

Then in this last part, God gave the answer He wanted the Jewish people to know about the fasts. Zechariah 8:18-23:

Then the word of the LORD of hosts came to me saying,

"Thus says the LORD of hosts, 'The fast of the fourth, the fast of the fifth, the fast of the seventh, and the fast of the tenth months will become joy, gladness, and cheerful feasts for the house of Judah; so love truth and peace.'

"Thus says the LORD of hosts, 'It will yet be that peoples will come, even the inhabitants of many cities. And the inhabitants of one will go to another saying, "Let us go at once to entreat the favor of the LORD, and to seek the LORD of hosts; I will also go." So many peoples and mighty nations will come to seek the LORD of hosts in Jerusalem and to entreat the favor of the LORD.'

"Thus says the LORD of hosts, 'In those days ten men from all the nations will grasp the garment of a Jew saying, "Let us go with you, for we have heard that God is with you."'"

Come soon, LORD Jesus!

SUMMARY AND CONCLUSION

Among other things in this chapter we learned: (1) Just from the size of the Scripture covered, this will be a shorter chapter. Zechariah 7–8 are short transitional chapters that, (2) bring us for a time into the real world of the people of Zechariah's time, (3) before the remaining extraordinary truths that eventually transform into the final prophecies of the Book of Zechariah 9–14. (4) Zechariah 7–8 is a definitive break in that the eight night visions have occurred in Zechariah 1–6. (5) Zechariah 7:12 best describes the spiritual status of the majority of the Jewish people during Zechariah's time with this condemning denouncement by God: "And *they* made *their hearts like flint* so that *they* could not hear the law and the words which the LORD of hosts had sent by His Spirit through the former prophets; therefore great wrath came from the LORD of hosts." (6) That sad spiritual condition of the majority of the Jewish people was their own doing—not God's doing.

(7) Chapter 8 is a transitional chapter that sets the stage for the incredible prophecies God reveals through His prophet. (8) Where Genesis 1–2 has 13 times some form of "and God says," (9) Zechariah 8 has **16 times** some form of "Thus says the LORD," with God placing emphasis on who the true source of the prophecies are—namely, Him and not Zechariah's thoughts. (10) God looks beyond the present bleak situation of those Jews who returned from the Babylonian exile with a promise in Zechariah 8:1–8 to tell of Zion/Jerusalem's future blessings that spring from the promise in Zechariah 8:3, "I will return to Zion and will dwell in the midst of Jerusalem." (11) In Zechariah 8:1–17 God gives the Jewish people very specific promises associated with His return, and (12) Zechariah 8:18-23 shows how the Gentiles will be affected by the return of the Lord.

DEEPER WALK STUDY QUESTIONS

(1) Name six ways Zechariah 7–8 are transitional chapters. Be specific and support your answer biblically.

(2) What did God call the people to do in Zechariah 7? Be specific and tell why is this important.

(3) Why does Zechariah 7:12 best describe the spiritual status of the majority of the Jewish people during Zechariah's time? Give five answers as to why this was a very serious matter.

(4) What does Zechariah 8, having some form of "Thus says the LORD" 16 times, emphasize? Why would God put that chapter where He has it? List four reasons each for these two questions. Support your answer biblically.

(5) Name five reasons Zechariah 8:3 is important. Explain and support your answer.

(6) Why is Zechariah 8 like Genesis 1–2? Give five reasons why this is important.

(7) Name twelve truths from Zechariah 8:1–17. Give 1 to 3 summary sentences of what God promises national Israel.

(8) Make up your own study question, answer it, and be able to give people five reasons why your question is important.

CHAPTER TEN

A THEOLOGICAL
WALK-THROUGH OF
ZECHARIAH 9–13

INTRODUCTION

So far, much of the Book of Zechariah has been about rebuilding God's Temple after the Jewish people had returned from the Babylonian exile. Zechariah and his fellow prophet Haggai had much exhortation and encouragement to offer the people. Eventually, after a few delays, the Temple of Yahweh was rebuilt and once again was functioning with the Levitical priesthood. This occurs while still in "the times of the Gentiles" (Luke 21:24), with no king sitting on David's throne. Jerusalem plays an important role in Zechariah, occurring over 30 times in the 14 chapters, and with God laying claim on the city in such verses as Zechariah 1:14: "So the angel who was speaking with me said to me, "Proclaim, saying, 'Thus says the LORD of hosts, "I am exceedingly jealous for Jerusalem and Zion,"" and Zechariah 3:1–2: "Then he showed me Joshua the high priest standing before the angel of the LORD, and Satan standing at his right hand to accuse him. And the LORD said to Satan, 'The LORD rebuke you, Satan! Indeed, the LORD who has chosen Jerusalem rebuke you! Is this not a brand plucked from the fire?'" Not only will we view the covenant-keeping God in action, we will pick up the next two "Appointed Times of Yahweh" from Leviticus 23, namely the fifth and sixth ones.

A BROAD SCRIPTURAL VIEW OF THE IMPORTANCE OF JERUSALEM IN UNDERSTANDING PROPHECY

There is no way to study the Book of Zechariah without some brief—but irreplaceable—doctrinal truths about Jerusalem. Many of these prophecies will be tied in with the return of King Jesus to earth and are therefore still unfulfilled prophecy. For instance, the prophet Zechariah and all who returned from the 70-year exile from Babylon returned to the same place, Jerusalem, but in totally different times. As we saw in the introduction, their ancestors had Jerusalem as the capital from David through centuries, with King Zedekiah being the last Davidic Covenant heir to sit on David's throne—including even up to the present time. No one has sat on David's Throne for about 2,600 years. And even though the phrase was not used until Luke 21:24, those who returned from the Babylonian Exile even up to today live in "the times of the Gentiles." And not only does Luke 21:24 give us that new term to use, it also gives us a new Trinity-determined time marker. So adding a little context to what Jesus is talking about, Luke 21:20–24 reveals events that we will come back to later in this chapter and elsewhere in this present book:

> "But when you see Jerusalem surrounded by armies, then recognize that her desolation is at hand. Then let those who are in Judea flee to the mountains, and let those who are in the midst of the city depart, and let not those who are in the country enter the city; because these are days of vengeance, *in order that all things which are written may be fulfilled* [*important to know this term*].
>
> "Woe to those who are with child and to those who nurse babes in those days; for there will be great distress upon the land, and wrath to this people,
>
> "And they will fall by the edge of the sword, and will be led captive into all the nations; *and Jerusalem will be trampled under foot by the Gentiles* **until the times of the Gentiles be fulfilled.**"

Here is our God-given time marker: as long as Jerusalem is trampled under foot by the Gentiles—which includes the day this book is written—it remains "the times of the Gentiles." Some of the last words of Luke 21:24 clearly reveal important matters: "and Jerusalem will be trampled under foot by the Gentiles until the times of the Gentiles be fulfilled." Even though Jerusalem will be trampled under foot by Gentiles for thousands of years, such trampling does have a termination point, and some of the few verses we will see and study later are tied into the return and reign of Jesus Christ. And while entire books are written on many of these verses or topics, we must limit ourselves, giving just enough evidence to show what is biblically sanctioned, and we will move on.

Initially, we know that God has chosen Jerusalem for His capital, as Psalm 132 so clearly demonstrates:

A Song of Ascents.

Remember, O LORD, on David's behalf,

All his affliction;
How he swore to the LORD,
And vowed to the Mighty One of Jacob,
"Surely I will not enter my house,
Nor lie on my bed;
I will not give sleep to my eyes,
Or slumber to my eyelids;
Until I find a place for the LORD,
A dwelling place for the Mighty One of Jacob."
Behold, we heard of it in Ephrathah;
We found it in the field of Jaar.
Let us go into His dwelling place;
Let us worship at His footstool.
Arise, O LORD, to Your resting place;
You and the ark of Your strength.
Let Your priests be clothed with righteousness;
And let Your godly ones sing for joy.

For the sake of David Your servant [*the proper Davidic Covenant Heir*],
Do not turn away the face of Your anointed [*the LORD's Messiah*].
The LORD has sworn to David,

A truth from which He will not turn back;
"Of the fruit of your body I will set upon your throne.
"If your sons will keep My covenant,
And My testimony which I will teach them,
Their sons also shall sit upon your throne forever."

For the LORD has chosen Zion;
He has desired it for His habitation.
"This is My resting place forever;
Here I will dwell, for I have desired it.
"I will abundantly bless her provision;
I will satisfy her needy with bread.
"Her priests also I will clothe with salvation;
And her godly ones will sing aloud for joy.
"There I will cause the horn of David to spring forth;
I have prepared a lamp for Mine anointed [*Messiah means the annointed One*].
"His enemies I will clothe with shame;
But upon himself his crown shall shine."

Psalm 132:13 best sums up the teaching of this psalm, where God chooses Jerusalem/Zion as His "resting place forever" and does so with the Davidic Covenant promises as the basis for a major part of Psalm 132:

For the LORD has chosen Zion;
He has desired it for His habitation.
"This is My resting place forever;
Here I will dwell, for I have desired it."

Jeremiah 31—the chapter that first has the New Covenant called by that name (Jer 31:31–34)—also has other parts to be fulfilled whenever the fulness of the New Covenant comes, and it is operative in the fullest sense, as Jeremiah 31:38–40 promises, with all the prophecies about this last part still unfulfilled and tied in ultimately with the return of King Jesus to earth:

"Behold, days are coming," declares the LORD, "when the city shall be rebuilt for the LORD from the Tower of Hananel to the Corner Gate. And the

measuring line shall go out farther straight ahead to the hill Gareb; then it will turn to Goah.

"And the whole valley of the dead bodies and of the ashes, and all the fields as far as the brook Kidron, to the corner of the Horse Gate toward the east, *shall be holy to the LORD; it shall not be plucked up, or overthrown anymore forever*."

Look what is promised by the LORD: (1) the city Jerusalem will be rebuilt for Him, (2) then it shall be holy to the LORD; (3) once it is rebuilt for the LORD, it shall not be plucked up, (4) or overthrown anymore forever. And in summary, as we saw in the introduction, Zechariah 3:2 simply says "And the LORD said to Satan, 'The LORD rebuke you, Satan! Indeed, the LORD who has chosen Jerusalem rebuke you! Is this not a brand plucked from the fire?'"

But before the fulness of the Godhead takes full possession of what is theirs, God allows Satan and the Antichrist to have it as part of their God-allowed rule: (1) Daniel 9:27: "And he will make a firm covenant with the many for one week, but in the middle of the week he will put a stop to sacrifice and grain offering; and on the wing of abominations will come one who makes desolate, even until a complete destruction, one that is decreed, is poured out on the one who makes desolate." (2) In a context that specifically deals with things related to Jesus' Second Coming (Matt. 24:1–3):

And Jesus came out from the temple and was going away when His disciples came up to point out the temple buildings to Him. And He answered and said to them, "Do you not see all these things? Truly I say to you, not one stone here shall be left upon another, which will not be torn down."

And as He was sitting on the Mount of Olives, the disciples came to Him privately, saying, "Tell us, when will these things be, and what will be the sign of Your coming, and of the end of the age?"

Later in this chapter both Jesus and the Holy Spirit, through the apostle Matthew, give this stern warning especially for the Jews, in Matthew 24:15: "Therefore when you see the ABOMINATION OF DESOLATION which was spoken of through Daniel the prophet, standing in the holy place (let the reader understand)....” However, Scripture does not reveal what the “abomination of desolation” is until 2 Thessalonian 2:3–4:

> Let no one in any way deceive you, for it [*the judgmental part of the Day of the Lord*] will not come unless the apostasy comes first, and the man of lawlessness is revealed, the son of destruction, who opposes and exalts himself above every so-called god or object of worship, **so that he takes his seat in the temple of God, displaying himself as being God.**

And there is only one place for the Temple of God to be, and that is in Jerusalem.

So, the Godhead has chosen Jerusalem; Satan and the future—and perhaps pending—Antichrist have chosen Jerusalem as well, and under sovereign control of the Godhead, He will allow them to have it. But all of these cannot occur at the same time. God allows Satan and his forces to have Jerusalem and the Temple. One more time reference written about events related to the last three-and-one-half years of the Tribulation, sometimes called “the Great Tribulation,” appears in Revelation, in the first two verses of chapter 11.

> And there was given me a measuring rod like a staff; and someone said, “Rise and measure the temple of God, and the altar, and those who worship in it.
>
> “And leave out the court which is outside the temple, and do not measure it, for it has been given to the nations/Gentiles [*the word “Gentiles” means nations*]; and they will tread under foot the holy city for forty-two months [*3 and ½ years*].

And look what is given to the unbelieving Gentiles: “and they will tread under foot the holy city [*Jerusalem*] for forty-two months [*3 and ½ years*].

KEY: As long as Jerusalem is trampled under foot, it *must still be* “the times of the Gentiles.” When the Lord Jesus Christ returns to earth, defeats Satan and his forces, and reclaims Jerusalem and the world, it will never, ever again be “the times of the Gentiles.”

But before Christ Jesus returns in Glory, they [*the unbelieving Gentiles*] will tread under foot the holy city for forty-two months [*3 and ½ years*]. Thus, this is the last three-and-a half years of "the times of the Gentiles."

Zechariah 9–13 is similar to Revelation 4:1: "After these things I looked, and behold, a door standing open in heaven, and the first voice which I had heard, like the sound of a trumpet speaking with me, said, 'Come up here, and I will show you what must take place after these things'"—which, in the context describes the events in Revelation 6–18. Zechariah 9–13 describes some parts in a different way and some parts in a similar way, the things which must take place before the King returns in the Glory of God.

A BROAD THEOLOGICAL
WALK THROUGH ZECHARIAH 9–11

Beginning with Zechariah 9–14, the emphasis will be placed more frequently on the future of Israel—including Jerusalem—with some bringing good news and some bringing bad news, but as we will see in an upcoming chapter, very much sets the biblical table for the Advents of the Messiah, both His first and second comings. Although Zechariah plays an important role in giving verses that reveal new revelation and disclosures by God, we must be selective in the verses we cover.

Most certainly fitting is Matthew 21:1–5, which includes a quote from Zechariah 9:9:

> And when they had approached Jerusalem and had come to Bethphage, to the Mount of Olives, then Jesus sent two disciples, saying to them, "Go into the village opposite you, and immediately you will find a donkey tied there and a colt with her; untie them, and bring them to Me.
>
> "And if anyone says something to you, you shall say, 'The Lord has need of them,' and immediately he will send them."
>
> Now this took place that what was spoken through the prophet might be fulfilled, saying,
>
> "SAY TO THE DAUGHTER OF ZION,
> 'BEHOLD YOUR KING IS COMING TO YOU,

GENTLE, AND MOUNTED ON A DONKEY,
EVEN ON A COLT, THE FOAL OF A BEAST OF BURDEN.'"

A few items to note with this: (1) look at the measures Jesus took to fulfill this effort, with His actions showing that He understood this with a literal-grammatical hermeneutic; (2) Deuteronomy 17:14–15 is the passage that states that God alone chooses who will be king of the Jewish people: "When you enter the land which the LORD your God gives you, and you possess it and live in it, and you say, 'I will set a king over me like all the nations who are around me,' you shall surely set a king over you whom the LORD your God chooses, one from among your countrymen you shall set as king over yourselves; you may not put a foreigner over yourselves who is not your countryman." (3) So the statement from Zechariah 9:9 is more than a generic "Behold your king;" this statement is an affirmation that the One riding on the donkey is God's personal—and eternal—choice to be Israel's king. (4) The fact that He was not accepted by most of the Jewish people during His first advent changes nothing, other than the time when He will begin His rule. Remember that Jesus the Messiah is the one who will save His people from their sins:

> But when he had considered this, behold, an angel of the Lord appeared to him in a dream, saying, "Joseph, son of David, do not be afraid to take Mary as your wife; for that which has been conceived in her is of the Holy Spirit.
>
> "And she will bear a Son; and you shall call His name Jesus, for it is He who will save His people from their sins" (Matt. 1:20–21).

(5) Jesus attended to matters and events, related to Zechariah 9:9, but He did nothing with regard to Zechariah 9:10, because they currently await Messianic fulfillment, noting again Zechariah 9:9:

> Rejoice greatly, O daughter of Zion!
> Shout in triumph, O daughter of Jerusalem!
> Behold, your king is coming to you;
> He is just and endowed with salvation,
> Humble, and mounted on a donkey,
> Even on a colt, the foal of a donkey.

IMPORTANT: Whoever the King of the Jews is—and we know Who He is—He *must* come first to Jerusalem with Himself "Endowed with salvation," as we just saw in Matthew 1:21, humble, mounted on a donkey with colt, the foal of donkey. If He does not do these biblical requirements, then He does not qualify as King of the Jews. As before, look how Jesus instructed His servants to get the necessary animals so that Scripture would be fulfilled that day.

Zechariah 9:9 has been fulfilled, every last bit of it, but Zechariah 9:10 awaits a future fulfillment when Jesus returns to Jerusalem in judgment mode. Jesus did not fulfill even one the smallest part of its requirements. These will be fulfilled at His Second Coming to earth:

And I will cut off the chariot from Ephraim,

And the horse from Jerusalem;
And the bow of war will be cut off.
And He will speak peace to the nations;
And His dominion will be from sea to sea,
And from the River to the ends of the earth.

The implements for war were not cut off by Him at that time, neither did He speak to the nations, nor begin His worldwide reign—which He will, at His Second Coming to earth—with the Euphrates River as the northern-most border, just as the Abrahmic Covenant requires.

CONSIDER: Zechariah 9:9 and 9:10 show that side-by-side pro-phetic verses may have their fulfillment separated by thousands of years. We will see another example later in the chapter. Time and context are usually the best ways to view this. Jesus Messiah is just as obligated to fulill every bit of Zechariah 9:10 at His Second Coming, as He was to fulfill the requirements of Zechariah 9:9 dur-ing His first Advent.

Zechariah 10:6 shows the broad view that God takes with national Israel:
"And I shall strengthen the house of Judah,
And I shall save the house of Joseph,
And I shall bring them back,
Because I have had compassion on them;
And they will be as though I had not rejected them,
For I am the LORD their God, and I will answer them.

Zechariah 10:6 is one of those verses about which we must ask: if God did not intend to show mercy on the Jewish people, why write it the way that He did? Furthermore, if this is a promise that pertains to the church (as many claim), then when and where did the church's rejection by God occur?—because whoever is in view for these verses must have seemed to have been rejected by Yahweh for a time: "And they will be as though I had not rejected them."

Many people are familiar with the following verses, but may not realize where they occur biblically, in Zechariah 11:11–13:

So it was broken on that day, and thus the afflicted of the flock who were watching me realized that it was the word of the LORD.
AND I SAID TO THEM, "IF IT IS GOOD IN YOUR SIGHT, GIVE ME MY WAGES; BUT IF NOT, NEVER MIND!" SO THEY WEIGHED OUT THIRTY SHEKELS OF SILVER AS MY WAGES. THEN THE LORD SAID TO ME, "THROW IT TO THE POTTER, THAT MAGNIFICENT PRICE AT WHICH I WAS VALUED BY THEM." SO I TOOK THE THIRTY SHEKELS OF SILVER AND THREW THEM TO THE POTTER IN THE HOUSE OF THE LORD.

Exodus 21:32 shows that this was the same low price to be paid for a gored slave: "If the ox gores a male or female slave, the owner shall give his or her master thirty shekels of silver, and the ox shall be stoned." The price was a reprehensible insult that Judas agreed was fair compensation for him to turn Jesus over to the religious officials, as seen in Matthew 26:14–16:

Then one of the twelve, named Judas Iscariot, went to the chief priests, and said, "What are you willing to give me to deliver Him up to you?" And they weighed out to him thirty pieces of silver.

And from then on he began looking for a good opportunity to betray Him.

Later, Matthew's crucifixion account is forever linked to Zechariah by its quotation of Zechariah 11:12–13, when Judas Iscariot tried to return the money (Matthew 27:1-10):

> And the chief priests took the pieces of silver [*that Judus had cast before them on the floor*] and said, "It is not lawful to put them into the temple treasury, since it is the price of blood." And they counseled together and with the money bought the Potter's Field as a burial place for strangers.
>
> For this reason that field has been called the Field of Blood to this day.
>
> Then that which was spoken through Jeremiah the prophet was fulfilled, saying, "AND THEY TOOK THE THIRTY PIECES OF SILVER, THE PRICE OF THE ONE WHOSE PRICE HAD BEEN SET by the sons of Israel; AND THEY GAVE THEM FOR THE POTTER'S FIELD, AS THE LORD DIRECTED ME."

A BROAD THEOLOGICAL WALK THROUGH ZECHARIAH 12–13

Let's fast-forward centuries to what God promises, because, as we have repeatedly seen, He had chosen Jerusalem and the Jewish people to be His forever. In Zechariah 12:1–9 He not only begins a long process to bring Jerusalem to Himself, but also begins working to fulfill the ancient promises about reclaiming the Jewish people to Himself:

> The burden of the word of the LORD concerning Israel.
>
> Thus declares the LORD who stretches out the heavens, lays the foundation of the earth, and forms the spirit of man within him, "Behold, I am going to make Jerusalem a cup that causes reeling to all the peoples around; and when the siege is against Jerusalem, it will also be against Judah. And it will come about in that day that I will make Jerusalem a heavy stone for all the peoples; all who lift it will be severely injured. And all the nations of the earth will be gathered against it.

"In that day," declares the LORD, "I will strike every horse with bewilderment, and his rider with madness. But I will watch over the house of Judah, while I strike every horse of the peoples with blindness. Then the clans of Judah will say in their hearts, 'A strong support for us are the inhabitants of Jerusalem through the LORD of hosts, their God.'

"In that day I will make the clans of Judah like a firepot among pieces of wood and a flaming torch among sheaves, so they will consume on the right hand and on the left all the surrounding peoples, while the inhabitants of Jerusalem again dwell on their own sites in Jerusalem. The LORD also will save the tents of Judah first in order that the glory of the house of David and the glory of the inhabitants of Jerusalem may not be magnified above Judah. In that day the LORD will defend the inhabitants of Jerusalem, and the one who is feeble among them in that day will be like David, and the house of David will be like God, like the angel of the LORD before them.

"And it will come about in that day that I will set about to destroy all the nations that come against Jerusalem.

But even beyond this, the Trinity begins working to fulfill ancient promises about reclaiming the Jewish people, as seen in the next verse, Zechariah 12:10:

"And I will pour out on the house of David and on the inhabitants of Jerusalem, the Spirit of grace and of supplication, so that they will look on Me whom they have pierced; and they will mourn for Him, as one mourns for an only son, and they will weep bitterly over Him, like the bitter weeping over a first-born."

Two vantage points occur in this one sentence: (1) so that they will look *on Me* whom they have pierced [*Jesus, the Son*], and (2) and they will mourn *for Him* [*third person*], as one mourns for an only son, and they will weep bitterly *over Him* [*third person*]—how the Jewish remnant will then see Jesus. But these things will not happen until God pours out on whatever Jews that He wants "the Spirit of grace and supplication." This is another way of saying that this is not more of the Mosaic Covenant, but rather "the Spirit of grace and supplication" of the New Covenant, so that the items noted earlier may be fulfilled as prophesied. Zechariah 13:1 continues the promise of God's cleansing that is necessary for anyone to be saved—Jew or Gentile—by the fountain of the New Covenant in the blood of Jesus the Messiah: "In that day a fountain will be opened for the house of David and for the inhabitants of Jerusalem, for sin and for impurity."

For time's sake, we must skip some verses in Zechariah that you can go back and read on your own. But Zechariah 13:7 is already familiar to those of you who read the Bible on a regular basis, whether you realized the source or not:

> "Awake, O sword, against My Shepherd,
> And against the man, My Associate,"
> Declares the LORD of hosts.
> "Strike the Shepherd that the sheep may be scattered;
> And I will turn My hand against the little ones.

Many of you are more familiar with the events accompanying the arrest of Jesus, as shown in Matthew 26:31: "Then Jesus said to them, 'You will all fall away because of Me this night, for it is written, 'I WILL STRIKE DOWN THE SHEPHERD, AND THE SHEEP OF THE FLOCK SHALL BE SCATTERED.'"

This was actually a protective scattering by God of some of His terrified sheep, so that Jesus would be the only One arrested that night from their group. The description of our loving Shepherd, as it has been written in John 13 about events a few hours earlier as the Passover meal began, still fits here: "Now before the Feast of the Passover, Jesus knowing that His hour had come that He should depart out of this world to the Father, having loved His own who were in the world, He loved them to the end."

THE FIFTH AND SIX
APPOINTED TIMES OF YAHWEH

We saw five times in Leviticus some form of "these are the appointed times of Yahweh." God took the Jewish calendar that He had made, but claimed seven appointed times—not of the Jews or Gentiles—but as the appointed times of Yahweh. We saw four of the appointed times in the spring, and

New Testament documentation that they are either already fulfilled or have been fulfilled.

Passover—"For Christ our Passover also has been sacrificed" (1 Cor 5:7).

Unleavened Bread—"Your boasting is not good. Do you not know that a little leaven leavens the whole lump of dough? Clean out the old leaven, that you may be a new lump, just as you are in fact unleavened." (1 Cor 5:6–8—context used in reference to an on-going sin problem in Corinth and the permeating nature of unchecked sin, with the call for a holy lifestyle). "Therefore let us celebrate the feast [*of Unleavened Bread, using it figuratively as an OT life lesson*]," not with old leaven, nor with the leaven of malice and wickedness, but with the unleavened bread of sincerity and truth."

First Fruits—"But now Christ has been raised from the dead, ***the first fruits of those who are asleep***. For since by a man came death, by a man also came the resurrection of the dead. For as in Adam all die, so also in Christ all shall be made alive. But each in his own order: ***Christ the first fruits***, after that those who are Christ's at His coming, then comes the end, when He delivers up the kingdom to the God and Father, when He has abolished all rule and all authority and power" (1 Cor 15:20–24—the chapter on the Resurrection).

Weeks/Pentecost—"And when the day of Pentecost had come, they were all together in one place" (Acts 2:1—All the events included: the pouring out of the Holy Spirit that Jesus had taught, Peter's first post-resurrection sermon, and the birth of the church)

There is a long period of "silence from God" before the next three feasts

KEY: From the previous section we can see/learn

(1) These first four of "the appointed times of Yahweh" each have a New Testament citation/documentation.

(2) It is not just any 4 out of 7 that are cited (such as numbers 1, 3, 5, 7). The first four in order are cited (numbers 1, 2, 3, 4).

(3) **Not one** of the last three appointed times of Yahweh is found **in the New Testament**.

(4) The last three appointed times of Yahweh are for national Israel/ the Jewish people in the Tribulation.

(5) We will study below the next two of the appointed times, and we will see that they are for the Tribulation and not for the present time.

CRUCIAL: When we come to Zechariah 13:8–9 and matching passages, although they are not mentioned specifically by name in this account, **two of the three Appointed Times of Yahweh in Leviticus were being fulfilled**, based on Zechariah 12:10: "And I will pour out on the house of David and on the inhabitants of Jerusalem, the Spirit of grace and of supplication, so that they will look on Me whom they have pierced," and Zechariah 13:1: "In that day a fountain will be opened for the house of David and for the inhabitants of Jerusalem, for sin and for impurity". As part of this comes Zechariah 13:8–9:

> "And it will come about in all the land,"
> Declares the LORD,
> "That two parts in it will be cut off and perish;
> But the third will be left in it.
> "And I will bring the third part through the fire,
> Refine them as silver is refined,
> And test them as gold is tested.
> They will call on My name,
> And I will answer them;
> I will say, 'They are My people,'
> And they will say, 'The LORD is my God.'"

> **The 5ᵗʰ Appointed Time is the Feast of Trumpets** when there is **a call to national Jewish repentance**—and that is important: individual sacrifices and offerings for individuals were found in Leviticus 1:1–6:7.
>
> **The 6ᵗʰ Appointed Time of Yahweh—the true Day of Atonement for National Israel/the Jewish people** will *not* be based on the Mosaic Covenant blood of bulls and goats, but the first true Day of Atonement will be based on the blood of the New Covenant, poured out by Jesus the Messiah: "And I will pour out on the house of David and on the inhabitants of Jerusalem, the Spirit of grace and of supplication, **so that they will look on Me whom they have pierced**." And totally unlike other times we have seen in Scripture, God will accept both the sacrifice—*and* the ones who offered it—the one-third Jewish remnant who truly heard and responded to *the 5ᵗʰ Appointed Time of Yahweh, the Feast of Trumpets* [call to national repentance for the Jewish people], who will have become holy to partake of *the 6ᵗʰ Appointed Time of Yahweh—the Day of Atonement*—and the ones who will partake of these appointed times of Yahweh, will do so during the latter part of the Tribulation.

The call for Jewish national repentance in the Feast of Trumpets becomes the fifth appointed time of Yahweh. Aspects of this may include the witness of the 144,000 (Rev 7:4–8; 14:1–5) and the special two witnesses (Rev 11:3–14), plus any other means or ways that God chooses to use. So, again, even though you do not have the term "the appointed time of Yahweh" for national repentance, there certainly is a call for the Jewish nation to repent before the LORD—and there certainly is a true biblical repentance with a spirit of grace and supplication for impurity.

Zechariah 13:8–9 offers details that we would not know otherwise, with the size of the destruction of the Jewish people, but also the size of the initial saving of the Jews during this time:

"It will come about in all the land,"
Declares the LORD,
"That two parts in it will be cut off and perish;
But the third will be left in it.

And Zechariah 13:9 verifies the true salvation of this initial remnant—the sixth "appointed time of Yahweh": the Day of Atonement—that will be multiplied many times over in the Millennial Kingdom:

"And I will bring the third part through the fire,
Refine them as silver is refined,
And test them as gold is tested.
They will call on My name,
And I will answer them;
I will say, 'They are My people,'
And they will say, 'The LORD is my God.'"

The Jewish remnant will do something it was previously prohibited from doing by the rabbis and others, namely, they "will call on My name," and in doing so the remnant saved by the Lamb will say, "The LORD is my God." And just as important—if not more—this initial remant, Jews called to repentance (the 5th Appointed Time of Yahweh), will enjoy true salvation (the 6th Appointed Time of Yahweh). God Himself verifies this by a twofold response to this people who will call on Him. After the people "call on My name," "I will answer them," and then God will say, "They are My people," and again, the newly redeemed remnant will say, "The LORD is my God." We could also remove the word "until"at that time, that Jesus foretold will not be removed until His Secon Coming to earth:

"O Jerusalem, Jerusalem, who kills the prophets and stones those who are sent to her! How often I wanted to gather your children together, the way a hen gathers her chicks under her wings, and you were unwilling. Behold, your house is being left to you desolate!

"For I say to you, from now on you shall not see Me ***until*** you say, 'BLESSED IS HE WHO COMES IN THE NAME OF THE LORD!'" (Matt 23:37-39; Psalm 118:26)

This—at the present time—remains an unfulfilled prophecy. After the Spirit of grace and supplication is poured out, the newly redeemed one-third will see Jesus their Messiah/Jesus their King, shall praise Him with this attestation—as they will do with many other appropriate verses— "Blessed is He who comes in the name of the LORD!"—and the "until" will be removed forever.

WHAT GOD HAD PREVIOUSLY PROMISED WHEN THE PROPER CALLING ON HIS NAME OCCURRED[14]

From *The Face and the Glory*, chapter 3, "The Peace," pp. 45–47

Yet still in the midst of this, none of these judgments were God's original design or desire. He sought to dwell among the people (Ex. 25:8), to meet with them above the Mercy Seat in the Ark of His Covenant (Ex. 25:20–22), and even more astounding, to consecrate His dwelling by His own glory (Ex. 29:43). Simply put, as He would eventually reiterate centuries later in Jeremiah 30:22 and so many other places in His Word: "And you shall be My people, and I will be your God."

Even more to the point is one particular instance of God's original desire. Before the nation left Mount Sinai after one year and twenty days (Num 10:11), and before the spies were sent out and the people again rebelled against God for the tenth time in their very short history of redemption (Num 13–14), in a theologically rich passage, the kindness of God's original design and intention are clearly seen in a blessing that He Himself desired for His people:

> Then the LORD spoke to Moses, saying, "Speak to Aaron and to his sons, saying, 'Thus you shall bless the sons of Israel. You shall say to them:
> The LORD bless you, and keep you;
> The LORD make His face shine on you, and be gracious to you;
> The LORD lift up His countenance on you, and give you peace.'

---

14 Greg Harris, *The Face and the Glory: Lessons on the Invisible and Visible God and His Glory* (The Woodlands, TX: Kress Biblical Resources, 2019). Used by permission.

"So they shall invoke My name on the sons of Israel, and I then will bless them." (Num 6:22–27)

Scholars erroneously call this "Aaron's Blessing" or "The Aaronic Blessing." Obviously, Aaron as the nation's first High Priest and his subsequent heirs would play an important part by God's original design in instilling this blessing, but even a casual reading shows that God is the one who will bless, with His name "The LORD" beginning each of the three lines of blessing. Also, each of the three lines contains two component parts resulting in a total of six combined elements of God's blessing. Twice, the blessings that God intended for the people relates directly to His face. "The LORD make His face [*paneh*] shine on you" (Num 6:25), followed by "The LORD lift up His countenance [*paneh*] upon you; and give you peace." Perhaps we are surprised when we first consider this blessing that God lifts up His face—not their faces—upon them. Actually, this is indeed a wonderful blessing because it demonstrates God's active and personal care and attention—and desire—to bless those who live in covenant obedience to Him, at this point in the context Jewish, but later also for the Gentiles, as His holy Word would repeatedly show.

No, this is not "Aaron's Blessing"—this is *the LORD's blessing* because it involves (twice) "His face." Or to reason differently, take away God's face and there will be no blessing. As we saw with Philippians 4, God includes Himself with the peace that He alone can give. So as stated before, these are not impersonal, by-product blessings that would merely happen; these are direct consequences of Yahweh's offering these promised blessings. As James 1:17 would later plainly show, "Every good thing given and every perfect gift is from above, coming down from the Father of lights, with whom there is no variation or shifting shadow"—all emerging from a true relationship with Him.

Although these verses are used at many weddings or are frequently displayed in believers' homes as plaques or in framed cross-stitched items, most times they are incomplete. Very few people quote or display the connected verse that is just as inspired, just as binding, and just as mandatory, namely Numbers 6:27: "So they shall invoke My name on the sons of Israel, and I then will bless them." All of the previous items involved the name of the LORD. It is only after God's name was properly invoked that the promise "and I will *then* bless them" would occur. This means that without the proper invoking of God's name, He would withhold these connected blessings until the Jewish nation did properly invoke His name in accordance with the stated command.

This mandated invocation of God's name is very personal with God and again is part of His original desire and design. So in descending order, note what this famous blessing entails: "The LORD" (three times), "His face" (twice) and "His name" (once). Remove any of these items—or add to them—and they are no longer God's blessings, rather they are reduced to something much less. And tragically, removing God's name is exactly what the Jewish nation eventually did.

(End of the first *The Face and the Glory* part.)

From *The Face and the Glory*, chapter 4, "The Name," pp. 60–62

How burdensome these man-made restraints were and are! How tragically sad for Jewish individuals who were/are taught that instead of using God's revealed name Yahweh, the covenant-keeping name of God, they are taught never to utter it. Instead of calling on the name of the LORD in prayer, Yahweh becomes an unknown name for God, unutterable and far-removed from them. Sadly, many Jewish people conclude that if they do not utter "Yahweh," then they must be considered righteous, and have no need for salvation—or a Savior.

And equally worse for national Israel are the far-reaching and tremendously damaging ramifications that not speaking this name entails. For instance, first, under such teaching, they collectively will never enjoy the intended blessing of Numbers 6:24–27:

> The LORD bless you, and keep you;
> The LORD make His face shine on you, and be gracious to you;
> The LORD lift up His countenance on you, and give you peace.

And remember the important next verse: "So they shall invoke My name on the sons of Israel, and I then will bless them."

It should be noted that "Yahweh" is used in each verse in the blessing of Numbers 6. God intended this as warmly personal, not the sterile and isolated, "The Name bless you and keep you. The Name make His face shine on you." Also, by not invoking God's name properly, national Israel cannot receive God's blessing (Num. 6:27). It will not be until Zechariah 12:10, when the LORD pours out His Spirit of grace and supplication, and they look on Him whom they have pierced, and mourn for Him as an only Son," that the Jewish nation collectively will be brought again into covenant obedience with Yahweh and become recipient of all that this blessing entails. Sadly, this will occur in the midst of the Tribulation, and much must occur before that takes place—such as the nation collectively receiving the Antichrist before they receive Jesus Christ (Dan 9:24–27; Matt 24:15–24).

The second tragedy regarding the Jewish people and the man-made prohibition regarding God's name is that it makes "The Temple of the LORD" take on an impersonal tone by being referred to as "The First Temple" or "The Second Temple." Whose temple? "We can't say." To this day it takes the eternal focus off of *the Lord's* Temple or The Temple *of the LORD* and makes it very impersonal. Even worse is that many people call it "Solomon's Temple" for the First Temple, and horribly, wretched, wretched "Herod's Temple" for the Second Temple. Read your Scripture cover-to-cover, beloved; I assure you that God never called His own Temple by these man-made designations. How profane, how non-honoring to the true God that the house that is called by His name" (Jer 7:11) is routinely called by someone else's name. You will not find this to be the case with any of the pagans in whose honor the temples were built. For instance, "The Temple of Baal," "The Temple of Diana," or "The Temple of Zeus" are names always used for those temples, but sadly, the name "The Temple of the LORD" is almost universally not used. Failure to use this name is of the evil one because it takes the focus away from God and His holy work and from His eternal promises. Satan never wants people to focus on the true God "who has placed His name there forever" (1 Kings 9:3), which, of course, includes even today. One would *never* understand the eternal significance of what has transpired—and will transpire—at this exact God-ordained place in Jerusalem without the proper use of God's name as God intended in His city Jerusalem which He Himself has chosen.

And finally, how utterly tragic for the Jewish people that most of them would not initially accept the Messiah who would come to them in the name of the LORD.

(End of the second *The Face and the Glory* part.)

We need to pause just for a moment where we left off at the end of Zechariah 13. With six of the seven "Appointed Times of Yahweh" having been fulfilled, and God's utter faithfulness and sovereignty exhibited time after time, that leaves only one unfulfilled of the "Appointed Times of Yahweh."

I wonder…does Zechariah 14 have anything to do with the seventh Appointed Time of Yahweh?

SUMMARY AND CONCLUSION

This is a longer, yet crucial, chapter, which means it has a longer summary. Some of what we have learned in this very important chapter, among other things: (1) the reminder biblically, even in the times of the Gentiles, that God has chosen Jerusalem to eventually be His. Zechariah 1:14: "So the angel who was speaking with me said to me, 'Proclaim, saying, "Thus says the LORD of hosts, 'I am exceedingly jealous for Jerusalem and Zion,'"'" and Zechariah 3:1–2: "Then he showed me Joshua the high priest standing before the angel of the LORD, and Satan standing at his right hand to accuse him. And the LORD said to Satan, 'The LORD rebuke you, Satan! Indeed, the LORD who has chosen Jerusalem rebuke you! Is this not a brand plucked from the fire?'" (2) There is no way to study the Book of Zechariah without some brief—but irreplaceable—doctrinal truths about Jerusalem. (3) For instance, the prophet Zechariah and all who returned from the 70-year exile from Babylon, returned to the same place, Jerusalem, but in totally different times. Their ancestors had Jerusalem as the capital from David through centuries, with King Zedekiah being the last Davidic Covenant heir to sit on David's throne—including up to the present time. (4) And even though the phrase was not used until Luke 21:24, those who returned from the Babylonian Exile until today live in "the times of the Gentiles."

(5) And not only does Luke 21:24 give us that new term to use, it also gives us a new Trinity-determined time marker: as long as Jerusalem is trampled under foot by the Gentiles—which includes today as I write—it remains the times of the Gentiles. (6) Some of the last words of Luke 21:24 clearly reveal important matters: "and Jerusalem will be trampled under foot by the Gentiles until the times of the Gentiles be fulfilled," and (7) even though Jerusalem will be trampled under foot by Gentiles for thousands of years, such trampling does end at some undisclosed point, and some of the few verses we will see and study later are tied in with the return and reign of Jesus Christ.

(8) A few select Scripture references out of many about the Godhead and Jerusalem provide added clarity. Psalm 132:13 best sums up the teaching of this psalm where God chooses Jerusalem/Zion as His capital and for His "resting place forever" and does so with the Davidic covenant promises as the basis for a major part of Psalm 132:

> For the LORD has chosen Zion;
> He has desired it for His habitation.
> "This is My resting place forever;
> Here I will dwell, for I have desired it."

(9) Jeremiah 31:38–40 specifies certain promises, with all the prophecies about this last part still unfulfilled and tied in ultimately with the return of King Jesus to earth. Note carefully what is promised by the LORD in this passage: (i) the city Jerusalem will be rebuilt for Him, (ii) then it shall be holy to the LORD; (iii) once it is rebuilt for the LORD, it shall not be plucked up, (iv) or overthrown anymore forever. And in summary, Zechariah 3:2 simply says "And the LORD said to Satan, 'The LORD rebuke you, Satan! Indeed, the LORD who has chosen Jerusalem rebuke you! Is this not a brand plucked from the fire?'"

But, (10) before the fulness of the Godhead takes full possession of what is God's, God allows Satan and the Antichrist to have Jerusalem as part of their rule (Dan 9:27; Matt 24:15; and 2 Thess 2:3–4). Also, one more time-reference in Revelation, written about events related to the last three-and-one-half years of the Tribulation, sometimes called "the Great Tribulation" in Revelation 11:1–2, concludes by stating "for it has been given to the nations/Gentiles and they will tread under foot the holy city for forty-two months." (11) As long as Jerusalem is trampled under foot, it *must still be* the "times of the Gentiles." When the Lord Jesus Christ returns to earth, defeats Satan and his forces, and reclaims Jerusalem and the world, it will never, ever again be "the times of the Gentiles."

(12) We also saw Zechariah used at what is erroneously called the "Triumphal Entry" in Matthew 21:1–5 which includes a quote from Zechariah 9:9:

> And when they had approached Jerusalem and had come to Bethphage, to the Mount of Olives, then Jesus sent two disciples, saying to them, "Go into the village opposite you, and immediately you will find a donkey tied there and a colt with her; untie them, and bring them to Me.
>
> "And if anyone says something to you, you shall say, 'The Lord has need of them,' and immediately he will send them."
>
> Now this took place that what was spoken through the prophet might be fulfilled, saying,
>
> "SAY TO THE DAUGHTER OF ZION,
> 'BEHOLD YOUR KING IS COMING TO YOU,
> GENTLE, AND MOUNTED ON A DONKEY,
> EVEN ON A COLT, THE FOAL OF A BEAST OF BURDEN.'"

We noted: (i) the measures Jesus took to fulfill this effort, with His actions showing that He understood this with a literal-grammatical hermeneutic. (ii) Deuteronomy 17:14–15 states that God alone chooses who will be king of the Jewish people. (iii) So the statement from Zechariah 9:9 is more than a broad, generic "Behold your king." This statement is an affirmation that the One riding on the donkey is God's personal—and eternal—choice to be Israel's king.

(13) Jesus attended to matters and events related to Zechariah 9:9, but He did nothing with regard to Zechariah 9:10, because those events currently await Messianic fulfillment, noting again that Zechariah 9:9 has been fulfilled, every last part of it:

> Rejoice greatly, O daughter of Zion!
> Shout in triumph, O daughter of Jerusalem!

> Behold, your king is coming to you;
> He is just and endowed with salvation,
> Humble, and mounted on a donkey,
> Even on a colt, the foal of a donkey.

(13) **But Zechariah 9:10 awaits a future fulfillment when Jesus returns to Jerusalem in judgment mode, because at the time Jesus entered Jerusalem riding on a donkey, He did not fulfill even one of the smallest parts of the following requirements. These will be fulfilled only at His Second Coming:**

> And I will cut off the chariot from Ephraim,
> And the horse from Jerusalem;
> And the bow of war will be cut off.
> And He will speak peace to the nations;
> And His dominion will be from sea to sea,
> And from the River to the ends of the earth.

The implements for war were not cut off by Him at that time, neither did He speak to the nations, nor begin His worldwide reign—which He will, at His Second Coming to earth, having the Euphrates River as the northern most border, just as the Abrahamic Covenant requires. Also, (14) Zechariah 9:9 and 9:10 show that side-by-side prophetic verses may have their fulfillment separated by thousands of years—thousands of years after the first before the other is fulfilled.

(15) Matthew's crucifixion account (27:7–10) is forever linked to Zechariah by its quotation of Zechariah 11:12–13, when Judas Iscariot tried to return the money:

> And the chief priests took the pieces of silver and said, "It is not lawful to put them into the temple treasury, since it is the price of blood." And they counseled together and with the money bought the Potter's Field as a burial place for strangers.
>
> For this reason that field has been called the Field of Blood to this day.
>
> Then that which was spoken through Jeremiah the prophet was fulfilled, saying, "AND THEY TOOK THE THIRTY PIECES OF SILVER, THE PRICE OF THE ONE WHOSE PRICE HAD BEEN

SET by the sons of Israel; AND THEY GAVE THEM FOR THE POTTER'S FIELD, AS THE LORD DIRECTED ME."

In the closing chapters of Zechariah, (16) the Trinity begins working to fulfill ancient promises about reclaiming the Jewish people, as seen in Zechariah 12:10:

> "And I will pour out on the house of David and on the inhabitants of Jerusalem, the Spirit of grace and of supplication, so that they will look on Me whom they have pierced; and they will mourn for Him, as one mourns for an only son, and they will weep bitterly over Him, like the bitter weeping over a first-born."

(17) We noted the two different identifications that occur in this one sentence: (1) so that they will look *on Me* whom they have pierced [*first person*], and (2) and they will mourn *for Him* [*third person*], as one mourns for an only son, and they will weep bitterly *over Him* [*third person*]. But these things will not happen until God pours out on those Jews whom He chooses "the Spirit of grace and supplication." (18) This is another way of saying that this is not more of the Mosaic Covenant, but rather "the Spirit of grace and supplication" of the New Covenant, so that the items noted earlier may be fulfilled as prophesied. (19) Zechariah 13:1 continues the promise of God's cleansing that is necessary for anyone to be saved—Jews in this context—by the fountain of the New Covenant in the blood of Jesus the Messiah: "In that day a fountain will be opened for the house of David and for the inhabitants of Jerusalem, for sin and for impurity."

For time's sake, we must skip some verses in Zechariah that you can go back and read on your own. (20) But Zechariah 13:7 is already familiar to those of you who read the Bible on a regular basis, whether you realized the source or not:

> "Awake, O sword, against My Shepherd,
> And against the man, My Associate,"
> Declares the LORD of hosts.
> "Strike the Shepherd that the sheep may be scattered;
> And I will turn My hand against the little ones.

Many of you are more familiar with the events accompanying the arrest of Jesus, as shown in Matthew 26:31: "Then Jesus said to them, 'You will all fall away because of Me this night, for it is written, 'I WILL STRIKE DOWN THE SHEPHERD, AND THE SHEEP OF THE FLOCK SHALL BE SCATTERED.'" This was actually a protective scattering by God of some of His terrified sheep, so that Jesus would be the only One arrested that night from their group.

(22) You can go to appropriate places for more information, but we were reminded from a previous chapter that five times Leviticus 23 contains some form of "these are the appointed times of Yahweh." God took the Jewish calendar that He had made, but added seven appointed times—not of the Jews or Gentiles—but the appointed times of Yahweh. We saw four of the appointed times in the spring, and the New Testament shows documentation that they are being fulfilled or already have been fulfilled.

Passover—"For Christ our Passover also has been sacrificed" (1 Cor. 5:7).

Unleavened Bread—1 Corinthians 5:6–8—The context of Feast of Unleavened Bread is used in reference to an on-going sin problem in Corinth and the permeating nature of unchecked sin, with the call for a holy lifestyle.

First Fruits—"But now Christ has been raised from the dead, *the first fruits of those who are asleep*." (1 Cor 15:20–24—the chapter on the Resurrection).

Weeks/Pentecost—"And when the day of Pentecost had come, they were all together in one place" (Acts 2:1—All the events included: the pouring out of the Holy Spirit that Jesus had taught, Peter's first post-resurrection sermon, and the birth of the church)

Followed by a long period of "silence from God."

We saw (24) it was crucial to understand key components each of the seven times of Yahweh: From the previous section we can learn: (i) These first four of the Appointed Times of Yahweh have a New Testament citation/documentation. (ii) Also, it is not just any four out of seven that are cited (such as numbers 1, 3, 5, 7). It is the first four in order (numbers 1, 2, 3,

4). (iii) While first four Appointed Times of Yahweh are cited and identified in the New Testament, **not one** *of the last three* Appointed Times of Yahweh is found anywhere (except the Day of Atonement in Hebrews, but there it is used in looking back and using in contrast and comparison with the New Covenant). (iv) The last three Appointed Times of Yahweh are specifically for national Israel/the Jewish people in the Tribulation. (v) We will study below the next two of the Appointed Times, and we will see that it is for the Tribulation and not for the present time.

It is crucial to understand that when we come to Zechariah 13:8–9 and matching passages, although they are not mentioned specifically by name in this account, **two of the three Appointed Times of Yahweh in Leviticus were being fulfilled**, based on Zechariah 12:10 ("And I will pour out on the house of David and on the inhabitants of Jerusalem, the Spirit of grace and of supplication, so that they will look on Me whom they have pierced") and Zechariah 13:1 ("In that day a fountain will be opened for the house of David and for the inhabitants of Jerusalem, for sin and for impurity." As part of this comes Zechariah 13:8–9:

"And it will come about in all the land,"
Declares the LORD,
"That two parts in it will be cut off and perish;
But the third will be left in it.
"And I will bring the third part through the fire,
Refine them as silver is refined,
And test them as gold is tested.
They will call on My name,
And I will answer them;
I will say, 'They are My people,'
And they will say, 'The LORD is my God.'"

The Fifth Appointed Time of Yahweh is the Feast of Trumpets when there is **a call to national Jewish repentance**—and that is important: individual sacrifices and offerings for individuals were found in Leviticus 1:1–6:7. **The Sixth Appointed Time of Yahweh—the true Day of Atonement** for National Israel/the Jewish people will *not* be based on the Mosaic Covenant blood of bulls and goats, but the first true day Day of Atonement will be based on the blood of the New Covenant, poured out by Jesus the Messiah: "And I will pour out on the house of David and on the inhabitants of Jerusalem, the Spirit of grace and of supplication, **so that they will look on Me whom they have pierced**." And totally unlike other times we have seen in Scripture, God will accept both the sacrifice *and* the ones who offered the sacrifice, the Jewish remnant, the one third who truly heard and responded to *the Fifth Appointed Time of Yahweh*, the Feast of Trumpets [call to national repentance for the Jewish people]. These will have become truly prepared to partake of *the Sixth Appointed Time of Yahweh*—the Day of Atonement—and they are the remnant who will partake of this Day of Atonement during the latter part of the Tribulation.

The calling for Jewish national repentance in the Feast of Trumpets becomes the Fifth Appointed Time of Yahweh. Aspects of this may include the witness of the 144,000 (Rev. 7:4–8; 14:1–5) and the special two witnesses (Rev. 11:3–14), plus any other means or ways that God chooses to use. So, again, even though you do not have the term "the Appointed Time of Yahweh" for national repentance, there certainly is a call for the Jewish nation to repent before the LORD—and there certainly is a true biblical repentance with a spirit of grace and supplication because of impurity.

Zechariah 13:8–9 offers details that we would not know otherwise, with the size of the destruction of the Jewish people, but also the size of the initial saving of the Jews during this time:

"It will come about in all the land,"
Declares the LORD,
"That two parts in it will be cut off and perish;
But the third will be left in it.

And Zechariah 13:9 verifies that true salvation of this initial remnant—the sixth of "the Appointed Times of Yahweh": the Day of Atonement—will come for the lost remnant of Jews that He will save in the Tribulation. As we will see in the next chapter, there God's salvation of the lost—Jew and and Gentile—will be multiplied many times over in the Millennial Kingdom:

"And I will bring the third part through the fire,
Refine them as silver is refined,

And test them as gold is tested.
They will call on My name,
And I will answer them;
I will say, 'They are My people,'
And they will say, 'The LORD is my God.'"

The Jewish remnant will do something that the rabbis and others previously prohibited it from doing, namely, they "will call on My name," and in doing so, the remnant saved by the Lamb will say this: "The LORD is my God." And just as important—if not more—is that this initial remant who was called to repentance (the fifth appointed time of Yahweh) will enjoy true salvation (the sixth appointed time of Yahweh). God Himself verifies this by a twofold response to this people who will call on Him. After the people "call on My name," "I will answer them," and then God will say, "They are My people," and again, the newly redeemed remnant will say "The LORD is my God." We could also remove the word "until" that Jesus used not many days before He died:

> "O Jerusalem, Jerusalem, who kills the prophets and stones those who are sent to her! How often I wanted to gather your children together, the way a hen gathers her chicks under her wings, and you were unwilling. Behold, your house is being left to you desolate!
>
> "For I say to you, from now on you shall not see Me *until* you say, 'BLESSED IS HE WHO COMES IN THE NAME OF THE LORD!'"—Psalm 118:26

After the Spirit of grace and supplication is poured out, the newly redeemed one-third will say of Jesus their Messiah/Jesus their King, "Blessed is He who comes in the name of the LORD!"—and the "until" will be removed forever.

DEEPER WALK STUDY QUESTIONS

(1) Show in Scripture Who desires Jerusalem, and give three truths for knowing why each one is important.

(2) As long as Jerusalem is trampled under foot, what do we know? Give three reasons why knowing this is important?

(3) Give eight biblical truths from Matthew 21:1–5 and Zechariah 9:9. Why is this account important biblically? Explain and support your answers.

(4) Give seven biblical truths from Zechariah 10:6. Support with Scripture and tell why they are important.

(5) Give eight biblical truths from Matthew 27:7–10 and Zechariah 11:12–13.

(6) Give seven biblical truths each for both Zechariah 12:10 and 13:1. Explain and be specific.

(7) Give 10 biblical truths for Zechariah 13:8–9.

(8) Where are the fifth and sixth appointed times of Yahweh, and why are they important? How would you answer someone who says, "The words *appointed times* are not found in the Bible for the fifth and the sixth feasts." Defend your answer with evidence that this is what God meant with five biblical supports for the fifth and six appointed times of Yahweh occuring.

(9) Write your own question and answer it, and tell why it is important. Be specific.

CHAPTER ELEVEN

THE RETURN OF THE KING IN GLORY: A THEOLOGICAL WALK-THROUGH OF ZECHARIAH 14

INTRODUCTION

When Jesus foretold the fifth of Five Theological Bombshells in Matthew 16:27–28, this may have seemed—as it did to me—an unimportant event at that time:

> "For the Son of Man is going to come in the glory of His Father with His angels; and WILL THEN RECOMPENSE EVERY MAN ACCORDING TO HIS DEEDS.

> "Truly I say to you, there are some of those who are standing here who shall not taste death until they see the Son of Man coming in His kingdom."

Choosing this statement as one of the more monumental ones that Jesus made during His Incarnation did not seem important at the time or later. After my decades of study, I believe that I can convince most Bible believers that one would be hard-pressed to find a better, more succinct six-word synopsis for the entire Bible than "The Glory of God Changes Everything"—and we will see that in the chapter before us. In this chapter many subsequent events and/or doctrines emerge from Jesus' return in glory. You will have a very limited, if not flawed, theology in the life and works of Jesus the Messiah unless you understand the significance of what returning in the Glory of God means and why these simple words will be earth-shattering when fulfilled. Many events with profound eternal consequences will also occur when these verses are fulfilled.

THE BIBLICAL RELEVANCE OF WHAT WE STUDIED IN THE PREVIOUS CHAPTER

In the previous chapter we saw that the fifth appointed time of Yahweh [*the Feast of Trumpets*] and the sixth [*the first Day of Atonement under the New Covvenent*] Appointed Time of Yahweh will be fulfilled in the future for national Israel's first true fellowship with the LORD. God will also be doing a great worldwide evangelistic work among the Gentiles during the Tribulation, as revealed in verses such as Matthew 24:14, "And this gospel of the kingdom shall be preached in the whole world for a witness to all the nations, and then the end shall come," and Revelation 7:9–17:

> After these things I looked, and behold, a great multitude, which no one could count, from every nation and all tribes and peoples and tongues, standing before the throne and before the Lamb, clothed in white robes, and palm branches were in their hands; and they cry out with a loud voice, saying,
>
> "Salvation to our God who sits on the throne, and to the Lamb."
>
> And all the angels were standing around the throne and around the elders and the four living creatures; and they fell on their faces before the throne and worshiped God,
>
> "Amen, blessing and glory and wisdom and thanksgiving and honor and power and might, be to our God forever and ever. Amen."
>
> And one of the elders answered, saying to me, "These who are clothed in the white robes, who are they, and from where have they come?"
>
> And I said to him, "My lord, you know." And he said to me, "These are the ones who come out of the great tribulation, and they have washed their robes and made them white in the blood of the Lamb. For this reason, they are before the throne of God; and they serve Him day and night

in His temple; and He who sits on the throne shall spread His tabernacle over them.

"They shall hunger no more, neither thirst anymore; neither shall the sun beat down on them, nor any heat; for the Lamb in the center of the throne shall be their shepherd, and shall guide them to springs of the water of life; and God shall wipe every tear from their eyes."

These verses are tremendously important in understanding both God and His greater work, and the entire world will be affected by such verses, but in this book, we are focusing primarily on the Jewish people in the Tribulation and the events that will follow, mentioning the Gentiles where applicable.

The fifth Appointed Time of Yahweh—the Feast of Trumpets—will be a call for national repentance, only this time, there will be a remnant of Jewish people who respond to the Lord God and be saved, as we see in such verses as Zechariah 12:10, "And I will pour out on the house of David and on the inhabitants of Jerusalem, the Spirit of grace and of supplication, so that they will look on Me whom they have pierced; and they will mourn for Him, as one mourns for an only son, and they will weep bitterly over Him, like the bitter weeping over a first-born." And Zechariah 13:1, "In that day a fountain will be opened for the house of David and for the inhabitants of Jerusalem, for sin and for impurity." Just note this, if you are already saved and are a part of the body of Christ, you have no need for the "Spirit of grace and of supplication" to be poured out on or among you, nor do you need a "a fountain ... opened for sin and for impurity," because if you truly are saved, the Holy Spirit has already done the same work in you, as Jesus revealed during the Last Supper in John 16:7–11:

"But I tell you the truth, it is to your advantage that I go away; for if I do not go away, the Helper shall not come to you; but if I go, I will send Him to you.

"And He, when He comes, will convict the world concerning sin, and righteousness, and judgment; concerning sin, because they do not believe in Me; and concerning righteousness, because I go to the Father, and you no longer behold Me; and concerning judgment, because the ruler of this world has been judged.

That the Jewish remnant of one-third of their entire population will exist—and what God promises for that remnant—is clearly demonstrated in Zechariah 12:10 ("And I will pour out on the house of David and on the inhabitants of Jerusalem") and 13:1 ("In that day a fountain will be opened for the house of David and for the inhabitants of Jerusalem, for sin and for impurity") where God pours out His Spirit on the remnant. Those who try to explain that all of these promises are made to the church bring their own unscriptural bias to the text by ignoring what God's Word says here and by replacing it with their own theology. We also saw in the previous chapter that under the Mosaic Covenant, individual Jewish people could do the separate offerings and sacrifices as found in Leviticus 1:1–6:7—but that is not at all that Zechariah 12–13 deals with. It includes The Feast of Trumpets—a call for *national* repentance; the Day of Atonement, looking for *national* atonement. And while countless observances have been made by national Israel in the past, all of them combined will not be as important as these particular ones during the ending of the Tribulation. We find out from Zechariah 13:8–9:

> "And it will come about in all the land,"
> Declares the LORD,
> "That two parts in it will be cut off and perish;
> But the third will be left in it.
> "And I will bring the third part through the fire,
> Refine them as silver is refined,
> And test them as gold is tested.
> They will call on My name,
> And I will answer them;
> I will say, 'They are My people,'
> And they will say, 'The LORD is my God.'"

For two-thirds of national Israel to perish during the Tribulation harmonizes (using only a small sampling of verses) with Scripture passages such as Isaiah 40:1–2, passages that John the Baptist never used as part of his preaching to the collective Jewish people because it was not yet time for these biblical promises to be fulfilled:

"Comfort, O comfort My people," says your God.
"Speak kindly to Jerusalem;
And call out to her, that her warfare has ended,
That her iniquity has been removed,
That she has received of the LORD's hand
Double for all her sins."

Likewise, by the time of Zechariah 14, Ezekiel 20:33–38 will have been fulfilled or will be in the process of being fulfilled:

"As I live," declares the Lord GOD, "surely with a mighty hand and with an outstretched arm and with wrath poured out, I shall be king over you.

"And I shall bring you out from the peoples and gather you from the lands where you are scattered, with a mighty hand and with an outstretched arm and with wrath poured out; and I shall bring you into the wilderness of the peoples, and there I shall enter into judgment with you face to face. As I entered into judgment with your fathers in the wilderness of the land of Egypt, so I will enter into judgment with you," declares the Lord GOD.

"And I shall make you pass under the rod, and I shall bring you into the bond of the covenant; and I shall purge from you the rebels and those who transgress against Me; I shall bring them out of the land where they sojourn, but they will not enter the land of Israel. Thus you will know that I am the LORD."

Just one personal note before moving on: I want to tell you up front that I do not understand the Trinity in a deep sense—but do not feel bad for me, because until we go to heaven, the same will be true for you. We definitely see in a mirror dimly on this one. Just for the record: saying that I do not understand something is not the same thing as saying I do not believe in the Trinity—far from it. I wholeheartedly believe in the Holy Trinity of the Godhead. But it is one of those subjects that, if you are saved, you currently see with only partial knowledge, as a fallen human, but one day you will see face to face. Let me put it this way: while fully accepting this as biblical truth, if I had been among the twelve apostles, I would have had a hard time understanding "I and the Father are One" (John 10:30), or John 14:9 where "Jesus said to him, 'Have I been so long with you, and yet you have not come to know Me, Philip? He who has seen Me has seen the Father; how do you say, "Show us the Father."'"

The reason I wrote that last part is because sometimes—such as in the Incarnation—we can clearly see dividing lines identifying God the Father, God the Son, and God the Holy Spirit. But other times, there seems to be a portion of overlap between Who does what, and you will see what I'm talking about presently.

WHAT KIND OF MESSIAH DID/ DO THE JEWS EXPECT?

There exist many distinct variations of Jews and their beliefs/doctrines and what they do or do not believe, so it is hard to group them all together—just as you would err considerably to group all Christians together with what they believe. But just for the sake of clarity, I think American Christians and those of other countries would define Orthodox Jews as those who believe "the Oracles of God" (what we call the Old Testament), and are practicing Jews, as best they can, not having access yet to God's Temple.

All of the following statements have been said to me by practicing Orthodox Jews at different times and places about what they believe. One, the Messiah has not yet come, so obviously Jesus cannot be God's Messiah. Two, they further believe that when the Messiah comes He will be an enlightened human being but not God; to call Him God is blasphemy. Three, coupled with the other stated beliefs, when Messiah does come, to worship Him would likewise be blasphemy. For the Orthodox Jews whom I have interacted with, I have asked about what sign(s) will accompany the advent of Messiah, and they have told me, there will be no signs— something with which God disagrees, giving hundreds of signs about the Messiah, such as Isaiah 7:14, "Therefore the Lord Himself will give you a sign: Behold, a virgin will be with child and bear a son, and she will call His name Immanuel." Those who believe there will be no signs given by God about His Messiah also say there will be only one grand, spectacular sign by which they will know how to identify the Messiah: the One who brings them world peace; that One will be the Messiah. Of course, Jesus the Messiah will eventually bring world peace, especially starting in Revelation 20, and ultimately in Revelation 21–22, but the neglect of believing the Scripture and making their own deductions as biblical doctrine sets the stage for the Jews to receive the Antichrist before they receive Jesus Christ.

So we will do this backward to get the wider biblical picture, but I use the word "backward" because we will also use New Testament verses as part of the components of our study, which the Orthodox Jews—at this point—would never receive as biblical truth. In Isaiah 6:1 the prophet writes, "In the year of King Uzziah's death, I saw the Lord sitting on a throne, lofty and exalted, with the train of His robe filling the temple." Later, Isaiah concludes in Isaiah 6:5,

> Then I said,
> "Woe is me, for I am ruined!
> Because I am a man of unclean lips,
> And I live among a people of unclean lips;
> For my eyes have seen the King, the LORD of hosts."

And then in John 12:37–41, see what the Apostle John wrote, especially the last verse:

> But though He had performed so many signs before them, yet they were not believing in Him; that the word of Isaiah the prophet might be fulfilled, which he spoke, "LORD, WHO HAS BELIEVED OUR REPORT? AND TO WHOM HAS THE ARM OF THE LORD BEEN REVEALED?"
>
> For this cause they could not believe, for Isaiah said again, "HE HAS BLINDED THEIR EYES, AND HE HARDENED THEIR HEART; LEST THEY SEE WITH THEIR EYES, AND PERCEIVE WITH THEIR HEART, AND BE CONVERTED, AND I HEAL THEM."

These things Isaiah said, because he saw His glory, and he spoke of Him. They would counter and say that this is New Testament/Christian teaching. So we will set this aside temporarily just for the sake of argument. The Messiah whom the Jews—and much of the world—are looking for is much more in keeping with Psalm 2:1–7,

Why are the nations in an uproar,
And the peoples devising a vain thing?
The kings of the earth take their stand
And the rulers take counsel together
Against the LORD and against His Anointed [*His Messiah*], saying,
"Let us tear their fetters apart
And cast away their cords from us!"
He who sits in the heavens laughs,
The Lord scoffs at them.
Then He will speak to them in His anger
And terrify them in His fury, saying,
"But as for Me [*God says*], I have installed My King [*Deut. 17—God chooses the King; My Davidic Covenant lineage*]

"I will surely tell of the decree of the LORD:
He said to Me, 'You are My Son,
Today I have begotten You.

That is the type of Messiah that many Jews have looked for and many continue to look for to this day. But there are other texts that we need to examine to help our understanding about God's Messiah.

SOME SAMPLE REFERENCES ON WHO THE MESSIAH WILL BE

Remove the Gospel of John references and use only the verses from Isaiah 6:5, and you still have Isaiah responding by saying:

"Woe is me, for I am ruined!
Because I am a man of unclean lips,
And I live among a people of unclean lips;
For my eyes have seen the King, the LORD of hosts."

This is a clear reference to Deity—not to humanity at this point—and if someone claims to believe the Oracles of God, this reference must be dealt with, and there will be other references. Although it is true that John 12 is

New Testament teaching, the basis for calling the Messiah the King, the LORD/Yahweh of hosts and speaking of His glory is Old Testament verses.

Here are a few more instances to note and to add to such usage—all found in Jeremiah—of the coming King, who will also be God. In Jeremiah 46:18, "As I live," declares the King, whose name is the LORD of hosts"; in 48:15, "Declares the King, whose name is the LORD of hosts"; and finally, Jeremiah 51:57, "Declares the King, whose name is the LORD of hosts." None of this is New Testament theology forced onto Old Testament theology; none of this could be accomplished by someone who will be "an enlightened and elevated man." So the King of Glory has to be a Godhead Member, and yet also has to be a Davidic Covenant heir, born of a virgin into the world He Himself created.

VERSES ABOUT THE DEITY OF THE MESSIAH AND HIS RETURNING IN GLORY

A very short list (we could add many more) begins our section with Psalm 24, a psalm of David that breaks down into two parts, with the second part asking and answering the question concerning Who the King of Glory is. We begin with the first six verses:

> A Psalm of David.
> The earth is the LORD's, and all it contains,
> The world, and those who dwell in it.
> For He has founded it upon the seas
> And established it upon the rivers.
> Who may ascend into the hill of the LORD?
> And who may stand in His holy place?
> He who has clean hands and a pure heart,
> Who has not lifted up his soul to falsehood
> And has not sworn deceitfully.
> He shall receive a blessing from the LORD
> And righteousness from the God of his salvation.
> This is the generation of those who seek Him,
> Who seek Your face—even Jacob. Selah.

And then go to this section of the psalm that no simple human being has had or ever will have the characteristics necessary to fulfill—the last verses of Psalm 24, verses 7–10,

> Lift up your heads, O gates,
> And be lifted up, O ancient doors,
> That the King of glory may come in!
> Who is the King of glory?
> The LORD strong and mighty,
> The LORD mighty in battle.
> Lift up your heads, O gates,
> And lift them up, O ancient doors,
> That the King of glory may come in!
> Who is this King of glory?
> The LORD of hosts,
> He is the King of glory. Selah.

Simply stated: when Jesus was claiming to return in the Glory of the Father, in Matthew 16— which is biblical truth—it is another way of claiming to be a Member of the Godhead. Who is the King of Glory? In this case the mere aspect of being David's son would not qualify Him to have the capacity to fulfill actions and/or attributes of the King of Glory, the LORD/Yahweh of hosts.

The Messiah returning in Glory or with the Glory of God does not begin with Jesus in Matthew. Rather there are multiple prophecies in the Old Testament that clearly show His returning in Glory/with Glory, and we will study only a few of these prophecies because of time and space limitations. When the Messiah returns to earth, one of the first things that He does is to defeat His enemies—the physical ones and the spiritual ones, as seen in Isaiah 24:21–23,

> So it will happen in that day,
> That the LORD will punish the host of heaven, on high,
> And the kings of the earth, on earth.
> And they will be gathered together
> Like prisoners in the dungeon,

And will be confined in prison;

And after many days they will be punished.

Then the moon will be abashed and the sun ashamed,

For the LORD of hosts will reign on Mount Zion and in Jerusalem,

And His glory will be before His elders.

Whether or not the Messiah returns in Glory/with Glory is not an insignificant matter. Ezekiel 39:21–29—and other verses—are used to prove Himself true to His Word, both to Jews and to Gentiles:

> "***And I will set My glory among the nations***; and all the nations will see My judgment which I have executed and My hand which I have laid on them.
>
> "And the house of Israel will know that I am the LORD their God from that day onward.
>
> "The nations will know that the house of Israel went into exile for their iniquity because they acted treacherously against Me, and I hid My face from them; so I gave them into the hand of their adversaries, and all of them fell by the sword.
>
> "According to their uncleanness and according to their transgressions I dealt with them, and I hid My face from them.'"
>
> Therefore thus says the Lord GOD, "Now I will restore the fortunes of Jacob and have mercy on the whole house of Israel; and I will be jealous for My holy name.
>
> "They will forget their disgrace and all their treachery which they perpetrated against Me, when they live securely on their own land with no one to make them afraid.
>
> "When I bring them back from the peoples and gather them from the lands of their enemies, then I shall be sanctified through them in the sight of the many nations.
>
> "Then they will know that I am the LORD their God because I made them go into exile among the nations, and then gathered them again to their own land; and I will leave none of them there any longer.

And then, there is the last verse of this segment that is also the last verse before the final section of Ezekiel (40–48), which deals with the Millennial

Temple and Priesthood. ***God Himself*** promises two eternally important works: (1) "I will not hide My face from them [the Jewish remnant and beyond] any longer, for (2) I will have poured out My Spirit on the house of Israel," declares the Lord GOD (Ezek. 39:29).

CONSIDER: If God did ***not*** mean that He will set His glory among the nations (Ezek. 39:21), and both the Jews and Gentiles, and if God promises to bring them back to the promised land, and that the Jews' punishment has ended (that means Isa. 40:1–2 will be completed, paraphrasing that the Jews and Jerusalem will be paid back double for their sins), then why use this language telling the Jews and Gentiles about God being vindicated? He indeed ***did*** mean it here and elsewhere that such promises are made. Also (1) what did God mean when He proclaimed these things, and (2) if you refuse to believe and accept these scriptures, how could you ever hope to understand ***anything*** God says in the Bible? What are the guidelines for understanding, if one rejects this?

For those who believe God's Word and allow it to speak for itself, ***we know***—not we think we perhaps may know. "For I will have poured out My Spirit on the house of Israel,' declares the Lord GOD" (Ezek. 39:29), means that **the fifth Appointed Time of Yahweh,** Zechariah 12:10 and 13:1 and the rest of chapter 13, **the Feast of Trumpets: a call for national Jewish repentance**, and **the sixth Appointed Time of Yahweh: the true Day of Atonement in the blood of the Lamb in the New Covenant,** will be fulfilled. This is when God receives the initial saved remnant back to Himself Zechariah 13:9, "And I will bring the third part through the fire, / Refine them as silver is refined, / And test them as gold is tested. / They will call on My name, / And I will answer them; / I will say, 'They are My people,' / And they will say, 'The LORD is my God.'" Isaiah 25:1 is a shorter version:

"plans formed long ago *with perfect faithfulness*"—Amen! Amen! Amen!

A couple more Scripture references for the LORD returning in Glory, the first one being Isaiah 4:2–6, fit in perfect harmony with other verses we have seen in our study:

> In that day the Branch of the LORD will be beautiful and glorious, and the fruit of the earth will be the pride and the adornment of the survivors of Israel.
>
> It will come about that he who is left in Zion and remains in Jerusalem will be called holy—everyone who is recorded for life in Jerusalem.
>
> **When the Lord has washed away** the filth of the daughters of Zion and purged the bloodshed of Jerusalem from her midst, by the spirit of judgment and the spirit of burning, **then** the LORD will create over the whole area of Mount Zion and over her assemblies a cloud by day, even smoke, and the brightness of a flaming fire by night; **for over all the glory will be a canopy.** There will be a shelter to give shade from the heat by day, and refuge and protection from the storm and the rain.

And second, after what we saw in Ezekiel 39 comes this promised event Ezekiel 43:1–5,

> Then he led me to the gate, the gate facing toward the east; **and behold, the glory of the God of Israel was coming from the way of the east. And His voice was like the sound of many waters; and the earth shone with His glory.**
>
> And it was like the appearance of the vision which I saw, like the vision which I saw when He came to destroy the city. And the visions were like the vision which I saw by the river Chebar; and I fell on my face [*as both earlier (Ezekiel 1:18 and 3:23) and again later (Ezekiel 44:4) when encountering God's glory*].

> **And the glory of the LORD came into the house by the way of the gate facing toward the east**.
>
> And the Spirit lifted me up and brought me [*Ezekiel, the trained priest*] into the inner court; **and behold, the glory of the LORD filled the house**.

We have seen clearly and beyond any reasonable doubt for those who believe and receive the Word of God that the LORD of hosts/Yahweh Sabaoth is the One Who returns in Glory. But two more uses remain that help connect certain matters and utterly confound the Orthodox Jews' theology, and confound similarly believing people, because the One Who returns will be the total opposite of who they are looking for. He will be what the Messiah should be.

THE RETURN OF THE KING IN ZECHARIAH 14 AND THE FINAL APPOINTED TIME OF YAHWEH

As we saw in Zechariah 12 and 13, during the Tribulation, two-thirds of Jewish people will be killed, but there will be a call to national repentance (the Feast of Trumpets as the Fifth Appointed Time of Yahweh), the Spirit of God poured out on a one-third remnant of the Jewish people who will participate in the true Day of Atonement (the Sixth Appointed Time of Yahweh), but with their participation based on what Jesus did in the New Covenant, not by their attempting to keep the Mosaic Covenant and earn their salvation by works.

Just to lead into the flow of this chapter, add the final two verses of chapter 13, verses 8 and 9:

> "And it will come about in all the land,"
> Declares the LORD,
> "That two parts in it will be cut off and perish;
> But the third will be left in it.
> "And I will bring the third part through the fire,
> Refine them as silver is refined,
> And test them as gold is tested.
> They will call on My name,

And I will answer them;
I will say, 'They are My people,'
And they will say, 'The LORD is my God.'"

This is the one-third Jewish remnant whom God will save during the Tribulation, but many more Jewish people—and Gentiles—will be born and saved during the Millennial Kingdom.

The following part of this chapter deals with some of the last part of the Battle of Armageddon, with the focus on Jerusalem, as seen in Zechariah 14:1–2,

> Behold, a day is coming for the LORD when the spoil taken from you will be divided among you. For I will gather all the nations against Jerusalem to battle, and the city will be captured, the houses plundered, the women ravished, and half of the city exiled, but the rest of the people will not be cut off from the city.

Three important items should be noticed: (1) "Behold, a day is coming *for the LORD*," because (2) He is the One orchestrating all of these matters, for "*I will gather* all the nations against Jerusalem to battle," and (3) Jerusalem will still be trampled underfoot by the Gentiles, at least for a short time, because the times of the Gentiles will be in its last days. The nations come to attack Jerusalem because God orders them there, and He will have brought all the nations to Jerusalem because it gives Him an opportunity to do what Zechariah 14:3 promises will occur: "Then the LORD will go forth and fight against those nations, as when He fights on a day of battle." And for those who think that Messiah will be only an enlightened man, Zechariah 14:4 refutes that—as do so many other verses in Scripture:

> And in that day His feet will stand on the Mount of Olives, which is in front of Jerusalem on the east; and the Mount of Olives will be split in its middle from east to west by a very large valley, so that half of the mountain will move toward the north and the other half toward the south.

Before moving on in Zechariah, let us again consider words from Acts 1:1-8 that we saw in the previous chapter of this book: (1) Jesus was "appearing to them over a period of forty days, and speaking of the things concerning the kingdom of God." (2) After the forty days of intensive training of the eleven (at that time), Jesus did not rebuke them when they were asking, "Lord, is it at this time You are restoring the kingdom to Israel?"—only about the matter of the timing for when that will happen, saying in Acts 1:7, "It is not for you to know times or epochs which the Father has fixed by His own authority." (3) All Jesus had to say is, "Don't you understand that these are spiritualized promises that I'm giving. There will be no Kingdom on earth. Haven't I been with you long enough for you to know that after forty days? Don't you know that the kingdom is only in your hearts?" Any such answer would have shut down any hope for the Kingdom promises from God—but again, Jesus did not correct their questions about the Kingdom, only about the timing. The King and His Kingdom are coming back to be established on earth with Jesusalem being the capital of His worldwide reign.

Consider also Acts 1:9–11,

> And after He had said these things, He was lifted up while they were looking on, and a cloud received Him out of their sight. And as they were gazing intently into the sky while He was departing, behold, two men in white clothing stood beside them; and they also said, "Men of Galilee, why do you stand looking into the sky? This Jesus, who has been taken up from you into heaven, will come in just the same way as you have watched Him go into heaven."

CRUCIAL: I have mused about this section of Scripture for many years, when the two angels, ask, "Men of Galilee, why do you stand looking into the sky?"—what else would they be looking at? (1) They have never seen anyone ascend, even Jesus. (2) For many, other than if God did things in private, this would be the last time each one saw Jesus until he went to heaven. (3) What else are they going to look? Are they going to say, "Hey, guys, look at this rock I found!" But let us let the two non-amillennialist angels finish their message in Acts 1:10–11, "And as they were gazing intently into the sky while He was departing, behold, two men in white clothing stood beside them; and they also said, 'Men of Galilee, why do you stand looking into the sky? This Jesus, who has been taken up from you into heaven, will come back in just the same way as you have watched Him go into heaven'"—which most definitely is not "whose kingdom is your heart." How do we know? Read Zechariah 14 and other places. King Jesus most definitely will not limit His return or kingdom to anyone's heart—unless that heart is a mountain east of Jerusalem.

Let us get back to the content and context of Zechariah 14:1–4,

> Behold, a day is coming for the LORD when the spoil taken from you will be divided among you. For I will gather all the nations against Jerusalem to battle, and the city will be captured, the houses plundered, the women ravished, and half of the city exiled, but the rest of the people will not be cut off from the city.
>
> Then the LORD will go forth and fight against those nations, as when He fights on a day of battle [just as Acts 1:10–11 requires: "And as they were gazing intently into the sky while He was departing, behold, two men in white clothing stood beside them; and they also said, 'Men of Galilee, why do you stand looking into the sky? This Jesus, who has been taken up from you into heaven, will come in just the same way as you have watched Him go into heaven"—which is exactly what Jesus will be doing at that time].
>
> And in that day His feet will stand on the Mount of Olives, which is in front of Jerusalem on the east; and the Mount of Olives will be split in its middle from east to west by a very large valley, so that half of the mountain will move toward the north and the other half toward the south.

I have been to Jerusalem numerous times, and everytime I have gone, the Mount of Olives is still in front of Jerusalem on the east. Also, the prophetic word in Zechariah is just as binding a prophetic word of God on what will happen as was the prophetic word in Matthew 21:1–5, which says Jesus *must* enter Jerusaelem in lowly manner so that Scripture might be fuffilled:

> And when they had approached Jerusalem and had come to Bethphage, to the Mount of Olives, then Jesus sent two disciples, saying to them, "Go into the village opposite you, and immediately you will find a donkey tied there and a colt with her; untie them, and bring them to Me.
>
> "And if anyone says something to you, you shall say, 'The Lord has need of them,' and immediately he will send them." Now this took place that what was spoken through the prophet might be fulfilled, saying, [in Zechariah 9:9]
>
> "SAY TO THE DAUGHTER OF ZION,
> BEHOLD YOUR KING IS COMING TO YOU,
> GENTLE, AND MOUNTED ON A DONKEY,
> EVEN ON A COLT, THE FOAL OF A BEAST OF BURDEN.'"

Zechariah 14:5–8 continues with vivid details about the Second Coming of the Lord:

> And you will flee by the valley of My mountains, for the valley of the mountains will reach to Azel; yes, you will flee just as you fled before the earthquake in the days of Uzziah king of Judah. Then the LORD, my God, will come, and all the holy ones with Him!
>
> And it will come about in that day that there will be no light; the luminaries will dwindle. For it will be a unique day which is known to the LORD, neither day nor night, but it will come about that at evening time there will be light.
>
> And it will come about in that day that living waters will flow out of Jerusalem, half of them toward the eastern sea and the other half toward the western sea; it will be in summer as well as in winter.

In Zechariah 14:9-11, note the biblical significance of Who will be King of the entire earth then, and very significant items as to what the rebuilding of Jerusalem will mean. Remember that God said in Deuteronomy 17:14–15 that He and He alone chooses Who will be King of the Jews. Look at this account of Whom He chooses:

And the LORD will be king over all the earth; in that day the LORD will be the only one, and His name the only one.

All the land will be changed into a plain from Geba to Rimmon south of Jerusalem; but Jerusalem will rise and remain on its site from Benjamin's Gate as far as the place of the First Gate to the Corner Gate, and from the Tower of Hananel to the king's wine presses.

And people will live in it, and there will be no more curse, for Jerusalem will dwell in security.

But note also, with *so* much occurring in this chapter, it is quite easy to miss the significance of Zechariah 14:10, "***All the land will be changed into a plain...***" So after the 1,000-year Millennial Kingdom, when Satan must be released, in Revelation 20:7–10, the plain that began with Jesus' return in Zechariah 14 is still there for this final assemblage for battle by Satan and those he will deceive:

And when the thousand years are completed, Satan will be released from his prison, and will come out to deceive the nations which are in the four corners of the earth, Gog and Magog, to gather them together for the war; the number of them is like the sand of the seashore.

And they came up on the broad plain of the earth and surrounded the camp of the saints and the beloved city, and fire came down from heaven and devoured them.

And the devil who deceived them was thrown into the lake of fire and brimstone, where the beast and the false prophet are also; and they will be tormented day and night forever and ever.

Just as Zechariah described it as all the land being changed into a plain, so it remains until the end of the Kingdom when Satan must be released for a short while.

Jeremiah 31 is the first chapter in the Bible that actually calls this next covenant by name, the New Covenant (Jer. 31:31–34), and we who are saved have received the incredible and irreplaceable parts of the New Covenant such as forgiveness of sins and having the Word implanted in our heart. But when the fulness of the New Covenant occurs, it will affect the entire world.

For instance, the fulness of the New Covenant will include the last verses of Jeremiah 31, verses 38–40:

> "Behold, days are coming," declares the LORD, "when the city shall be rebuilt for the LORD from the Tower of Hananel to the Corner Gate. And the measuring line shall go out farther straight ahead to the hill Gareb; then it will turn to Goah. And the whole valley of the dead bodies and of the ashes, and all the fields as far as the brook Kidron, to the corner of the Horse Gate toward the east, [and Jerusalem] **shall be holy to the LORD; it shall not be plucked up, or overthrown anymore forever.**"

Although there is other Scripture that could have been used, we need to use only Jeremiah 31:40 and the last part of Luke 21:24 to see what has happened: "and Jerusalem will be trampled under foot by the Gentiles until the times of the Gentiles be fulfilled." So with the promise that Jerusalem will be rebuilt for the Lord, and will never ever be "plucked up" or "overthrown any more forever," this means that the times of the Gentiles will be over forever and ever as well. Also, the part in Zechariah 14:11 about "there will be no more curse," does not relate to the entire world and the end of time as we know it, but rather only to the city of Jerusalem—in harmony with Jeremiah 31:38–40, "and there will be no more curse, for Jerusalem will dwell in security." As we will soon see, there will still be sin, the curse and the effects of the curse in some of the remaining verses of Zechariah 14, so this cannot be the same as such verses as Revelation 22:3, "And there shall no longer be any curse; and the throne of God and of the Lamb shall be in it, and His bond-servants shall serve Him." Those promises will eventually be fulfilled, but only after Satan's temporary release from the abyss, the final rebellion, and the Great White Throne judgment found in Revelation 20 where afterward, people are cast eternally into hell.

Just to complete where we are headed in the text, we will include Zechariah 14:12–15,

> Now this will be the plague with which the LORD will strike all the peoples who have gone to war against Jerusalem; their flesh will rot while they stand on their feet, and their eyes will rot in their sockets, and their tongue will rot in their mouth.

And it will come about in that day that a great panic from the LORD will fall on them; and they will seize one another's hand, and the hand of one will be lifted against the hand of another.

And Judah also will fight at Jerusalem; and the wealth of all the surrounding nations will be gathered, gold and silver and garments in great abundance.

So also like this plague, will be the plague on the horse, the mule, the camel, the donkey, and all the cattle that will be in those camps.

THE SEVENTH APPOINTED TIME OF YAHWEH AND TWO MORE USAGES ABOUT WHO THE KING IS

It is fitting that this last of the seven Appointed Times of Yahweh from Leviticus 23 occurs on the heels of the fifth Appointed Time of Yahweh (the Feast of Trumpets—a call to Jewish *national* repentance) and the sixth Appointed Time (the Day of Atonement—a call to Jewish *national* atonement). This is accomplished with the New Covenant blood, not the Mosaic Covenant, and these events will be taking place with the return of the Lord (Zech 14:1–4).

We will include Zechariah 14:16–21 so we can see it, and work backward for some of its vital parts:

Then it will come about that any who are left of all the nations that went against Jerusalem will go up from year to year to worship the King, the LORD of hosts, and to celebrate the Feast of Booths.

And it will be that whichever of the families of the earth does not go up to Jerusalem to worship the King, the LORD of hosts, there will be no rain on them.

And if the family of Egypt does not go up or enter, then no rain will fall on them; it will be the plague with which the LORD smites the nations who do not go up to celebrate the Feast of Booths.

This will be the punishment of Egypt, and the punishment of all the nations who do not go up to celebrate the Feast of Booths. In that day there will be inscribed on the bells of the horses, "HOLY TO THE

LORD." And the cooking pots in the LORD's house will be like the bowls before the altar.

And every cooking pot in Jerusalem and in Judah will be holy to the LORD of hosts; and all who sacrifice will come and take of them and boil in them. And there will no longer be a Canaanite in the house of the LORD of hosts in that day.

Many have pointed out through the years that this cannot be the eternal state or heaven because sin, sinners, and punishment still exist—none of which are present in Revelation 21–22, where the verses speak about the blessing and description of the eternal state. And the verses from Zechariah 14 cannot refer to our present time, because the Lord has not returned in glory and Jerusalem has not been rebuilt for the Lord—holy, and never again overthrown, and the Mount of Olives is still intact.

And it is pertinent to note the (generally standardized) theology of the Orthodox Jews and its components about the descriptive encapsulation of how they view the Messiah, briefly:

(1) The Messiah has not come yet, therefore Jesus cannot be the Messiah.

(2) When the Messiah comes, He will be an elevated human being, but not a Godhead Member; to call Him God is blasphemy.

(3) Since He is not God, to worship the Messiah is a blasphemous act.

Now with those three tenets, look carefully at Zechariah 14:16–17 and see how much it differs from the teaching of the Orthodox Jews, viewed with the background of the seventh of seven Appointed Times of Yahweh, the Feast of Tabernacles/Booths:

Then it will come about that any who are left of all the nations that went against Jerusalem will go up from year to year **to worship the King, the LORD of hosts**, and **to celebrate the Feast of Booths**.

And it will be that whichever of the families of the earth **does not go up to Jerusalem to worship the King, the LORD of hosts**, there will be no rain on them.

(1) Look who the King is: Yahweh Sabaoth / the LORD of hosts (occurs two times).

(2) Look at what the nations are commanded to do: worship the King (also used twice).

(3) This is to be done on a year after year basis as part of the seventh of the Appointed Times of Yahweh: the Feast of Tabernacles/Booths.

(4) Look at the punishment for those who do not go up to Jerusalem for the Feast of Tabernacles/Booths: God will withhold the rain that He sends (Matt 5:45).

Orthodox Jews have no answers to these questions other than by either ignoring them or allegorizing the text. To put this another way, the Orthodox Jews and anyone else who holds the earlier description, have no answer to this (at the present time) about Zechariah 14, and who the King will be after He returns in Glory.

Succinctly put, the seventh of the seven Appointed Times of Yahweh is the Millennial Kingdom for 1,000 years on earth. We will read one more item before closing this chapter, and hopefully read with biblically fresh eyes. First Corinthians 15:20–26 reveals:

> But now Christ has been raised from the dead, the first fruits of those who are asleep. For since by a man came death, by a man also came the resurrection of the dead. For as in Adam all die, so also in Christ all shall be made alive. But each in his own order: Christ the first fruits, after that those who are Christ's at His coming,
>
> *then comes the end, when He delivers up the kingdom to the God and Father [at the end of 1,000 years], when He has abolished all rule and all authority and power.*
>
> For He must reign until He has put all His enemies under His feet. [Psalm 110:1]
>
> The last enemy that will be abolished is death.

Even so, come Lord Jesus!

SUMMARY AND CONCLUSION

For our study, in this chapter we learned: (1) In Matthew 16:26–27 is "the fifth theological bombshell," one in which Jesus Christ promised to return in the Glory of His Father. (2) The best succinct six-word synopsis for the entire Bible is "The Glory of God Changes Everything." (3) In the previous chapter we saw, among other things, that the fifth and the sixth Appointed Times of Yahweh [*the Feast of Trumpets and the true Day of Atonement*], will be fulfilled in the future for national Israel. (4) God will also be doing a great worldwide evangelistic work among the Gentiles during the Tribulation, as revealed in verses such as Matthew 24:14. One-third of the population of Jews and massive numbers of Gentiles will be saved then (Rev. 7:9–17). (5) Our focus for this chapter and for most of the book is on the Jewish people, especially in the Tribulation.

(6) The fifth Appointed Time of Yahweh—the Feast of Trumpets—will be a call for national repentance of the Jewish people, only this time, there will be a remnant of Jewish people who respond to the Lord God, as we see in such verses as Zechariah 12:10—a work God promises during the Tribulation, but not before, "And I will pour out on the house of David and on the inhabitants of Jerusalem, the Spirit of grace and of supplication, so that they will look on Me whom they have pierced; and they will mourn for Him, as one mourns for an only son, and they will weep bitterly over Him, like the bitter weeping over a first-born." And, Zechariah 13:1, "In that day a fountain will be opened for the house of David and for the inhabitants of Jerusalem, for sin and for impurity." (7) If you are already saved, you do not need any fountain of cleansing because the same Holy Spirit has already done that for you (John 16:7–11). (8) We also saw in the previous chapter that under the Mosaic Covenant, individual Jewish people could offer the separate offerings and sacrifices as found in Leviticus 1:1–6:7, but (9) the Feast of Trumpets and the Day of Atonement in Zechariah 12–13 call for *national* repentance. The Day of Atonement offers *national* atonement for those Jews who will receive both Him as Messiah, and the true atonement that He offers in His blood of the New Covenant, already shed.

(10) Zechariah 13:8 reveals that two-thirds will be killed, but 13:9 shows that one-third of the Jewish people have a different future:

But the third will be left in it.
"And I will bring the third part through the fire,
Refine them as silver is refined,
And test them as gold is tested.
They will call on My name,
And I will answer them;
I will say, 'They are My people,'
And they will say, 'The LORD is my God.'

(11) Isaiah 40:1-2 is loaded with compassion that will be poured out in the future. (For instance, John the Baptist could not use this verse as part of his message. He always started with Isaiah 40:3. His use of Isaiah 40 followed his being asked about his identity and his message.) Isaiah 40:1–2 is applicable only to the future, because that is when these things will occur:

"Comfort, O comfort My people," says your God.
"Speak kindly to Jerusalem;
And call out to her, that her warfare has ended,
That her iniquity has been removed,
That she has received of the LORD's hand
Double for all her sins."

(12) The Messiah whom the Orthodox Jews and other such sects are looking for is an elevated human, and according to them, the Messiah will not be God, nor is the Messiah to be worshipped; this is utter blasphemy for them. (13) The Messiah whom the Jews—and much of the world—are looking for is much more in keeping with Psalm 2:1–7,

Why are the nations in an uproar,
And the peoples devising a vain thing?
The kings of the earth take their stand
And the rulers take counsel together
Against the LORD and against His Anointed [*His Messiah*], saying,
"Let us tear their fetters apart
And cast away their cords from us!"
He who sits in the heavens laughs,
The Lord scoffs at them.

Then He will speak to them in His anger
And terrify them in His fury, saying,
"But as for Me [*God says*], I have installed **My King** [*Deut. 17—God chooses the King; My Davidic Covenant lineage*]

(14) Several verses, such as Isaiah 6:5, caused Isaiah to respond by crying out:

"Woe is me, for I am ruined!
Because I am a man of unclean lips,
And I live among a people of unclean lips;
For my eyes have seen the King, the LORD of hosts."

(15) This is a clear reference to Deity—not to humanity—and if someone claims to believe the Oracles of God, this reference and others must be dealt with.

(16) We will do a sampling of other verses to show the attributes of the King Messiah, and none of the verses that we use have characteristics that can be attributed to some enlightened—but still fallen—man, as Psalm 24:7–10 corroborates:

Lift up your heads, O gates,
And be lifted up, O ancient doors,
That the King of glory may come in!
Who is the King of glory?
The LORD strong and mighty,
The LORD mighty in battle.
Lift up your heads, O gates,
And lift them up, O ancient doors,
That the King of glory may come in!
Who is this King of glory?
The LORD of hosts,
He is the King of glory. Selah.

(17) We saw earlier in this chapter, that when Jesus was claiming that He will return in the Glory of the Father, in Matthew 16—and this is true—then it is another way of claiming to be a Member of the Godhead. Who is

the King of Glory? In this case merely being David's son would not enable Him to fulfill the qualifications of the King of Glory, the LORD /Yahweh of hosts. (18) The same is true for the three passages in Jeremiah that show Deity characteristics and name. Jeremiah 46:18, "'As I live,' declares the King, whose name is the LORD of hosts" and also two chapters over in 48:15, "Declares the King, whose name is the LORD of hosts." And finally, Jeremiah 51:57, "Declares the King, whose name is the LORD of hosts." (19) None of this is New Testament theology forced onto Old Testament theology; none of these are verses from which we "take a part here and another part there" and concoct theology to make it say something that it does not say. Declares who? "Declares the King"—and what is His name?—"whose name is the LORD of hosts." (20) None of this could be accomplished by someone who will be "an enlightened and elevated man." Therefore, the King of Glory has to be a Godhead Member, and yet also has to be a Davidic Covenant heir, born of a woman into the world He Himself created.

(21) We have seen clearly and beyond any reasonable doubt for those who believe and receive the Word of God that the Lord of hosts/Yahweh Sabaoth is the One who returns in Glory. But two more uses remain that help connect certain matters and utterly confound the Orthodox Jews' theology, and theology of similarly believing people, because the One who returns will be the total opposite of whom they are looking for and what the Messiah should be. For instance, (22) Zechariah 14:1–2 opens with, "Behold, a day is coming for the LORD when the spoil taken from you will be divided among you. For I will gather all the nations against Jerusalem to battle, and the city will be captured, the houses plundered, the women ravished, and half of the city exiled, but the rest of the people will not be cut off from the city." Three important items should be noticed: (i) "Behold, a day is coming *for the LORD*," because (ii) He is the One orchestrating all of these matters, for "*I will gather* all the nations against Jerusalem to battle," and (iii) Zechariah 14:2 with Jerusalem still trampled underfoot by the Gentiles, is, at least for a short time, the times of the Gentiles. However, (23) the nations come to attack Jerusalem because God orders them there, and He will have brought all the nations to Jerusalem because it gives Him an opportunity to do what Zechariah

14:3 promises will occur: "Then the LORD will go forth and fight against those nations, as when He fights on a day of battle." And for those who think that Messiah will be only an enlightened man, Zechariah 14:4 refutes that—as do many other verses in Scripture:

> And in that day His feet will stand on the Mount of Olives, which is in front of Jerusalem on the east; and the Mount of Olives will be split in its middle from east to west by a very large valley, so that half of the mountain will move toward the north and the other half toward the south.

We also learned (24) the prophetic word in Zechariah is just as binding a prophetic word of God on what will happen as was the prophetic word in Matthew 21:1–5. Jesus *must* enter Jerusalem in a lowly manner so that Scripture might be fulfilled. Then other prophecies about a future reign by the Lord Jesus Christ should be expected also in the sense they are presented. (25) Note the biblical significance of Zechariah 14:9–11 regarding Who will be King of the entire earth then, and very significant items as to what the rebuilding of Jerusalem will mean, and remember that God said in Deuteronomy 17:14–15 that He and He alone chooses who will be King of the Jews—and look at this account of Whom He chooses:

> And the LORD will be king over all the earth; in that day the LORD will be the only one, and His name the only one.
>
> All the land will be changed into a plain from Geba to Rimmon south of Jerusalem; but Jerusalem will rise and remain on its site from Benjamin's Gate as far as the place of the First Gate to the Corner Gate, and from the Tower of Hananel to the king's wine presses.
>
> And people will live in it, and there will be no more curse, for Jerusalem will dwell in security.

We observed (26) that it is fitting for this last of the seven Appointed Times of Yahweh from Leviticus 23 to occur on the heels of the fifth Appointed Time of Yahweh (the Feast of Trumpets—a call to Jewish *national* repentance) and the sixth Appointed Time (the Day of Atonement—a call to Jewish *national* atonement). We noted that these are accomplished with the New Covenant blood, not the Mosaic Covenant, and these events will be taking place with the return of the Lord (Zech 14:1–4). (27) We include

Zechariah 14:16–21 so we could see it and work a little bit backward for some of its vital parts:

> Then it will come about that any who are left of all the nations that went against Jerusalem will go up from year to year to worship the King, the LORD of hosts, and to celebrate the Feast of Booths.
>
> And it will be that whichever of the families of the earth does not go up to Jerusalem to worship the King, the LORD of hosts, there will be no rain on them.
>
> And if the family of Egypt does not go up or enter, then no rain will fall on them; it will be the plague with which the LORD smites the nations who do not go up to celebrate the Feast of Booths.
>
> This will be the punishment of Egypt, and the punishment of all the nations who do not go up to celebrate the Feast of Booths. In that day there will be inscribed on the bells of the horses, "HOLY TO THE LORD." And the cooking pots in the LORD's house will be like the bowls before the altar.
>
> And every cooking pot in Jerusalem and in Judah will be holy to the LORD of hosts; and all who sacrifice will come and take of them and boil in them. And there will no longer be a Canaanite in the house of the LORD of hosts in that day.

And (28) it is pertinent to note the (generally standardized) theology of the Orthodox Jews and its components based on the descriptive encapsulation of how they view the Messiah, briefly:

—The Messiah has not come yet, therefore Jesus cannot be the Messiah.

—When the Messiah comes, He will be an elevated human being, but not a Godhead Member; to call Him God is blasphemy.

—Since He is not God, to worship the Messiah is a blasphemous act.

Now with those three tenets, (29) look carefully at Zechariah 14:16–17 and how much it differs from the teaching of the Orthodox Jews, viewed with the background of the Feast of Tabernacles/Booths being the seventh of seven Appointed times of Yahweh:

Then it will come about that any who are left of all the nations that went against Jerusalem will go up from year to year **to worship the King, the LORD of hosts**, and **to celebrate the Feast of Booths**.

And it will be that whichever of the families of the earth **does not go up to Jerusalem to worship the King, the LORD of hosts**, there will be no rain on them.

—Look who the King is: Yahweh Sabaoth / the LORD of hosts (occurs two times).

—Look at what the nations are commanded to do: worship the King (also used twice).

—This is to be done on a year-to-year basis as part of the seventh Appointed Time of Yahweh: the Feast of Tabernacles/Booths.

—Look at the punishment for those who do not go up to Jerusalem for the Feast of Tabernacles/Booths: God will withhold the rain that He sends (Matt 5:45).

(30) Orthodox Jews have no answers to these questions other than by either ignoring such texts or allegorizing them. To put this another way, the Orthodox Jews and others who hold the earlier description, have no answer (at the present time) about Zechariah 14, and who the King will be after He returns in Glory. (31) Succinctly put, the seventh of the seven Appointed Times of Yahweh is the Millennial Kingdom for 1,000 years on earth, and (32) it ends with the Son giving the Kingdom to the Father, as 1 Corinthians 15:20–26 reveals.

DEEPER WALK STUDY QUESTIONS

(1)   How does Zechariah 13 set the stage for what happens in Zechariah 14? What happens (broadly) in Zechariah 13?

(2)   How does Zechariah 13:8–9 set the stage for the events of Zechariah 14?

(3)   After Zechariah 13 has been fulfilled, how can verses such as Isaiah 40:1–2 start being fulfilled? Explain and support biblically.

(4) Name six pertinent truths from Psalm 24:7–10. Why are these truths important? Explain with two to three sentences.

(5) Name four ways Zechariah 14:1–2 show the Godhead at work. Be specific and support your answers.

(6) What happens in Zechariah 14:3–4? Name four biblical truths from there.

(7) Give six biblical truths from Zechariah 14:9–11. Why are these important? Explain in detail.

(8) List 8 biblical truths from Zechariah 14:16–21. Tell in one sentence each why each one is important.

(9) How are such verses as Zechariah 14:16–21 such problem verses for groups like Orthodox Jews. Explain, support with Scripture and tell why this is very important.

(10) Summarize what is the seventh Appointed Times of Yahweh, and why is this important?

(11) Make up your own study question, answer it, and be able to give people five reasons why your question was important.

CHAPTER 12

WILL THERE BE SACRIFICES IN THE MILLENNIAL KINGDOM, AND HOW CAN THAT BE?

As we come to the final chapter of *The King and His Glory: From His Return to Earth All the Way Into the Eternal State*, I was thinking about the best way to present the larger-than-normal chapter. As with all the other books, readers come with varying degrees of Bible knowledge, from the newborn Christian to the educated layman, students, and professors around the world. As with all matters related to this book, I prayed through how to best write this chapter and felt led by the Lord to do this in a question and answer format. I think that by using this method, we can disperse much more biblical understanding in a logical sequence so that not only will many questions and answers be given, but also that those who have only a basic knowledge of Old Testament customs and commands hopefully will have a clearer understanding of them.

Q AND A ABOUT THE SACRIFICES PAST AND PRESENT AND THE PRIESTHOOD.

QUESTION: *We have such a broad range of readers and what they know or do not know about the sacrificial system. The vast majority of people—Jews and Christians—have no idea of the theological or historical framework about the Temple and Jerusalem.*

So before addressing the sacrifices in the millennial kingdom, let's go back to the beginning for a few important items. Why are there no sacrifices today? For instance, why can't some major city such as New York City or Paris suffice? Why not build a Temple there or elsewhere instead of in Jerusalem?

When national Israel was on the precipice of becoming a nation in the land that God had given them, God gave some very specific commands in Deuteronomy 16:1–2:

> "Observe the month of Abib and celebrate the Passover to the LORD your God, for in the month of Abib the LORD your God brought you out of Egypt by night. You shall sacrifice the Passover to the LORD your God from the flock and the herd, **in the place where the LORD chooses to establish His name**.

But then God restricts some possible actions in Deuteronomy 16:5–6:

> "You are not allowed to sacrifice the Passover in any of your towns which the LORD your God is giving you; **but at the place where the LORD your God chooses to establish His name,** you shall sacrifice the Passover in the evening at sunset, at the time that you came out of Egypt.

The Tabernacle functioned before the Temple of Yahweh did, but it was portable. Two of several chapters that show this are Joshua 3 and 4, with the nation of Israel getting ready to cross the flooded Jordan and to enter into the promised land. Mark well that the ark of the covenant—the innermost part of the Holy of Holies—was portable, and as long as the leaders and the priests carried it exactly as God had instructed them to do, as verses from Joshua 3–4 show, it was no danger to them. The Jewish people were entering the promised land, with a flooded river in front of them, as Joshua 3:14–17 reveals, and as it had been with the Red Sea before them, God had to perform a miracle so that national Israel could cross:

> So when the people set out from their tents to cross the Jordan with the priests carrying the ark of the covenant before the people, and when those who carried the ark came into the Jordan, and the feet of the priests carrying the ark were dipped in the edge of the water (for the Jordan overflows all its banks all the days of harvest), the waters which were flowing

down from above stood and rose up in one heap, a great distance away at Adam, the city that is beside Zarethan; and those which were flowing down toward the sea of the Arabah, the Salt Sea, were completely cut off.

So the people crossed opposite Jericho. And the priests who carried the ark of the covenant of the LORD stood firm on dry ground in the middle of the Jordan while all Israel crossed on dry ground, until all the nation had finished crossing the Jordan.

After the people crossed the Jordan, Joshua placed twelve memorial stones in the dry Jordan River so that generations to come would know/be told about the significance of this miracle by God, as seen in Joshua 4:15–18:

> Now the LORD said to Joshua,
>
> "Command the priests who carry the ark of the testimony that they come up from the Jordan."
>
> So Joshua commanded the priests, saying, "Come up from the Jordan."
>
> It came about when the priests who carried the ark of the covenant of the LORD had come up from the middle of the Jordan, and the soles of the priests' feet were lifted up to the dry ground, that the waters of the Jordan returned to their place, and went over all its banks as before.

The Tabernacle could be moved, but not the Temple—the Jews had not had a temple up to this point in their history. When David first spoke to Nathan the prophet about building a permanent house for God, there came this (most likely surprising) prohibition by God in 2 Samuel 7:4–7:

> But in the same night the word of the LORD came to Nathan, saying,
>
> "Go and say to My servant David, 'Thus says the LORD, "Are you the one who should build Me a house to dwell in? For I have not dwelt in a house since the day I brought up the sons of Israel from Egypt, even to this day; but I have been moving about in a tent, even in a tabernacle.
>
> "Wherever I have gone with all the sons of Israel, did I speak a word with one of the tribes of Israel, which I commanded to shepherd My people Israel, saying, 'Why have you not built Me a house of cedar?'"'"

Eventually the House of the LORD would be built precisely where God wanted it built, but it would cost severely, as David took a census contrary to God's will and was punished by God for doing so. We must skip much of what is in the chapter, but I hope that you will be able to go back and read carefully this fundamental chapter:[15]

QUESTION: *We understand that the Jewish people were not allowed to build the Temple of Yahweh anywhere they desired, but how did they know that the Temple was built where God wanted it to be built, and why is it important to know this information?*

From The Stone and the Glory of Israel, p. 29:

Everything about Second Samuel 24 and its parallel chapter First Chronicles 21 is perplexing at face value. In this account King David ordered his general Joab to conduct a census, an act that had been done at various times before in the history of Israel. In fact, much of the Book of Numbers is basically a census of the Exodus generation. Yet, when David took his census, everything was different. First Chronicles 21:7 states, "God was displeased with this thing, so He struck Israel." Why would God be displeased? Also, how could David's military commander Joab sense God's displeasure beforehand by warning David, "Why does my Lord seek this thing? Why should he be a cause of guilt to Israel?" (1 Chron 21:3). Nonetheless, David prevailed. The census was taken, followed by God's punishment of the king and his nation.

(End of *The Stone and the Glory of Israel* portion)

At this point God intervened to make sure that His Temple would be built exactly where He wanted it to be built, as we will see in the next section. He left nothing for chance—and remember, we have time to give only the abbreviated version of what happened and why. The other relevant books referred to throughout this book give much more biblical truth than we could insert here. I highly recommend that you read them if you are interested in knowing the story with many deeper truths therein.

---

15 See Greg Harris, *The Stone and the Glory of Israel: An Invitation for the Jewish People to Meet Their Messiah* (The Woodlands, TX: Kress Biblical Resources, 2016). Used by permission. This portion is taken from chapter two, "The Place."

Just by means of a reminder, in the Pentateuch (which was earlier than David), the Jews were/are not allowed to sacrifice anywhere they wanted to, but rather God was very precise about where they were allowed to do their sacrifices, beginning in Deuteronomy 16:1–2:

> "Observe the month of Abib and celebrate the Passover to the LORD your God, for in the month of Abib the LORD your God brought you out of Egypt by night. You shall sacrifice the Passover to the LORD your God from the flock and the herd, *in the place where the LORD chooses to establish His name*.

But then God restricts some possible actions in Deuteronomy 16:5–6:

> "You are not allowed to sacrifice the Passover in any of your towns which the LORD your God is giving you; *but at the place where the LORD your God chooses to establish His name,* you shall sacrifice the Passover in the evening at sunset, at the time that you came out of Egypt.

And as we have already seen and will see, God is still just as clear as to the one place on the entire earth where the Temple of Yahweh is to be rebuilt and to function again.

From the Stone and the Glory of Israel, pp. 30–34

Once David completed his census, God struck Israel. David confessed to God, "I have sinned greatly, in that I have done this thing. But now, please take away the iniquity of Your servant, for I have done very foolishly" (1 Chron 21:8). The Lord then commanded His prophet to proclaim God's Word to David:

> The LORD spoke to Gad, David's seer, saying, "Go and speak to David, saying, Thus says the LORD, 'I offer you three things; choose for yourself one of them, which I will do to you.'"
>
> So Gad came to David and said to him, "Thus says the LORD, 'Take for yourself either three years of famine, or three months to be swept away before your foes, while the sword of your enemies overtakes you, or else three days of the sword of the LORD, even pestilence in the land, and

the angel of the LORD destroying throughout all the territory of Israel.' Now, therefore, consider what answer I shall return to Him who sent me."

David said to Gad, "I am in great distress; please let me fall into the hand of the LORD, for His mercies are very great. But do not let me fall into the hand of man" (1 Chron 21:9–13).

The account reveals that 70,000 men of Israel died from the pestilence that God had sent (1 Chron 21:14). Beyond this, "God sent an angel to Jerusalem to destroy it; but as he was about to destroy it, the LORD saw and was sorry over the calamity, and said to the destroying angel, 'It is enough; now relax your hand.' And the angel of the LORD was standing by the threshing floor of Ornan the Jebusite" (21:15). Jebus was the ancient name for Jerusalem; thus the inhabitants were called Jebusites.

The utter seriousness of the situation became evident when "David lifted up his eyes and saw the angel of the LORD standing between earth and heaven with his drawn sword in his hand stretched out over Jerusalem. Then David and the elders, covered with sackcloth, fell on their faces" (1 Chron 21:16). David then said to God, "Is it not I who commanded to count the people? Indeed, I am the one who has sinned and done very wickedly, but these sheep, what have they done? O LORD my God, please let Your hand be against me and my father's household, but not against Your people that they should be plagued" (21:17). The angel of the LORD then commanded Gad to tell David that he "should go up and build an altar to the LORD on the threshing floor of Ornan the Jebusite" (21:18). Even in the midst of divine chastisement, God sovereignly directed the events so that David went back to the exact designated place that God had chosen.

The account continues in First Chronicles 21:19–25:

> So David went up at the word of Gad, which he spoke in the name of the LORD.
>
> Now Ornan turned back and saw the angel, and his four sons who were with him hid themselves. And Ornan was threshing wheat. As David came to Ornan, Ornan looked and saw David, and went out from the threshing floor and prostrated himself before David with his face to the ground.

Then David said to Ornan, "Give me the site of this threshing floor, that I may build on it an altar to the LORD; for the full price you shall give it to me, that the plague may be restrained from the people."

Ornan said to David, "Take it for yourself; and let my Lord the king do what is good in his sight. See, I will give the oxen for burnt offerings and the threshing sledges for wood and the wheat for the grain offering; I will give it all."

But King David said to Ornan, "No, but I will surely buy it for the full price; for I will not take what is yours for the LORD, or offer a burnt offering which costs me nothing."

So David gave Ornan 600 shekels of gold by weight for the site.

First Chronicles 21:26 notes, "Then David built an altar to the LORD there and offered burnt offerings and peace offerings. And he called to the LORD and He answered him with fire from heaven on the altar of burnt offering" [i.e., God accepted this offering].

Usually, when we read lengthy Old Testament accounts, we know what took place generally, but rarely do we make the connections that God reveals in Scripture. For David and the nation of Israel, this event became an act of judgment tendered with divine mercy. Interestingly, David responded somewhat like Jacob had centuries earlier in Genesis, saying, "This is the house of the LORD God, and this is the altar of burnt offering for Israel" (1 Chron 22:1). Even more importantly, it is from this account that the Temple preparations began:

So David gave orders to gather the foreigners who were in the land of Israel, and he set stonecutters to hew out stones to build the house of God. David prepared large quantities of iron to make the nails for the doors of the gates and for the clamps, and more bronze than could be weighed; and timbers of cedar logs beyond number, for the Sidonians and Tyrians brought large quantities of cedar timber to David.

David said, "My son Solomon is young and inexperienced, and the house that is to be built for the LORD shall be exceedingly magnificent, famous and glorious throughout all lands. Therefore now I will make preparation for it." So David made ample preparations before his death (1 Chron 22:2–5).

Yet, tucked away, almost without notice, is a one-sentence revelatory nugget that draws the entire account together. Nothing about this episode with David and the census and God's response merely happened haphazardly. God *led* David to the place, leading for three days as God had previously led Abraham for three days. Strategically, God led David to the exact place where He had led Abraham centuries before. Second Chronicles 3:1 uncovers a three-word goldmine: "Then Solomon began to build the house of the LORD in Jerusalem *on Mount Moriah,* where the LORD had appeared to his father David, at the place that David had prepared on the threshing floor of Ornan the Jebusite."

Moriah—the place where God appears. Note this same significance in 2 Chronicles 3:1: "Mount Moriah, where the LORD *appeared* to his father David"—again with a play on words from the verb part of the word Moriah.

The Samaritans, of which the woman of John 4 was representative, were wrong. God had selected Mount Moriah in Jerusalem—not Shechem in Samaria. Only twice does Moriah appear in the entire Bible: each instance depicts God's specific leading; each time requires God's specified sacrifice at His designated place. Both references look beyond the immediate participants to the greater work of God.

On Moriah: God will prepare (literally, "see") for Himself a lamb (Gen. 22:8).

Abraham named the place "The LORD will provide."

As it is said to this day, both proverbially and prophetically: "On the mountain of the LORD it will be provided" (Gen. 22:14).

Moriah: the place where God will provide for Himself a Lamb.

Moriah: the place where God will provide for us.

Moriah: the place where the Lord appeared to David (2 Chron. 3:1), becomes the Temple mount God chose to inhabit—*and* to place His name there forever (2 Chron. 7:16).

Moriah: the place to see God becomes the promised place where the LORD will appear. As His Holy Word would later reveal, "'And the LORD, whom you seek, will suddenly come to His Temple, and the messenger of the covenant, in whom you delight, behold, He is coming,' says the LORD of hosts" (Mal. 3:1).

Each element is true historically.

Each element is true for the future—especially in view of the Stone of Israel, whose dwelling it actually is.

(End of *The Stone and the Glory of Israel* portion)

That place is generally not referred to as Moriah today, but it is tremendously important to know that the place where God led Abraham earlier is the same place to which God led David with strict instructions about where God's Temple would be built.

QUESTION: *All of these items we studied are important, but some people claim that if these events ever occurred at all, they occurred from 2,000 to 3,000 years ago. How do we know that this still matters to God and still has any future relevance for national Israel and the rest of the world?*

Second Chronicles 7:1–3 has the Temple of the LORD dedication service:

> Now when Solomon had finished praying, fire came down from heaven and consumed the burnt offering and the sacrifices; and the glory of the LORD filled the house. And the priests could not enter into the house of the LORD, because the glory of the LORD filled the LORD's house.
>
> And all the sons of Israel, seeing the fire come down and the glory of the LORD upon the house, bowed down on the pavement with their faces to the ground, and they worshiped and gave praise to the LORD, saying, "Truly He is good, truly His lovingkindness is everlasting."

Later on the same night that the Temple had been dedicated, God appeared to Solomon, in 2 Chronicles 7:15–16, saying:

> "Now My eyes shall be open and My ears attentive to the prayer offered in this place.

"For now I have chosen and consecrated this house that *My name may be there forever,* and My eyes and My heart will be there *perpetually*."

The answer is, as God alone chose and will choose the King of Israel, so He chose the accepted place of worship as well. Among other places, Psalm 132:1–14 gives one more reference to the chosen place in one of the Psalms of Ascents that the Jewish people would sing along the way to special holiday observances, such as Passover:

A Song of Ascents.

Remember, O LORD, on David's behalf, /All his affliction; /How he swore to the LORD, And vowed to the Mighty One of Jacob, "Surely I will not enter my house, / Nor lie on my bed; I will not give sleep to my eyes, / Or slumber to my eyelids; / Until I find a place for the LORD, /A dwelling place for the Mighty One of Jacob."

Behold, we heard of it in Ephrathah; / We found it in the field of Jaar. Let us go into His dwelling place; / Let us worship at His footstool. Arise, O LORD, to Your resting place; / You and the ark of Your strength. / Let Your priests be clothed with righteousness; / And let Your godly ones sing for joy.

For the sake of David Thy servant, / Do not turn away the face of Your anointed.

The LORD has sworn to David, / A truth from which He will not turn back; / Of the fruit of your body I will set upon your throne.

"If your sons will keep My covenant,

And My testimony which I will teach them,

Their sons also shall sit upon your throne forever."

For the LORD has chosen Zion [a hill in Jerusalem];

He has desired it for His habitation.

"This is My resting place forever; /

Here I will dwell, for I have desired it."

These—among many other things—are reasons that the Middle East with the Temple Mount in Jerusalem is a perpetual tinderbox ready to explode, and it eventually will explode, but only as God permits it during the Tribulation. Now God has promised that He will dwell in His resting place forever, but the seven-year Tribulation period must occur before God takes His proper place and position—all in accordance with God's design and desire. God has chosen Jerusalem, but so has Satan, and ultimately the Antichrist will also choose Jerusalem (Rev 11:2; 2 Thessalonians 2:3–4) before being finally vanquished forever.

QUESTION: *For people, such as Orthodox Jews who believe the Oracles of God [one of the names the Jews use to refer to their Scriptures], why does having the Temple Mount—and the rebuilt Temple—incite such a strong and passionate desire? Or to put this differently, why will having the Temple of God be so important to them as a people?*

The short answer is, along with the other necessary conditions already mentioned, that currently there is no one functioning as high priest, and even if one were functioning as high priest, he could not do what the Oracles of God command under the Mosaic Covenant because he would have to perform those duties where God directs in Jerusalem, as we saw in Zechariah 3:1–2:

> Then he showed me Joshua the high priest standing before the angel of the LORD, and Satan standing at his right hand to accuse him.
>
> And the LORD said to Satan, "The LORD rebuke you, Satan! Indeed, the LORD who has chosen Jerusalem rebuke you! Is this not a brand plucked from the fire?

There are many verses where you can find that Satan and the Antichrist have also chosen Jerusalem, which God tolerates for a short time, right before the return to earth of the Lord Jesus Christ. This is why Jerusalem is and will remain an incredibly contentious subject. Since the destruction of the Temple of Yahweh for the second time in AD 70, the Jews have not been able to observe a biblically accurate Passover or Day of Atonement because they do not have access to the Temple Mount, which—as we saw—is the only place in the entire world where the Jews could start their sacrificial system again. Many Jewish people yearn for such a blessing from God.

Also, many people will point to polls and surveys that show that there are many who are non-practicing of their Jewish religion. Some of the polls may be accurate, but current information on what Jews believe is totally irrelevant to what happens during the seven-year Tribulation. The Jews who try to live the Jewish life do so without access to the Temple Mount that the Muslims currently occupy. Currently, many Jews look at their Jewishness as something totally historical—with no theological importance—but God has much more in store for this city and for the Jewish people, especially when He pours out His Spirit on the one-third remnant and brings them to Himself (Zech 12:10: 13:1, 9–10).

QUESTION: *You seem confident that there will be sacrifices during the Tribulation. Why is that?*

I am as confident about the sacrifices being restored as God is. So was Daniel, after his heavenly messenger Gabriel brought him holy and divine information, in Daniel 9:20–23:

> Now while I was speaking and praying, and confessing my sin and the sin of my people Israel, and presenting my supplication before the LORD my God in behalf of the holy mountain of my God, while I was still speaking in prayer, then the man Gabriel, whom I had seen in the vision previously, came to me in my extreme weariness about the time of the evening offering.
>
> And he gave me instruction and talked with me, and said, "O Daniel, I have now come forth to give you insight with understanding.
>
> "At the beginning of your supplications the command was issued, and I have come to tell you, for you are highly esteemed; so give heed to the message and gain understanding of the vision."

This is the same Gabriel who appeared twice in Luke 1 to deliver wonderful news, first about the birth of the Forerunner of the Messiah, and then about the arrival and birth of the Messiah Himself—although very few people knew it at the time. And Zacharias, the future father of the biblically-required Forerunner for the Messiah, who would be called John the Baptist, received a rebuke and punishment after questioning the truthfulness of what Gabriel told him—Luke 1:18–20:

> Zacharias said to the angel, "How will I know this for certain? For I am an old man and my wife is advanced in years."

The angel answered and said to him, *"I am Gabriel, who stands in the presence of God*, and I have been sent to speak to you and to bring you this good news.

"And behold, you shall be silent and unable to speak until the day when these things take place, because you did not believe my words, which will be fulfilled in their proper time."

Back in Daniel 9, Gabriel, who still stands in the presence of God, had been sent out with God's message, not concerning the near future of Jerusalem, but concerning what would be revealed later in Scripture as the last seven years of the times of the Gentiles—the Tribulation—with the last part being three and one-half years, as revealed in Daniel 9:20–23:

Now while I was speaking and praying, and confessing my sin and the sin of my people Israel, and presenting my supplication before the LORD my God in behalf of the holy mountain of my God, while I was still speaking in prayer, then the man Gabriel, whom I had seen in the vision previously, came to me in my extreme weariness about the time of the evening offering. He gave me instruction and talked with me and said, "O Daniel, I have now come forth to give you insight with understanding.

"At the beginning of your supplications the command was issued, and I have come to tell you, for you are highly esteemed; so give heed to the message and gain understanding of the vision."

At this time, Gabriel disclosed to Daniel the prophet matters about national Israel and the last part of the Tribulation, and we must for time's sake limit this to the last verse (you can read all of Daniel 9, if you like):

"And he will make a firm covenant with the many for one week [it does not say what kind of firm covenant or with whom it will be made, but most likely the Antichrist will make a covenant allowing the Temple to be rebuilt], *but in the middle of the week* [*of seven years*] *he* [the Antichrist] *will put a stop to sacrifice and grain offering: and on the wing of abominations will come one who makes desolate, even until a complete destruction, one that is decreed, is poured out on the one who makes desolate."*

At some time, there must be **the start of the offerings during the Tribulation in order for the Antichrist to stop the offerings midway through the seven-year Tribulation**. This eventuality is important because it is presented in the context that has to do with the apostles asking Jesus about His coming, and it is in the same context where Jesus foretells of the Abomination of Desolation and (short version) instructs those, especially Jews, who will be living at that time in Matthew 24:15-16—as does the Holy Spirit Himself through Matthew the apostle:

> "Therefore when you see the ABOMINATION OF DESOLATION which was spoken of through Daniel the prophet, standing in the holy place (let the reader understand), then those who are in Judea must flee to the mountains.

Later, the Holy Spirit, by means of the Apostle Paul, explained in 2 Thessalonians 2:3–4 what "the Abomination of Desolation" is, and why God the Son and God the Holy Spirit warned people about it so strongly:[16]

> Let no one in any way deceive you, for it will not come unless the apostasy comes first, and the man of lawlessness is revealed, the son of destruction, who opposes and exalts himself above every so-called god or object of worship, so that he takes his seat in the temple of God [that is, *the rebuilt temple during the Tribulation*], displaying himself as being God.
>
> Do you not remember that while I was still with you, I was telling you these things?

So in its simplest definition, the abomination of desolation begins when the Antichrist takes his seat in the Temple of Yahweh for the last three and one-half years of the Tribulation, and at that time Satan indwelling the Antichrist will demand worldwide worship of them alone.

---

16 See Greg Harris, *The Bible Expositor's Handbook (OT/NT)* (Nashville: B & H Academic, 2020), Chapter 26: "Seven Astounding Doctrinal Truths from 2 Thessalonians 2," 457–493. Used by permission. That chapter has much more important and relevant information than we could cover here, from some of the Bible's most helpful verses for understanding biblical truths about the Tribulation.

QUESTION: *Initially, when the Temple of God will be rebuilt in the Tribulation, and the sacrifices made by the Jews/the high priest/the other priests begin being offered again, will God accept the sacrifices that will be done by the Jewish people for the first time in about 2,000 years, and if not, why would God not accept them?*

As much as this may surprise some of you, **Yahweh will not accept the sacrifices done by the Jewish people during the Tribulation**. And let us not forget that from Genesis 4:1–8, the first chapter after the Fall and the ensuing judgments, comes the world's first rejected offering to God, from what consequently becomes the world's first false religion, with one offering being accepted and one being rejected by Him:

> Now the man had relations with his wife Eve, and she conceived and gave birth to Cain, and she said, "I have gotten a manchild with the help of the LORD." And again, she gave birth to his brother Abel. And Abel was a keeper of flocks, but Cain was a tiller of the ground.
>
> So it came about in the course of time that Cain brought an offering to the LORD of the fruit of the ground.
>
> And Abel, on his part also brought of the firstlings of his flock and of their fat portions. And the LORD had regard for Abel and for his offering; but for Cain and for his offering He had no regard. So Cain became very angry and his countenance fell.
>
> Then the LORD said to Cain, "Why are you angry? And why has your countenance fallen? If you do well, will not your countenance be lifted up? And if you do not do well, sin is crouching at the door; and its desire is for you, but you must master it."
>
> And Cain told Abel his brother. And it came about when they were in the field, that Cain rose up against Abel his brother and killed him.

Instead of "mastering sin," First John 3:9–12 reveals that the work of Cain was not just his own doing:

> No one who is born of God practices sin, because His seed abides in him; and he cannot sin, because he is born of God. By this the children of God and the children of the devil are obvious: anyone who does not practice righteousness is not of God, nor the one who does not love his brother.

For this is the message which you have heard from the beginning, that we should love one another; not as Cain, who was of the evil one and slew his brother. And for what reason did he slay him? Because his deeds were evil, and his brother's were righteous.

From Cain's sinful, futile offering to our present time and forever, God is under no obligation to accept any sacrifice or offering made to Him. Two reasons in particular point to this as being the correct answer about why God will not accept such sacrifices in the first part of the Tribulation at His Temple carried out by the Levitical priesthood in accordance to what and how the Pentateuch directs: (1) the New Covenant has already been ratified by the Godhead in the blood of Jesus, and (2) because of this, there is a changing in the position of the high priests—and God permits only one high priest to function at a time. We know from Psalm 110:4 that our Lord Jesus Christ "will be a priest forever." What we do not learn until the Book of Hebrews is that not only will there be a priest, but Jesus already is—if you are saved—our High Priest. Tens, if not hundreds, of thousands of priests will be functioning in the Tribulation, **but** by God's design, only one high priest is to be operative at the time. Hebrews makes it very clear who our High Priest already is and how long He will continue to be. Here is only a sample, Hebrews 4:14–16:

> Therefore, **since we have** [*present tense*] **a great high priest** who has passed through the heavens, Jesus the Son of God, let us hold fast our confession. For we do not have a high priest who cannot sympathize with our weaknesses, but One who has been tempted in all things as we are, yet without sin. Therefore let us draw near with confidence to the throne of grace, so that we may receive mercy and find grace to help in time of need.

Hebrews 6:19–20 is important to our topic as to our High Priest's longevity of service:

> This hope we have as an anchor of the soul, a hope both sure and steadfast and one which enters within the veil, where Jesus has entered as a forerunner for us, **having become a high priest forever** according to the order of Melchizedek.

We will close this section with two accompanying passages. Hebrews 7:26–27 shows Jesus' attributes that make Him eternally qualified to be High Priest forever:

> For it was fitting for us to have such a high priest, holy, innocent, undefiled, separated from sinners and exalted above the heavens; who does not need daily, like those high priests, to offer up sacrifices, first for His own sins and then for the sins of the people, because this He did once for all when He offered up Himself.

QUESTION: *Why would the offerings in the Tribulation not being accepted by God, if they will be making them under the Mosaic Covenant as a Levitical high priest? Studies in genetics are making it closer and closer to be sure the right man is chosen; the high priest in the Tribulation will be from Levi—just as God's Word says, so why would the offerings not be accepted?*

"Just as God's Word says," would be more accurately written as "just as God's Word says about the Mosaic Covenant and the Levitical priesthood." As we will see shortly, the problem here is not the Levitical priesthood. We remember that Jesus began His High Priesthood ministry *after* His Ascension—*not* during the Incarnation—as Hebrews 7:11–14 explains:

> Now if perfection [*i.e. completion*] was through the Levitical priesthood (for on the basis of it the people received the Law), what further need was there for another priest to arise according to the order of Melchizedek, and not be designated according to the order of Aaron?
>
> For when the priesthood is changed, of necessity there takes place a change of law also. For the one concerning whom these things are spoken belongs to another tribe, from which no one has officiated at the altar.
>
> For it is evident that our Lord was descended from Judah, a tribe with reference to which Moses spoke nothing concerning priests [*under the Mosaic Covenant*].

We have seen from other passages that Jesus is currently functioning as High Priest, and because He has begun, He will continue forever. Those well-intended Jews can go through the motions, but as before, though some of the sacrifices will likely be offered with good intentions, Yahweh will not and cannot accept them. As we saw in a different chapter, it would have been sinful for Jesus to act as Priest or High Priest before His death—as it was for His ancestor, King Uzziah, whom God struck with leprosy for his high-handed sin of sacrificing as a priest in Yahweh's Temple.

A few major doctrines to add to this will help. If people remove the redeeming work accomplished by the Messiah—which orthodox Jews and many others do—all they will have left to approach the Holy God is the Mosaic Covenant—and they attempt this after the death, resurrection, and ascension of Jesus the Messiah.

Romans 9–11 is one section in Scripture, and Paul's context for these three very important chapters begins with the Jewish people in Romans 9:1–5:

> I am telling the truth in Christ, I am not lying, my conscience testifies with me in the Holy Spirit, that I have great sorrow and unceasing grief in my heart. For I could wish that I myself were accursed, separated from Christ for the sake of my brethren, my kinsmen according to the flesh, who are Israelites, to whom belongs the adoption as sons, and the glory and the covenants and the giving of the Law and the temple service and the promises, whose are the fathers, and from whom is the Christ according to the flesh, who is over all, God blessed forever. Amen.

Later in the chapter, the Holy Spirit through the apostle Paul lists sins that many Jewish people kept/keep sinning on an ongoing basis. At its heart is a system of works shown in Romans 9:30–10:4:[17]

> What shall we say then? That Gentiles, who did not pursue righteousness, attained righteousness, even the righteousness which is by faith; but Israel, pursuing a law of righteousness, did not arrive at that law.
>
> Why? Because they did not pursue it by faith, but as though it were by works. They stumbled over the stumbling stone, just as it is written, [*Note the two more uses of the numerous "Messianic Stone Prophecies" that were first given*

---

17 See *The Bible Expositor's Handbook (OT/NT)*, Chapter Twelve: "And How Shall They Hear Without a Preacher?" 389–431, for the biblical trail to this incredibly important section of Scripture. For those who want the scholastic material and much detail, see the journal article by Gregory H. Harris, "And How Shall They Hear Without a Preacher?" A Biblical Theology of Romans 9–11." *The Master's Seminary Journal* 30:2 (Fall 2019): 227–55.

in Genesis 49:24. National Israel's rejecting of the Messiah the Stone is still part of that nation's unforgiven sins against God] [18]

"BEHOLD, I LAY IN ZION A STONE OF STUMBLING AND A ROCK OF OFFENSE, AND HE WHO BELIEVES IN HIM WILL NOT BE DISAPPOINTED."

Brethren, my heart's desire and my prayer to God for them is for their salvation.

For I testify about them that they have a zeal for God, but not in accordance with knowledge. For not knowing about God's righteousness and seeking to establish their own, they did not subject themselves to the righteousness of God. For Christ is the end of the law for righteousness to everyone who believes.

These same sins will be committed by the priesthood and the high priest and most of the Jewish people during the Tribulation—especially at the beginning of it—and many will be just as guilty as their ancestors were who rejected the Stone of Israel (Gen. 49:24) as being the true Messiah sent by God.

So at that time they will think that everything is in the best situation, for world peace has arrived, but they will horribly and erroneously under-estimate what will be happening. God still allows only one high priest to function at a time. Hebrews 6:19–20, as we saw earlier, proclaims Jesus the Messiah's longevity of service as High Priest:

This hope we have as an anchor of the soul, a hope both sure and stead-fast and one which enters within the veil, where Jesus has entered as a forerunner for us, ***having become a high priest forever*** according to the order of Melchizedek.

And finally, Hebrews 8:1–2 adds these cogent points about what the redeemed already have:

---

18 See Greg Harris, *The Stone and the Glory of Israel: An Invitation for the Jewish People to Meet Their Messiah* (The Woodlands, TX: Kress Biblical Resources, 2016), beginning with chapter one, "The Stone," for the incredible "Messianic Stone Prophecies" that play an important part in the first and second comings of Jesus the Messiah to earth, as well as the time in between.

> *Now the main point* in what has been said is this: *we have such a high priest, who has taken His seat at the right hand* of the throne of the Majesty in the heavens, a minister in the sanctuary and in the true tabernacle, which the Lord pitched, not man.

And never again will there be any high priest other than Jesus the Messiah. The blood He shed at the ratification of the New Covenant is the only basis for salvation anywhere from Genesis 1 into the eternal state. It is the source for the fountain of cleansing sin in such verses as Zechariah 12:10 and 13:1.

SO HOW WILL THE PRIESTHOOD FUNCTION DURING THE MILLENNIAL KINGDOM?

NOTE: Entire books and dissertations have been written about Ezekiel 40–48 and Zechariah 14 concerning the restarting of the sacrificial system, with arguments for or against it. There is no way we can begin to cover all of the arguments in this last part of the book, but before turning away from this sacrificial system as a possibility—as very many people already have done without considering even the possibility that these sacrifices will exist—let's at least see what the Bible has to say about this.

QUESTION: *How do we know that sacrifices in the Millennial Kingdom will not be the reinstitution of the Mosaic Covenant?*

If people used any part of the Mosaic Covenant, they had to use *all* of it, if such were God's design for it to be used. The Mosaic Covenant cannot be divided into separate pieces; it is an either-or proposition. So, to begin with, there are only four feasts for the Millennial Kingdom found in Scripture, instead of seven, such as we have clearly seen in Leviticus 23 as the appointed times of Yahweh. The first feast of the Millennial sacrifices listed (Ezek 45:18–20) is not found in the Mosaic Covenant, but rather it seems to be some kind of New Year festival:

'Thus says the Lord G OD, "**In the first month, on the first of the month**, you shall take a young bull without blemish and cleanse the sanctuary. The priest shall take some of the blood from the sin offering and put it on the door posts of the house, on the four corners of the ledge of the altar and on the posts of the gate of the inner court.

"Thus you shall do on the seventh day of the month for everyone who goes astray or is naive; so you shall make atonement for the house.

Passover and the Feast of Unleavened Bread is within the Mosaic Covenant and the Millennial Kingdom Sacrifices, as seen in Ezekiel 45:21–24:

"In the first month, on the fourteenth day of the month, you shall have the Passover, a feast of seven days; unleavened bread shall be eaten.

"On that day the prince shall provide for himself and all the people of the land a bull for a sin offering.

"During the seven days of the feast he shall provide as a burnt offering to the L ORD seven bulls and seven rams without blemish on every day of the seven days, and a male goat daily for a sin offering. He shall provide as a grain offering an ephah with a bull, an ephah with a ram and a hin of oil with an ephah.

Here is an important item: The future sacrificial system contains no Pentecost, no Feast of Trumpets, and certainly no Day(s) of Atonement; but there is within both systems the Feast of Booths/Tabernacles, which was also the seventh of seven appointed times of Yahweh. Zechariah 14:4 reveals Jesus the Messiah as King over all the earth after His feet hit the Mount of Olives and He defeats His enemies. The Feast of Tabernacles/ Booths occurs in Ezekiel 45:25: "In the seventh month, on the fifteenth day of the month, at the feast, he shall provide like this, seven days for the sin offering, the burnt offering, the grain offering and the oil."

Also, the Mosaic Covenant required that the priests and High Priest be *only* from the tribe of Levi: the New Covenant priesthoods are also from the tribe of Levi. However, Jesus is to be both King and High Priest, as we have seen frequently from Zechariah 6:12–13:

> "Then say to him, 'Thus says the LORD of hosts, "Behold, a man whose name is Branch, for He will branch out from where He is; and He will build the temple of the LORD.
>
> "Yes, it is He who will build the temple of the LORD, and He who will bear the honor and sit and rule on His throne. Thus, He will be a priest on His throne, and the counsel of peace will be between the two offices.'"

Under the Mosaic Covenant no king [*tribe of Judah/Davidic Covenant*] could attempt to qualify biblically as a priest, such as King Uzziah foolishly and sinfully attempted, without a strong reaction and punishment from God. No priest [*tribe of Levi*] could ever reign on David's throne as king, because that too would be a high-handed sin and would warrant strong reaction and punishment from God. So, this is additional verification that the priesthood in the Millennial Kingdom is not the rebuilding of the Mosaic Covenant. Very simply put, no one but the Messiah qualifies to fulfill Zechariah 6:12–13 to usher in the time when "the counsel of peace will be between the two offices."

QUESTION: *So who is the priesthood under the Millennial Kingdom guidelines?*

Special honor is given to the sons of Zadok because of the covenant that God made with Phinehas in Numbers 25. Some of the determinants for future sacrifices that will eventually occur go back to a sort of tucked away (to many) passage, Numbers 25:1–5, beginning with the wilderness generation of the Jews openly and brazenly sinning:

> While Israel remained at Shittim, the people began to play the harlot with the daughters of Moab. For they invited the people to the sacrifices of their gods, and the people ate and bowed down to their gods. So Israel joined themselves to Baal of Peor, and the LORD was angry against Israel.
>
> The LORD said to Moses, "Take all the leaders of the people and execute them in broad daylight before the LORD, so that the fierce anger of the LORD may turn away from Israel."
>
> So Moses said to the judges of Israel, "Each of you slay his men who have joined themselves to Baal of Peor."

The punishment for such sin was harsh and was carried out with all the tribes looking on, to see the punishment following the sin and the positive result of that punishment for the sin. Then, in one of the all-time bad timings to do something, another son of Israel and a Midianite [*a Gentile tribe*] woman commit the exact same sin within the presumed protection of their tent. However, this time, action was taken against them by Phinehas, as stated in Numbers 25:6–13:

> Then behold, one of the sons of Israel came and brought to his relatives a Midianite woman, in the sight of Moses and in the sight of all the congregation of the sons of Israel, while they were weeping at the doorway of the tent of meeting. When Phinehas the son of Eleazar, the son of Aaron the priest, saw it, he arose from the midst of the congregation and took a spear in his hand, and he went after the man of Israel into the tent and pierced both of them through, the man of Israel and the woman, through the body. So the plague on the sons of Israel was checked. Those who died by the plague were 24,000.

The actions that Phinehas took resulted in God doing and saying the following:

> Then the LORD spoke to Moses, saying,
> "Phinehas the son of Eleazar, the son of Aaron the priest, has turned away My wrath from the sons of Israel in that he was jealous with My jealousy among them, so that I did not destroy the sons of Israel in My jealousy.
> "Therefore say, **'Behold, I give him My covenant of peace; and it shall be for him and his descendants after him, a covenant of a perpetual priesthood**, because he was jealous for his God and made atonement for the sons of Israel.'"

With this background, it should be not surprising to find some collaborating promises in Jeremiah 30–33. We begin with Jeremiah 30:1–2, which gives some very precise historical markers to note:

> The word that came to Jeremiah from the LORD in the tenth year of Zedekiah king of Judah, which was the eighteenth year of Nebuchadnezzar.

Now at that time the army of the king of Babylon was besieging Jerusalem, and Jeremiah the prophet was shut up in the court of the guard, which was in the house of the king of Judah ..."

God made specific promises concerning the lineage of two very important tribes among the twelve Jewish tribes in Jeremiah 33:14–22:

"Behold, days are coming,'" declares the LORD, 'when I will fulfill the good word which I have spoken concerning the house of Israel and the house of Judah. In those days and at that time I will cause a righteous Branch of David to spring forth; and He shall execute justice and righteousness on the earth. In those days Judah will be saved and Jerusalem will dwell in safety; and this is the name by which she will be called: the LORD is our righteousness."

"For thus says the LORD, 'David shall never lack a man to sit on the throne of the house of Israel; **and the Levitical priests shall never lack a man before Me** to offer burnt offerings, to burn grain offerings and to prepare sacrifices continually.'"

The word of the LORD came to Jeremiah, saying,

"Thus says the LORD, 'If you can break My covenant for the day and My covenant for the night, so that day and night will not be at their appointed time, then My covenant may also be broken with David My servant so that he will not have a son to reign on his throne, **and with the Levitical priests, My ministers**.

As the host of heaven cannot be counted and the sand of the sea cannot be measured, so I will multiply the descendants of David My servant **and the Levites who minister to Me.**'"

The Book of Ezekiel begins with this notation in Ezekiel 1:3, "the word of the LORD came expressly to Ezekiel the priest ..." so when God gives Ezekiel visions of the Temple in Ezekiel 1 and in later chapters, to use a modern analogy, it would be as though you are saying "Ezekiel the mechanic went to a car garage." Ezekiel spent many years in training for the priesthood, but he never got the opportunity to serve because of the exile. But with his training, he could tell how much the Temple was used with the Mosaic Covenant directions and how much was used with the

New Covenant directions. Ezekiel 40–48 specifies matters relating to the return to the earth of the Lord in Glory, and Ezekiel 40:1–2 begins this section with very specific time markers:

> In the twenty-fifth year of our exile, at the beginning of the year, on the tenth of the month, in the fourteenth year after the city was taken, on that same day the hand of the LORD was upon me and He brought me there. In the visions of God He brought me into the land of Israel and set me on a very high mountain, and on it to the south there was a structure like a city.

So in the fourteenth year after the fall of Jerusalem—during the times of the Gentiles—God Himself initiates what will happen in the future, and in some cases, He gives the reasons for why certain things will be happening. In Ezekiel 40–46, God gives Ezekiel visions of the Millennial Kingdom Temple and aspects of worship never done before.

Some groups will be rewarded for their ancestors' faithfulness, but others will be punished for their ancestors' iniquity. For instance, in Ezekiel 44:9–14 God judged the wicked activity of their ancestors thusly:

> Thus says the Lord GOD, "No foreigner uncircumcised in heart and uncircumcised in flesh, of all the foreigners who are among the sons of Israel, shall enter My sanctuary.
>
> "But the Levites who went far from Me when Israel went astray, who went astray from Me after their idols, shall bear the punishment for their iniquity. Yet they shall be ministers in My sanctuary, having oversight at the gates of the house and ministering in the house; they shall slaughter the burnt offering and the sacrifice for the people, and they shall stand before them to minister to them.
>
> "Because they ministered to them before their idols and became a stumbling block of iniquity to the house of Israel, therefore I have sworn against them," declares the Lord GOD, "that they shall bear the punishment for their iniquity.
>
> "And they shall not come near to Me to serve as a priest to Me, nor come near to any of My holy things, to the things that are most holy;

but they will bear their shame and their abominations which they have committed.

"Yet I will appoint them to keep charge of the house, of all its service and of all that shall be done in it.

And in total contrast comes this commendation for one special group, as seen in Ezekiel 44:15–17:

> "But the Levitical priests, the sons of Zadok, who kept charge of My sanctuary when the sons of Israel went astray from Me, shall come near to Me to minister to Me; and they shall stand before Me to offer Me the fat and the blood," declares the Lord GOD.
>
> "They shall enter My sanctuary; they shall come near to My table to minister to Me and keep My charge.
>
> "It shall be that when they enter at the gates of the inner court, they shall be clothed with linen garments; and wool shall not be on them while they are ministering in the gates of the inner court and in the house.

There are two other verses of reward to the sons of Zadok for previous faithfulness. Ezekiel 44:15 says: "But the Levitical priests, the sons of Zadok, who kept charge of My sanctuary when the sons of Israel went astray from Me, shall come near to Me to minister to Me; and they shall stand before Me to offer Me the fat and the blood," declares the Lord GOD. Ezekiel 48:11 says: "It shall be for the priests who are sanctified of the sons of Zadok, who have kept My charge, who did not go astray when the sons of Israel went astray as the Levites went astray."

Now when the lineage is expanded, look who is related to whom, as Ezra 7:1–5:

> Now after these things, in the reign of Artaxerxes king of Persia, *there went up* Ezra son of Seraiah, son of Azariah, son of Hilkiah,
> son of Shallum, **son of Zadok**, son of Ahitub,
> son of Amariah, son of Azariah, son of Meraioth,
> son of Zerahiah, son of Uzzi, son of Bukki,
> son of Abishua, **son of Phinehas**, son of Eleazar, **son of Aaron the chief priest**.

God is totally faithful in keeping His Covenant that He made with Phinehas, back in Numbers 25, and that covenant will be completely fulfilled through the sons of Zadok in the future—when Jesus returns.

QUESTION: *What happens at the end of the 1,000 years of the Millennial Kingdom?*

First Corinthians 15:20–27 reveals the Trinity's answer:

> But now Christ has been raised from the dead, the first fruits of those who are asleep. For since by a man came death, by a man also came the resurrection of the dead.
>
> For as in Adam all die, so also in Christ all shall be made alive. But each in his own order: Christ the first fruits, after that those who are Christ's at His coming,
>
> **then comes the end, when He delivers up the kingdom to the God and Father**, when He has abolished all rule and all authority and power.
>
> For He must reign until He has put all His enemies under His feet.
>
> The last enemy that will be abolished is death.
>
> For HE HAS PUT ALL THINGS IN SUBJECTION UNDER HIS FEET. But when He says, "All things are put in subjection," it is evident that He is excepted Who put all things in subjection to Him.

Having completed the judgment of Satan and of those who are in final rebellion, and the Great White Throne Judgment (Rev. 20:11–15), most of Revelation 21–22 is a brief description of the new heavens, the new earth and the New Jerusalem. Revelation 21:1–4 begins:

> And I saw a new heaven and a new earth; for the first heaven and the first earth passed away, and there is no longer any sea. And I saw the holy city, new Jerusalem, coming down out of heaven from God, made ready as a bride adorned for her husband.
>
> And I heard a loud voice from the throne, saying, "Behold, the tabernacle of God is among men, and He shall dwell among them, and they shall be His people, and God Himself shall be among them, and He shall wipe away every tear from their eyes; and there shall no longer be any

death; there shall no longer be any mourning, or crying, or pain; the first things have passed away."

Revelation 21:21–22 is the first time this description will be true, but only after the Son delivers up the kingdom to the God the Father (1 Cor 15:24)—but not before then, and not until the seventh of the seven Appointed Times of Yahweh is complete:

> And the twelve gates were twelve pearls; each one of the gates was a single pearl. And the street of the city was pure gold, like transparent glass. And I saw no temple in it, for the Lord God, the Almighty, and the Lamb, are its temple.

And the covenant promise that God made to Phinehas will be complete, and with no temple in heaven, there will be no need for the priesthood, unlike the situation in Zechariah, where sin and punishment are still present, with a priesthood and one High Priest. After the Lord Jesus Christ returns from heaven to the Mount of Olives (Zech 14:3–4), and after He subjugates His enemies, then "the LORD will be king over all the earth; in that day the LORD will be the only one, and His name the only one;" however, sin still exists on earth at that time as Zechariah 14:16–19 shows, so this cannot be about heaven, as some claim:

> Then it will come about that any who are left of all the nations that went against Jerusalem will go up from year to year to worship the King, the LORD of hosts, and to celebrate the Feast of Booths.
>
> And it will be that whichever of the families of the earth does not go up to Jerusalem to worship the King, the LORD of hosts, there will be no rain on them. If the family of Egypt does not go up or enter, then no rain will fall on them; it will be the plague with which the LORD smites the nations who do not go up to celebrate the Feast of Booths.
>
> This will be the punishment of Egypt, and the punishment of all the nations who do not go up to celebrate the Feast of Booths.

Remember that this is one of the legitimate times for the Messiah to receive the worship that is due Him, as is shown in the Scripture that two times contains the phrase "to worship the King, the LORD of hosts" (Zech

14:16–17). A king who is merely the Son of David would not be worthy of worship. This One must be Son of God/Trinity member, in order to be worshiped—and He is.

QUESTION: *What was the biggest surprise to you personally as you were writing the book, particularly about the biblical content you were learning/relearning?*

I'll limit these to four items, and it was very much a learning experience for me because I had never taught a class on Zechariah, and much of the material I had not looked at—looked at in a true study sense, not just reading passages from my Bible—since my study preparation and taking the Th.D. exams long ago at Dallas Theological Seminary

First, I was surprised how many times "just plain out in the open" were verses with lines similar to "My eyes have seen the King, the LORD of Hosts," (Isa. 6:5; twice in Zech. 14.) The other references that we saw give us about seven to eight times that this is plain in Scripture. We also saw verses such as Ezekiel 20:33, "As I live," declares the Lord GOD, "surely with a mighty hand and with an outstretched arm and with wrath poured out, I shall be king over you." Psalm 24:7–11 has three times:

> Lift up your heads, O gates,
> And be lifted up, O ancient doors,
> That the King of glory may come in!
> Who is the King of glory?
> The LORD strong and mighty,
> The LORD mighty in battle.
> Lift up your heads, O gates,
> And lift them up, O ancient doors,
> That the King of glory may come in!
> Who is this King of glory?
> The LORD of hosts,
> He is the King of glory. Selah.

For those of you who have Jewish friends who have been taught, or even the most trained rabbi, these verses will silence people just as much as Jesus' use of one verse from Psalm 110. Now, of course, this would be for those who believe in the Bible/the Oracles of God. In other words, Yahweh Himself is not hidden; these verses occur many times that are easily seen in the Old Testament—not the New Testament. God left them no other answer.

Second, I realized how much clearer the church being a "mystery" became to me. As some of you might have known, I had never heard of it until I went to seminary. So many of you are like I was, but a *mystery* biblically is not the Sherlock Holmes variety. A mystery in the OT is something about which God gave just a little bit of revelation, or no revelation at all. And what I saw much clearer than ever before—especially with the seven "appointed times of Yahweh"—is why many people would have a hard time understanding the "mystery" or even acknowledging that the church exists (looking from a Jewish perspective), as is seen in Colossians 1:25–27:

> Of this church I was made a minister according to the stewardship from God bestowed on me for your benefit, so that I might fully carry out the preaching of the word of God, that is, the mystery which has been hidden from the past ages and generations, but has now been manifested to His saints, to whom God willed to make known what is the riches of the glory of this mystery among the Gentiles, which is Christ in you, the hope of glory.

Ephesians 3:1–7:

> For this reason I, Paul, the prisoner of Christ Jesus for the sake of you Gentiles—if indeed you have heard of the stewardship of God's grace which was given to me for you; that by revelation there was made known to me the mystery, as I wrote before in brief. By referring to this, when you read you can understand my insight into the mystery of Christ, which in other generations was not made known to the sons of men, as it has now been revealed to His holy apostles and prophets in the Spirit; to be specific, that the Gentiles are fellow heirs and fellow members of the body, and fellow partakers of the promise in Christ Jesus through the gospel, of which I was made a minister, according to the gift of God's grace which was given to me according to the working of His power.

Third, the synchronization of Scripture is perfect when it is left to interpret itself and with absolutely no artificial hermeneutic thrust onto it. A verse I have used many times is Isaiah 25:1, which speaks of "Plans formed long ago, with perfect faithfulness." I have taught "These Are the Appointed Times of Yahweh," in many classes, and there have been numerous times for someone, or even the entire class, to erupt in something along the lines of, "These truths cannot have been made by different committees over centuries," as much of liberal theology claims. It speaks for itself. Also, God directed me to an entirely different approach—as He has over the decades on numerous occasions. It was a lot of work, but I knew doing it was very important work.

Fourth, how worshipful it was for me to write "Merry Christmas, Adam and Eve!" That was such a close time with our Savior and Shepherd that I did not want the writing session to end, but I had "miles to go before I sleep"[19] at that time.

SUMMARY AND CONCLUSION

For our study in this chapter we learned, among other things, (1) In Deuteronomy 16:1–2 and 16:5–6 God instructed and restricted the Jews on where they were to build His Temple:

> "You are not allowed to sacrifice the Passover in any of your towns which the LORD your God is giving you; **but at the place where the LORD your God chooses to establish His name,** you shall sacrifice the Passover in the evening at sunset, at the time that you came out of Egypt (Deut 16:5–6).

(2) One of the major differences between worship at the Tabernacle and worship at the Temple was that the Tabernacle functioned before the Temple of Yahweh did, and it was portable (e.g. Josh 3–4); God's Temple would not be. (3) Up to 2 Samuel 7, never in Israel's history did God command that a permanent structure be built for Him, as we saw in such verses as Deuteronomy 16:5–6, that—*in God's mind*—*a major role the Temple would serve was that it would be "at the place where the LORD your God chooses to establish His name."* (4) The angel of the LORD then commanded Gad to tell David that he "should go up and build an altar to the LORD on the threshing floor of

---

19 The quotation is from Robert Frost's poem "Stopping By Woods on a Snowy Evening."

Ornan the Jebusite" (1 Chron. 21:18). Even in the midst of divine chastisement, God sovereignly directed the events so that David went back to the exact designated place that God had chosen.

(5) After all the buying of the land from Ornan the Jebusite (with Jebus being the ancient name for what would become Jerusalem), the Angel of the LORD was prepared to slay those in Jerusalem. First Chronicles 21:26 notes, "Then David built an altar to the LORD there and offered burnt offerings and peace offerings. And he called to the LORD and He answered him with fire from heaven on the altar of burnt offering" [i.e., God accepted this offering]. Usually, when we read lengthy Old Testament accounts, we know generally what took place, but rarely do we make the connections that God reveals in Scripture. For David and the nation of Israel, this event became an act of judgment tempered with divine mercy. (6) Interestingly, David responded somewhat like Jacob had centuries earlier in Genesis, saying, "This is the house of the LORD God, and this is the altar of burnt offering for Israel" (1 Chron. 22:1). Even more importantly, it is from this account that the Temple preparations began.

(7) Yet, tucked away, almost without notice, is a one-sentence revelatory nugget that draws the entire account together. Nothing about this episode with David and the census and God's response happened haphazardly. God *led* David to the place, leading for three days as God had previously led Abraham for three days. Strategically, God led David to the exact place where He had led Abraham centuries before. (8) Second Chronicles 3:1 uncovers a three-word goldmine: "Then Solomon began to build the house of the LORD in Jerusalem *on Mount Moriah,* where the LORD had appeared to his father David, at the place that David had prepared on the threshing floor of Ornan the Jebusite."

We know from the Bible that (9) later on the same night that the Temple had been dedicated, God appeared to Solomon, in 2 Chronicles 7:15–16, saying:

> "Now My eyes shall be open and My ears attentive to the prayer offered in this place.

"For now I have chosen and consecrated this house that *My name may be there forever,* and My eyes and My heart will be there *perpetually*."

(10) Further, we know from Psalm 132:13–14:

> *For the LORD has chosen Zion;*
> *He has desired it for His habitation.*
> *"This is My resting place forever;*
> *Here I will dwell, for I have desired it."*

(11) These—among many other things—are reasons that the Middle East with the Temple Mount in Jerusalem is a perpetual tinderbox ready to explode—and it eventually will explode, but only as God permits it during the Tribulation, and not until God Himself brings these events about.

(12) For those Jews who believe the Oracles of God, there is a passionate desire to have the Temple rebuilt on the Temple Mount. Because sacrifices must be at the place that God has chosen, the place must be on ancient Moriah, in Jerusalem, with a high priest and a Levitical priesthood operative, especially for Passover and the Day of Atonement. (13) However, the sacrifices will not begin until the Temple is rebuilt in the Tribulation, as the Scripture repeatedly shows, and as was shown to Daniel after his heavenly messenger Gabriel brought him holy and divine information, in Daniel 9:20–23:

> Now while I was speaking and praying, and confessing my sin and the sin of my people Israel, and presenting my supplication before the LORD my God in behalf of the holy mountain of my God, while I was still speaking in prayer, then the man Gabriel, whom I had seen in the vision previously, came to me in my extreme weariness about the time of the evening offering.
>
> And he gave me instruction and talked with me, and said, "O Daniel, I have now come forth to give you insight with understanding.
>
> "At the beginning of your supplications the command was issued, and I have come to tell you, for you are highly esteemed; so give heed to the message and gain understanding of the vision."

Later (14) Gabriel will play an important role in proclaiming matters pertaining to the birth of the Messiah's forerunner and of Jesus; however, this time Gabriel appeared to Daniel the prophet and revealed matters about national Israel. You can read all of Daniel 9, if you like. For time's sake we limited our study to the last verse:

> "*And he will make a firm covenant with the many for one week* [*does not say what the firm covenant will be or with whom it will be made, but it might be with the Antichrist to allow the Temple to be rebuilt*], but in the middle of the week [*of seven years*] **he will put a stop to sacrifice and grain offering**: and on the wing of abominations will come one who makes desolate, even until a complete destruction, one that is decreed, is poured out on the one who makes desolate."

For the Antichrist to stop the offerings midway through the seven-year Tribulation, there must be the start of the offerings at some time during the Tribulation. And in a context concerning Jesus' Second Coming to earth (such as we saw in Zechariah), Matthew 24:1–3 begins thusly:

> Jesus came out from the temple and was going away when His disciples came up to point out the temple buildings to Him. And He said to them, "Do you not see all these things? Truly I say to you, not one stone here will be left upon another, which will not be torn down."
>
> As He was sitting on the Mount of Olives, the disciples came to Him privately, saying, "Tell us, when will these things happen, and what will be the sign of Your coming, and of the end of the age?"

The answer that Jesus gives is extremely important, (15) if for no other reason than how it is presented in the Bible, and it is where Jesus speaks of the coming Abomination of Desolation (short version) in Matthew 24:15-16, with even the Holy Spirit doing something He very rarely does:

> "Therefore when you see the ABOMINATION OF DESOLATION which was spoken of through Daniel the prophet, standing in the holy place (let the reader understand) [The Holy Spirit *adds emphasis* to the spoken words of Jesus Messiah], then those who are in Judea must flee to the mountains."

The Holy Spirit, by means of the Apostle Paul, later explained in 2 Thessalonians 2:3–4 what "the Abomination of Desolation is," and why God the Son and God the Holy Spirit warned people about it:

> Let no one in any way deceive you, for it will not come unless the apostasy comes first, and the man of lawlessness is revealed, the son of destruction, who opposes and exalts himself above every so-called god or object of worship, so that he takes his seat in the temple of God [*the rebuilt temple of the Tribulation*], displaying himself as being God.
>
> Do you not remember that while I was still with you, I was telling you these things?

We learned one of the most startling (for some) truths from our studies: (16) *Yahweh will not accept the sacrifices done by the Jewish people during the Tribulation.* While this may seem a harsh response by God, beginning in Genesis 4 comes the world's first rejected offering to God—Cain's offering—in consequently what was the world's first false religion, when Abel's offering was accepted by God, but Cain's offering was rejected by God. We also saw in regard to the offerings in the Tribulation, (17) that two reasons in particular point to this as being the right answer about God not accepting such sacrifices in the first part of the Tribulation at His Temple carried out by the Levitical priesthood in accordance to what and how the Pentateuch directs: (i) the New Covenant has already been ratified by the blood of Jesus, and (ii) because of this, there is a change in the high priesthood—and God permits only one high priest to function at a time. We know from Psalm 110:4 that our Lord Jesus Christ "will be a Priest forever." Also, (18) this tremendously important doctrine that God does not reveal until the Book of Hebrews is not only that there will be a priest, but Jesus already is—if you are saved—our High Priest, as revealed in Hebrews 4:14: "Therefore, **since we have** [*present tense*] **a great high priest** who has passed through the heavens, Jesus the Son of God, let us hold fast our confession." (19) Hebrews 6:19–20 discloses something that has not been true for any time in the history of high priests or for anyone who will briefly occupy that position in the Tribulation, namely, our High Priest's longevity of service:

This hope we have as an anchor of the soul, a hope both sure and steadfast and one which enters within the veil, where Jesus has entered as a forerunner for us, **having become a high priest forever** according to the order of Melchizedek.

We also learned (20) that the Mosaic Covenant had one high priest at a time, and that is what the Jews will try to establish again. (21) Also, the Holy Spirit through the Apostle Paul explains very specific sins the Jewish people committed and would perform again—and similarly to the rich, young ruler—Judaism became not something of God's design, but at its heart were those seeking to be justified under the Mosaic Covenant under a "works-righteousness system," as we saw in Romans 9:30–10:4. These are some of the major sins committed by those who seek justification on this basis:

> What shall we say then? That Gentiles, who did not pursue righteousness, attained righteousness, even the righteousness which is by faith; but Israel, pursuing a law of righteousness, did not arrive at that law.
>
> Why? Because they did not pursue it by faith, but as though it were by works. They stumbled over the stumbling stone, just as it is written. [*We noted the two more of the numerous "Messianic Stone Prophecies" that were first given in Genesis 49:24. National Israel's rejecting of the Messiah the Stone is still part of that nation's unforgiven sins against God*]
>
> "BEHOLD, I LAY IN ZION A STONE OF STUMBLING AND A ROCK OF OFFENSE, AND HE WHO BELIEVES IN HIM WILL NOT BE DISAPPOINTED."
>
> Brethren, my heart's desire and my prayer to God for them is for their salvation.
>
> For I testify about them that they have a zeal for God, but not in accordance with knowledge. For not knowing about God's righteousness and seeking to establish their own, they did not subject themselves to the righteousness of God.
>
> For Christ is the end of the law for righteousness to everyone who believes.

(22) Hebrews 6:19–20, as we saw earlier, shows Jesus the Messiah's longevity of service as High Priest:

> This hope we have as an anchor of the soul, a hope both sure and steadfast and one which enters within the veil, where Jesus has entered as a forerunner for us, *having become a high priest forever* according to the order of Melchizedek.

(23) And finally, Hebrews 8:1–2 adds these cogent points about what the redeemed already have:

> *Now the main point* in what has been said is this: *we have such a high priest, who has taken His seat at the right hand* of the throne of the Majesty in the heavens, a minister in the sanctuary and in the true tabernacle, which the Lord pitched, not man.

(24) To sum up this section on the Mosaic offerings given under the Mosaic Covenant not being accepted by God: never again will there be any high priest other than Jesus the Messiah, and He became so with His own blood that He shed at the ratification of the New Covenant, which is the only basis for salvation anywhere from Genesis 1 into the eternal state.

In a very important section, (25) Ezekiel 40–48 reveals most of God's answers about the Millennial Kingdom Temple which will be in Jerusalem and concerning filling His Temple again with His Glory—something that cannot be true for the Tribulation Temple: (26) This is with the understanding of the events already revealed about Jesus' return that we saw in Zechariah 14 and other passages.

(27) How do we know that sacrifices in the Millennial Kingdom will not be offered under the Mosaic Covenant? Again, most of the material God gave us to answer this and related questions is in Ezekiel 40–48. First, there are only four feasts in the Millennial Kingdom, instead of seven such as we have in Leviticus as the Appointed Times of Yahweh, and the first feast listed (Ezek 45:18–20) seems to be some kind of Millennial Kingdom New Year festival, not found in the Mosaic Covenant. The second Millennial feast (Passover) and the Feast of Unleavened Bread are within the Mosaic Covenant and the Millennial Kingdom Sacrifices.

(28) In Ezekiel 40–46, God gives Ezekiel visions of the Millennial Kingdom Temple and aspects of worship never done before. Based on their ancestors' behaviors, some groups from the tribe of Levi will be rewarded for their faithfulness and others will be punished for their iniquity. For instance, in Ezekiel 44:9–14, God judged the wicked behavior of their ancestors thusly, with very specific reasons given:

> Thus says the Lord GOD, "No foreigner uncircumcised in heart and uncircumcised in flesh, of all the foreigners who are among the sons of Israel, shall enter My sanctuary.
>
> "But the Levites who went far from Me when Israel went astray, who went astray from Me after their idols, shall bear the punishment for their iniquity. Yet they shall be ministers in My sanctuary, having oversight at the gates of the house and ministering in the house; they shall slaughter the burnt offering and the sacrifice for the people, and they shall stand before them to minister to them.
>
> "Because they ministered to them before their idols and became a stumbling block of iniquity to the house of Israel, therefore I have sworn against them," declares the Lord GOD, "that they shall bear the punishment for their iniquity.
>
> "And they shall not come near to Me to serve as a priest to Me, nor come near to any of My holy things, to the things that are most holy; but they will bear their shame and their abominations which they have committed.
>
> "Yet I will appoint them to keep charge of the house, of all its service and of all that shall be done in it.

(29) And in total contrast comes this commendation for one special group, as seen in Ezekiel 44:15–17:

> "But the Levitical priests, the sons of Zadok, who kept charge of My sanctuary when the sons of Israel went astray from Me, shall come near to Me to minister to Me; and they shall stand before Me to offer Me the fat and the blood," declares the Lord GOD.
>
> "They shall enter My sanctuary; they shall come near to My table to minister to Me and keep My charge.

"It shall be that when they enter at the gates of the inner court, they
shall be clothed with linen garments; and wool shall not be on them while
they are ministering in the gates of the inner court and in the house.

(30) So also are two verses of previous faithfulness, in Ezekiel 44:15, "But
the Levitical priests, the sons of Zadok, who kept charge of My sanctuary
when the sons of Israel went astray from Me, shall come near to Me to
minister to Me; and they shall stand before Me to offer Me the fat and the
blood," declares the Lord GOD, and this is followed by one more example
of their faithfulness rewarded, as revealed in Ezekiel 48:11: "It shall be
for the priests who are sanctified of the sons of Zadok, who have kept My
charge, who did not go astray when the sons of Israel went astray as the
Levites went astray."

DEEPER WALK STUDY QUESTIONS

(1) Why can't the Jews build a Temple to God at some place other than
Jerusalem? Why is this important and what does that mean in regard
to Jerusalem in both now and future world events?

(2) How do we know that the place where the Jews chose to build the
Temple was where God wanted it? Explain with at least six biblical
supports.

(3) The Angel of the LORD led them to the place where the Trinity had
fore-ordained for the Temple of Yahweh to be built. What was the
Angel of the LORD about to do and why? How does this show—initially—the exact place where God wanted the Temple to be built?

(4) How do we see God's sovereignty in the selection of where His Temple
would be? Name ten biblical truths, support each one with Scripture,
and make sure that at least three of those truths have Moriah in them.

(5) Name ten biblical truths from 2 Chronicles 7 and Psalm 132 that prove biblically the eternal aspect of what God displays there. Support each answer with biblical support and tell why each one of your answers is important.

(6) Why is having the rebuilt Temple so important to people such as the Orthodox Jews? Name eight reasons and support them biblically.

(7) Name eight ways and support each one with Scripture why the sacrifices will begin and end during the Tribulation.

(8) Name ten spiritual truths from Daniel's (and others') encounters with Gabriel. Why is this important prophetically? Be specific and support your answers.

(9) From Daniel 9, Matthew 24, and 2 Thessalonians 2:1–4, develop a small biblical theology on "the Abomination of Desolation." Have at least six items, and then tell why they are important biblically.

(10) How do we know biblically that God will not accept the religious sacrifices made by the Jews in the Tribulation? Name six biblical reasons, support your answers, and tell why this is important.

(11) From what we saw in Hebrews 5–7 about the priesthood and high priesthood, what are ten biblical truths we can learn from these chapters? Be specific and support your answers biblically.

(12) Why is having a High Priest so important to our walk now, and why will the high priesthood be important in the Tribulation? Explain and support your answer biblically. Also, list five reasons biblically that show that God will not stop the ministry of His next true priest after the Tribulation.

(13) Give four reasons biblically that show Jesus could not have functioned as a high priest under the Mosaic Covenant. Be specific and support your answer biblically. Also, from the passages that we saw in Romans 9:30–10:4, list the sins attributed to Jewish unbelievers: past, present, and some into the future.

(14) How do we know that there will be sacrifices during the Millennial Kingdom? Give five supports for your answer from the Bible.

(15) Who is Phinehas, what did he do and what was God's reward for his action? Be specific, especially about what God promised him. How do the Sons of Zadok fit in with the covenant that God made with Phinehas? Give four answers and support each one biblically.

The word which Isaiah the son of Amoz saw concerning Judah and Jerusalem.

Now it will come about that
In the last days,
The mountain of the house of the LORD
Will be established as the chief of the mountains,
And will be raised above the hills;
And all the nations will stream to it.
And many peoples will come and say,
"Come, let us go up to the mountain of the LORD,
To the house of the God of Jacob;
That He may teach us concerning His ways,
And that we may walk in His paths."
For the law will go forth from Zion,
And the word of the LORD from Jerusalem.
And He will judge between the nations,
And will render decisions for many peoples;
And they will hammer their swords into plowshares, and their spears into pruning hooks.
Nation will not lift up sword against nation,
And never again will they learn war.

—Isaiah 2:1–4

In that day the Branch of the LORD will be beautiful and glorious, and the fruit of the earth will be the pride and the adornment of the survivors of Israel.

And it will come about that he who is left in Zion and remains in Jerusalem will be called holy—everyone who is recorded for life in Jerusalem. When the Lord has washed away the filth of the daughters of Zion, and purged the bloodshed of Jerusalem from her midst, by the spirit of judgment and the spirit of burning, then the LORD will create over the whole area of Mount Zion and over her assemblies a cloud by day, even smoke, and the brightness of a flaming fire by night; for over all the glory will be a canopy.

And there will be a shelter to give shade from the heat by day, and refuge and protection from the storm and the rain.

—Isaiah 4:2–6

Then he showed me Joshua the high priest standing before the angel of the LORD, and Satan standing at his right hand to accuse him.

And the LORD said to Satan, "The LORD rebuke you, Satan! Indeed, the LORD who has chosen Jerusalem rebuke you! Is this not a brand plucked LORD from the fire?"

—Zechariah 3:1–2

"Then say to him, 'Thus says the LORD of hosts, "Behold, a man whose name is Branch, for He will branch out from where He is; and He will build the temple of the LORD.

"Yes, it is He who will build the temple of the LORD, and He who will bear the honor and sit and rule on His throne. Thus, He will be a priest on His throne, and the counsel of peace will be between the two offices."

—Zechariah 6:12–13

"As I live," declares the Lord GOD, "surely with a mighty hand and with an outstretched arm and with wrath poured out, I shall be king over you."

—Ezekiel 20:33

A Psalm of David.

The earth is the LORD's, and all it contains,
The world, and those who dwell in it.
For He has founded it upon the seas
And established it upon the rivers.
Who may ascend into the hill of the LORD?
And who may stand in His holy place?
He who has clean hands and a pure heart,
Who has not lifted up his soul to falsehood
And has not sworn deceitfully.
He shall receive a blessing from the LORD
And righteousness from the God of his salvation.
This is the generation of those who seek Him,
Who seek Your face —even Jacob.   Selah.

Lift up your heads, O gates,
And be lifted up, O ancient doors,
That the King of glory may come in!
Who is the King of glory?
The LORD strong and mighty,
The LORD mighty in battle.
Lift up your heads, O gates,
And lift them up, O ancient doors,
That the King of glory may come in!
Who is this King of glory?
The LORD of hosts,
He is the King of glory. Selah.

—Psalm 24

Now to the King eternal, immortal, invisible, the only God, be honor and glory forever
and ever. Amen.

—1 Timothy 1:17

BARE-BONES REVIEW OF THE SEVEN APPOINTED TIMES OF YAHWEH, SUMMARY SHEET

Some form of "the Appointed Times of Yahweh" occurs six times in **Leviticus 23** (vv. 2 [twice], 4 [twice], 37, and 44) where God introduces seven times that are eternally important to Him, as He reveals in the rest of Scripture.

All of these (1) were given at first to the Jews only, (2) were part of the Mosaic Covenant that was ratified in Exodus 24, and (3) the phrase appears at the beginning and ending of the chapter.

The first four appointed times of Yahweh and their New Testament fulfillment:

(1) **God's Passover** (Lev 23:5): 1 Corinthians 5:7: "For *Christ our Passover* also has been sacrificed."

(2) **The Feast of Unleavened Bread** (Lev 23:6–8): 1 Corinthians 5:6–8: includes *the second of the seven appointed times of Yahweh*:

(3) **The Feast of the First Fruits of Your Harvest, or just Feast of First Fruits** (Lev 23:9–14): 1 Corinthians 15:20–23. Christ has been raised from the dead, the first fruit of those who are asleep.

(4) **The Feast of Weeks** (Lev 23:15–22): the last appointed time in the spring; later in history it picks up a new name, **Pentecost,** and this will include the birth of the church: Acts 2:1–5.

KEY: After the first four appointed times of Yahweh, there was "**a long time of silence from God**" (from their vantage point); that is, from the last of spring until late September/October, nothing else was given to the people in this festival cycle from God. We currently live in this period of a long silence from God, which may be ending soon.

(5) **The Feast of Trumpets** (Lev 23:23–25): *a call for Jewish national repentance* during the Tribulation. Obviously, this remains unfulfilled prophecy at present.

(6) **The Real Day of Atonement** (Lev. 23:26–32): **a call for Jewish national atonement**. This will be **the first true Day of Atonement** under the blood of the New Covenant as shown in Zechariah 13:8–9.

(7) **The Last of the Seven Appointed Times of Yahweh: the Feast of Booths/Tabernacles** (Lev. 23:34-44): *This is the millennial kingdom reign after the Messiah has returned to Earth to reign from Jerusalem over the entire world* as seen in Zechariah 14; Revelation 20; plus many other passages.

www.ingramcontent.com/pod-product-compliance
Lightning Source LLC
Chambersburg PA
CBHW062149080426
42734CB00010B/1621

* 9 7 8 1 9 3 4 9 5 2 6 2 7 *